The Repressed Expressed:
Novel Perspectives on African and Black Diasporic Literature

Edited by

**Bill F. Ndi
Adaku T. Ankuma
Benjamin Hart Fishkin**

Langaa Research & Publishing CIG
Mankon, Bamenda

Publisher:
Langaa RPCIG
Langaa Research & Publishing Common Initiative Group
P.O. Box 902 Mankon
Bamenda
North West Region
Cameroon
Langaagrp@gmail.com
www.langaa-rpcig.net

Distributed in and outside N. America by African Books Collective
orders@africanbookscollective.com
www.africanbookscollective.com

ISBN-10: *9956-764-62-0*

ISBN-13: *978-9956-764-62-4*

© Bill F. Ndi, Adaku T. Ankuma, Benjamin Hart Fishkin 2017

All rights reserved.
No part of this book may be reproduced or transmitted in any form or by any means, mechanical or electronic, including photocopying and recording, or be stored in any information storage or retrieval system, without written permission from the publisher

Dedication

To all British Southern Cameroonians killed and or maimed on their territory as they express their resistance to oppression from *La République du Cameroun*. No drop of your blood will go in vain.

Bill F. Ndi

To all who are being persecuted in various parts of the world for daring to stand up for what they believe.

Adaku T. Ankumah

To the loving memory of Stanley Hochman; the best, kindest and most compassionate uncle, mentor and teacher a person can hope to find.

Benjamin Hart Fishkin

The Editors

Bill F. Ndi, Associate Professor of English and Foreign Languages at Tuskegee University, Tuskegee, Alabama, USA, earned his Doctorate from the University of Cergy-Pontoise in 2001. He is a poet, playwright, storyteller, literary critic, translator, historian of ideas and mentalities as well as an academic who has held teaching positions in several universities in Australia, France and elsewhere. His areas of teaching and research comprise among others English Languages and literatures, French, Professional, Technical and Creative Writing, World Literatures, Applied/Historical Linguistics, Literary History, Media and Communication Studies, Peace/Quaker Studies and Conflict Resolution, History of Internationalism, History of Ideas and Mentalities, Translation & Translatology, 17th Century and Contemporary Cultural Studies. He has published extensively in these areas. His publications include numerous scholarly works on Early Quakerism and translation of Early Quaker writings. He has also published poetry and plays in both the French and the English languages. Professor Bill F. Ndi has 18 published volumes of poetry of which 5 are in French, a play and 4 works in translation. He is co-editor of *Outward Evil, Inward Battle: Human Memory in Literature* with Adaku T. Ankumah, Benjamin Hart Fishkin, and Festus Fru Ndeh as well as co-editor of *Fears, Doubts, and Joys of not Belonging* with Adaku T. Ankumah and Benjamin Hart Fishkin. His most recent edited work is *Secret, Silences, and Betrayals*. Also, he has served as a National Endowment for the Humanities' scholar.

Adaku T. Ankumah, Interim Chair and Professor of English at Tuskegee University, received her PhD in Comparative Literature from the University of Wisconsin-Madison with a minor in drama. Her dissertation and initial research interests focused on revolutionary playwrights from the African Diaspora, such as Kenyan Ngugi wa Thiong'o, Martiniquais writer Aimé Césaire, and African American Amiri Baraka, who use their creative efforts to work for the destruction of what they consider to be the colonial/capitalist foundation of post-colonial Africa. Ngugi's play *The Trial of Dedan Kimathi*, a play that examines the arrest and trial of one of the famous leaders of the Mau Mau revolt against the British in Kenya in the 1950's, has been the subject of her published research. She has also done research on the role of women in revolutionary theatre, voicelessness of African women, and gender and politics in the works of African women authors like Mariama Bâ, Ama Ata Aidoo and Tsitsi Dangarembga.

Professor Ankumah's recent research interest includes the writings of women in the African diaspora. This includes research on memory in literature and its role in helping those dealing with painful, fragmented pasts forge a wholesome future in Edwidge Danticat's *The Dew Breaker*. She has also examined memory and resistance in the poetry of South African performer and writer Gcina Mhlophe. She recently edited *Nomenclatural Poetization and Globalization*. Also, she co-edited, with Bill F. Ndi, Benjamin Hart Fishkin and Festus Fru Ndeh, *Outward Evil Inward Battle: Human Memory in Literature,* and with Bill F Ndi and Benjamin Hart Fiskin: *Fears, Doubts, and Joys of not Belonging.*

Benjamin Hart Fishkin, Associate Professor of English at Tuskegee University specializes in teaching Nineteenth Century British Literature. He holds a Ph.D. from the University of Alabama where he served as a Junior Fellow in The Blount Undergraduate Initiative. In his research, he has emphasized Nineteenth Century British Literature through each phase of his education. Prior to earning his Doctorate from the University of Alabama in May of 2009, he obtained a BA in English and Film from the University of Michigan, Ann Arbor, and an MA from Miami University, Oxford, Ohio where he examined the interest of Charles Dickens in the theatre and how the stage influenced his novel writing. He has published *The Undependable Bonds of Blood: The Unanticipated Problems of Parenthood in the Novels of Henry James*. He co-edited *Outward Evil Inward Battle: Human Memory in Literature* with Adaku T. Ankumah, Bill F. Ndi, and Festus Fru Ndeh, and *Fears, Doubts and Joys of not Belonging* with Adaku T. Ankumah and Bill F. Ndi. His recent research interests include, besides his growing interest in Anglophone Cameroon literature, the problems of marriage and the American family, and the relationship between the Blues and the single-parent home in the works of William Faulkner, August Wilson, and F. Scott Fitzgerald.

Authors

Adaku T. Ankumah is Professor of English at Tuskegee University and chairs the Department of Modern Languages, Communication and Philosophy. She holds a Ph.D. from the University of Wisconsin-Madison. Her areas of interest include women's literature (with a focus on African and Diaspora women) and the short story genre.

Antonio J. Jimenez-Munoz is lecturer at the University of Oviedo, Spain. His research takes on the influence of Romantic literature and culture upon the present. His main line of research deals with the influence of Romantic legacies in modern poetry and art and particularly the material continuity of Romantic modes of expression in contemporary art-forms. His fields of interest are Literary Criticism, Theory, and World Poetry. Before his current position, he was a Teaching Fellow at the universities of Kent at Canterbury-UK (2001-2004) and Hull-UK (2004-2006), after graduating in English Studies at the University of Cordoba (Spain) in 2001.

Benjamin Hart Fishkin is an Associate Professor of English at Tuskegee University, where he specializes in teaching Nineteenth Century British Literature. He holds a Ph.D. from the University of Alabama where he served as a Junior Fellow in The Blount Undergraduate Initiative.

Bill F. Ndi, teaches at Tuskegee University. He has numerous scholarly publications on Early Quakerism and translation of Early Quaker writings. He has also published extensively in both the French and the English languages. These publications include scholarly articles and book chapters, poetry, and plays. Professor Bill F. Ndi has 18 volumes of poetry of which 5 are in French, a play and 4 works in translation.

Emmanuel Fru Doh holds a Ph.D. from the University of Ibadan and has taught in colleges and universities in Cameroon and the United States since 1990. Poet, novelist, social and literary critic, his research interests, with a remarkable interdisciplinary approach, include Africa's literatures, cultures, and politics; the African diaspora; and colonial and postcolonial literatures. Besides fictional and poetic works, Doh has published numerous substantial scholarly works, including *Africa's political Wasteland: The Bastardization of Cameroon*, and *Stereotyping Africa: Surprising Answers to Surprising Questions, Anglophone-Cameroon Literature: An Introduction, The Obasinjom Warrior: The Life and Works of Bate Besong*. Also worthy of mention is a significant book chapter in *Fears, Doubts, and Joys of not Belonging*: "Bill F. Ndi's Social Angst and Humanist Vision: Politics Alienation and the Quest for Freedom in *K'cracy, Trees in the Storm and Other Poems*". He is currently teaching in the Department of English at Century College in Minnesota.

Rhonda Collier is an Associate Professor of English at Tuskegee University, where she also serves as the Interim Director of the TU Global Office. She is a Fulbright Scholar, who studied at the Universidad de São Paulo in Brazil. She received her Ph.D. in Comparative Literature from Vanderbilt University in Nashville, TN. She also holds a B.S. and a Master's degree in Industrial Engineering from the University of Tennessee, Knoxville and Georgia Tech respectively. She has published in the areas of Afro-Brazilian, Afro-Cuban, African-American, and global hip hop studies. At Tuskegee, she focuses on American literature and composition courses with an emphasis on service-learning. Her work "Mothering Cuba: The Poetics of Afro-Cuban Women" appears in *Another Black Like Me: The Construction of Identities and Solidarity in the African Diaspora* (Cambridge Scholar Press, 2015). Her upcoming work will focus on Afro-German hip hop. She discusses art as a space of forgiveness and reconciliation. She is passionate about education abroad and cross-cultural student engagement.

Richard Evans is assistant professor of English at Tuskegee University in Tuskegee, Alabama. Educated in classics at the University of South Carolina, the American School of Classical Studies at Athens and Columbia University, Dr. Evans holds a Ph.D. in comparative literature with research interests in ancient and medieval literatures, theories of translation and linguistic relativity.

He has published numerous academic book reviews, essays promoting the study of Classical Greek in schools, and articles on Greek and Roman authors in the Dictionary of Literary Biography and articles on various topics in classical literature.

Yosimbom Hassan Mbiydzenyuy holds a PhD in Literature from the University of Yaoundé 1 Cameroon. Currently, he teaches in the Department of English, University of Buea, Cameroon. His PhD thesis explores "Identity Dynamics in Cameroon Literature". His current research interests and projects focus on the links between Postcolonial and Postmodern theories, and how their interplay shapes and nurtures multiple-layered identity formation and performance in postcolonial societies, especially Cameroon. Also, he is keen on researching Latin American epistemological foundations such as Transmodernity, Coloniality, Decoloniality, Pluriversality, etc. and how they could be used to de-/re-construct postcolonial African societies.

Table of Contents

Introduction... **xiii**

Chapter 1
Francis Nyamnjoh's *The Disillusioned African:*
a Philosophy of Liberation.. 1
Yosimbom Hassan Mbiydzenyuy

Chapter 2
The Playwright as Whistleblower:
Drama and the Expression of the Repressed
in Cameroon.. 25
Emmanuel Fru Doh

Chapter 3
Bill F. Ndi's *Gods in the Ivory Towers*:
An Expression of Universal Academic Tragedy................... 53
Richard Evans

Chapter 4
Francis Nyamnjoh's *Soul's Forgotten*:
A Rejection of Poor Education and Failing
Democracy.. 71
Benjamin Hart Fishkin

Chapter 5
Nyamnjoh's *Homeless Waters:*
Juvenile Rebellion and Old Age Recollection..................... 91
Bill F. Ndi

Chapter 6
Rising from the Ashes: Conflict and
Repression in Bill F. Ndi's Poetry................................121
Antonio Jimenez-Munoz

Chapter 7
Yearning for a Distance: Prophetic Narrative
in Zora Neale Hurston's *Jonah's Gourd Vine* (1934)...............143
Rhonda Collier

Chapter 8
The Plight of a Woman Expressed in
Jing's *Tale of an African Woman*....................................... 161
Adaku T. Ankumah

Chapter 9
Emmanuel Fru Doh's *Nomads: The Memoirs of a S
outhern Cameroonian*: Censorship, Treachery and
Instability in Former British Southern Cameroons...............181
Benjamin Hart Fishkin

Chapter 10
Francis B. Nyamnjoh's *A Nose for Money*:
Airing Devoiced Thoughts.. 201
Bill F. Ndi

Index..225

Introduction

The world is increasingly becoming a global village in which cultures, peoples, ideas, traditions, lifestyles, religions, beliefs and philosophical systems, thoughts and forms of (mis)representation and presentation crisscross. This crisscrossing of these values brings into contact forces of repression and the will to express all that which is repressed. This is because their coming into contact does not translate into an all accepting world of expression without restraint. All too often, people are faced with issues where expressing themselves, and freely too, could determine life and or death. Consequently, forms of censorship (including self-censorship) have developed over the span of human history. Such censorships have impinged on the ways and manners in which realities are perceived, confronted or expressed and translated. It is no surprise that social anthropologists argue that "[t]he lived lives of those who are not of the dominant race, place, culture, class, place or age are often swept to the sidelines of scholarship—and given voice in alternative spaces such as music and literature" (Nyamnjoh, qtd. in *Alternation* 19, 1.68). Leading from this is the proverbial pen and the sword contest which some individuals have posited, through the use/misuse of their rights or might, that the pen is mightier than the sword. Charles R. Larson in his exploration of the ordeal of the African writer, highlights such repressive malaise permeating every aspect of "Publishing the Truth," to borrow a Quaker terminology. This repression, he makes clear, is not only on the African front as its impact has gripped even foreign publishers with the fear of repercussions. He writes:

> [...] African publishers [...] in some cases edit[ing] out potentially offensive passages in novels, so that these works will be approved by their governments for the classroom. Writers identify several levels of this growing form of censorship. First, they themselves may not write what they would like to because of the fear of repression by their governments. Their local publishers are likely to excise passages deemed offensive for sexual, political, and/or religious reasons. Even worse, publishers

outside Africa fear repercussions for books that may be deemed politically incorrect, for a variety of reasons. (62-63)

The difficult creative circumstances of writers worldwide, and their relentlessness in their creative endeavor raise hopes that the adage saying the pen is mightier than the sword could be extended to imply that the written word is more powerful than the canon as literature takes this famous maxim and extends it towards its logical conclusion. Literature serves as a project or mechanism to subvert, rebel, refute, and transcend the conscious and unconscious silencing of voices. From their very origin, literary texts have been motivated by discords, and they tend to litigate them. Such power struggles and the resistance they engender have been highlighted by Foucault in *An Introduction to the History of Sexuality*. In this seminal work, he observes:

> Where there is power, there is resistance, and yet, or rather consequently, this resistance is never in a position of exteriority in relation to power [...] a multiplicity of points of resistance: these play a role of adversary, target, support, or handle in power relations. These point of resistance are everywhere in the power network. (95-96)

The multiple points of resistance become the underpinnings of the discords, which in themselves, are too painful not to write. The cost of repressing one's thoughts is immeasurable and creates so many spiritual problems that expressing one's conscience, wet with perspiration for all the world to see, is the only way to avoid going insane or suffering from an implosion. Hence, the insatiable desire to communicate translates into a variety of exchanges not just of a blissful and worry-free life but that of the repressed burdens weighing heavily on the writers' minds. This notion of "variety of communication" comforts the assertion that "writing is not a uniform thing" but "a complex practice that emerges in specific places, assumes a variety of forms, and changes in many ways over time" (qtd. in Scholes, Comley and Peritz 4).

The plethora of writings surrounding us obfuscates every single sense that can be made of it all (Scholes, Comley and Peritz 4). However, the predicament of the Anglophone Cameroonians, much like the Celtic Tiger in the cage of Northern Ireland or African Americans in the USA, or the Native American on a reservation in the state of Washington/North Dakota, or the Buddhist monks in Tibet whose freedoms are limited, is that they must construct a thought process that will surmount social, cultural, political, and religious attempts to keep them obsequious, obedient, and silent. Comprehending how individuals in the globalized and globalizing world, marked by restraint and political correctness, deal with problems of identity that are shaped by systematic rejection, exclusion, discrimination, and the pains such engender become the *raison d'être* of exploring texts that communicate self, knowledge, and power to overcome any form of repression, either extraneously imposed or self-imposed. It takes so much energy to censor one's impulses. How does a repressed population stay intellectually vigorous and how do writers in different parts of the globe, trapped in this, handle the similar temptation of avoiding to complain because they are too afraid to speak? Do they delve into their own psyche and/or society's to probe and say the truth with resolve no matter what? Or will the writer in the face of repression be afraid of society, i.e. what Vaclav Havel styles as a very "mysterious animal with many hidden faces and potentiality"? (qtd. in Elshtain 7). Or again, would the writer follow Elshtain's claim that "in order for the truth to be told, it must be recognized" (36)? If "cowards," indeed, "die many times before their death," according to Shakespeare's Julius Caesar in Act 2 Scene 2 of his tragedy of the same name (Shakespeare 954), are cowards their own jailors and, more to the point, do they do a better job of it than the powers that be?

This book encompasses a world of perspectives from different contexts in which any free expression of thoughts may have a serious social, political, historical and gendered significance, and/or be viewed as an unacceptable infringement of cultural and traditional heritage. Then too, for other individuals, highlighting the collocation of the expression process where repression reigns supreme becomes a signifier of hybridity marked by "one vital distinction to draw between forms of domination [which lie] in the kinds of indignities the exercise of power routinely produces" (Scott 7). Thus the idea that the pleasure or displeasure to express such indignities might have nothing to do with the actual sentiments expressed, might in turn, be the object of representation and not self-representation of and by language itself. And to this, Bakhtin upholds that "to a greater or lesser extent, every novel is a dialogized system made up of the images of 'languages,' styles and consciousnesses that are concrete and inseparable from language" (240).

However, for many individuals, the expression of the repressed becomes important in that it signifies "living freedom" and serves as representation, that is, the expression of which freedom very often translates into the image that their inner thoughts and narratives signify. They replicate who these individuals are in conjunction with whom they pass for and how they are positioned within the society and the global world. These variations in the expression of the repressed also lead to different identity constructs and account for the differing language use by writers to shape and inject meaning into the world that surrounds us. Exploring the expression of the repressed becomes akin to 17th Century Quaker ideal of *Proclaiming or Publishing the Truth* or again the Bahktinian celebration of the diversity of behavior in human interaction as well as the Barthesian desire "to change systems: no longer to unmask, no longer to interpret, but to make consciousness itself a drug, and thereby to accede to the perfect vision of reality, to the great bright dream, to prophetic love" (60).

Furthermore, the idea of these collective essays has its genesis in a simple, yet observable fact that from the time humans are born till death, they have Rousseau's proverbial chain around them. Unfortunately, this work reveals more than proverbial limitations. *The Repressed Expressed* reveals limits that not even Rousseau would have imagined in *The Social Contract*. There are always visible and invisible constraints upon what humans say or do. It would not be presumptuous to state *ipso facto* that life is governed by dos and don'ts. Even Milton in his speech for the liberty of unlicensed printing to the parliament, quotes the following poem:

> This is true liberty, when free-born men,
> Having to advise the public, may speak free,
> Which he who can, and will, deserves high praise;
> Who neither can, nor will, may hold his peace:
> What can be juster in a state than this?

Euripid. Hicetid. (qtd. in William Kerrigan, John Rumrich, and Stephen M. Fallon 175)

Thus the poem highlights the need for "free-born men, / Having to advise the public, may speak free," and one may question: What about people born of lower and "unfree" estate? Since the publication of *Aeropagetica* advocating free press and/or speech, freedom seems not to have found landing ground among all people; not even in the most advanced democracies where "dos" and "don'ts" still dictate what, when, where, why and how people are allowed total freedom to express even that which society frowns upon. Foucault must have had this in mind when he highlighted that "much is at stake in the way we use language i.e. individuals' prestige and society's concepts of "right" and "true" of power and knowledge (qtd. In Scholes, Comley and Peritz 1). Foucault's stance, to quote Elshtain, "brings to mind Hannah Arendt's critics who attacked her revelation of Jewish participation in helping the Nazi's execute their dirty job" (37). They attacked her on the basis that such a revelation was "either not true or not true in the way she claimed, or that it was truth that should not be told because it would embolden the forces of evil and undermine the forces of good" (37).

As a result, in our endeavor, we expressly refuse to take communication for granted because the shared understanding between writers and readers must be incessantly created and recreated. This is especially the case given that repression is a social contradiction in a global dispensation despite which liberties and freedoms are heralded while leaving literature and myth, as Lévi-Strauss would have it, as "resolutions of real social contradictions" (qtd. in Eagleton 97). This is further bolstered by J.C. Scott's claim that "the disparity between public action and offstage discourse depends heavily […] on the severity of the domination […] the more involuntary, demeaning, onerous, and extractive it is, the more it will foster a counter discourse starkly at odds with its official claim" (134). That is why, "For sociologists and anthropologists, dipping into fiction can bring voice to silenced spaces and help science bridge rather than reinforce socially constructed difference" (*Alternation* 19, 1 (2012) 68). This underlines why Ngugi wa Thiong'o also draws attention with the following understatement:

Even the contradictions of the ages are comparable. Those in the midst of the European Renaissance could view it as an expression of both hope and hopelessness. Erasmus of Rotterdam, for instance, alternated between denouncing it as corruption ("When was there ever more tyranny? When did avarice reign more largely and less punished?") and lauding it as the "near approach of a golden age," the dawn of a new world, making him wish he could grow young again; and even then he went back to denouncing it as the "irremediable confusion of everything." (*Something Torn and New* 79)

Therefore, *The Repressed Expressed* stems from whence neither repression nor its expression can be taken for granted and not even when such contradictions are hailed as "near approach of a golden age," or denounced as the "irremediable confusion of everything." Exploring "the repressed expressed" brings to mind early Quaker literature which according to Ndi, "[...] comes across as a vehicle for [an] ideology behind which seem[s] to lurk a functional and operational logic characteristic of the movement" (qtd. in *Outward Evil Inward Battle: Human Memory in Literature* 10) and also "foreground... both intrinsic and extrinsic concerns that they have for those who would read [their] works in the future" (qtd. in *Outward Evil Inward Battle: Human Memory in Literature* 8) which finally leaves the reader with, in the words of Ngugi wa Thiong'o, "the vitality, strength, and beauty of resistance." (*Decolonising the Mind* ix).

Following Ngugi's claim, the example of actress, screenwriter, playwright and sex symbol Mae West, who frequently upset authorities, comes to mind. When a judge allegedly asked her if she was trying to show contempt for this court, she replied, "No No' I'm doin' my best to hide it!" (Web) However mirthful this may sound, Ms. West, in her irrepressible vaudevillian style, has stumbled on the political reality that turns out to be one of the cornerstones of this book project. There is a need to conceal, to cover, to hide and to self-censor one's true feelings and nowhere is this more prevalent than in alleged democracies around the world. The subjects of this study have had their thought processes assaulted by obstacles, burdens and impediments which are purposely intended to derail them. Nonetheless, the various writers under study seem to sit above the fray and do just what William E. Buckler underscores of Milton's indefatigable campaign for free press. He highlights how Milton's "genius gives to [his works] a peculiar charm, an air of nobleness and freedom which distinguishes them from other writings of the same class" (7). This raises the hope that "…once every reactive ideology had disappeared, consciousness were finally to become this: the abolition of the manifest and latent, of the appearance and the hidden" (Barthes 60-61).

The Repressed Expressed is about how hard it is to build a community in a nation that no longer has the beneficial qualities of hope and transparency. Moreover, it is our hope to inform the reader that this lack of stability and order among the populous is a universal problem. We can all, wherever we may be, hear about democracy and experience treachery. Instead of enjoying life the way we wish it would be, we all too often must endure an unpleasant reality that is rarely placed upon paper in any language. The various writers in this collection address, in one way or another, the dangers of silence, complacency and indifference to the inherent worth of the individual so much "…so that a long series of verbal contentions […] may suddenly explode into some generalized revulsion: a crying jag […] before the other's flabbergasted eyes will suddenly wipe out all the efforts […] of a carefully controlled language" (Barthes 44). At its most, this collection is about the restoration of human decency. It brings to the fore the strength of imagination over the weight of obstacles, burdens, and impediments in their bid to suffocate any form of expression geared at unveiling troubling and undesirable truths about institutions, nations, polities, or entities. To accomplish this, every nation needs a verbal and written accounting of what has been lost in a monologue which according to Barthes, "is […] pushed back to the very limits of humanity: in archaic tragedy, in certain forms of schizophrenia" (204-205). The nation needs an unvarnished look at its own history.

Post-colonialism has placed the African in a fog, and there is no promise that it will lift anytime soon. What is necessary is to look even farther afield. These types of problems are troublesome, and this is no time to be bashful, so wherever people feel politically or educationally limited they need a pilot for their soul to provide commentary and courage. Consequently, there is need for this in-depth study to counter the fading away of human identity and dignity.

Authoritarian repression has existed in many countries around the world and Ngugi highlights this:

> The avarice, tyranny, and confusion that appalled Erasmus of Rotterdam apply also to postcolonial Africa, where diseases, famines, and massacres beset places like Rwanda, Darfur, Liberia, and Sierra Leone. Hope and hopelessness still contend for domination of the African soul as they did for that of the European soul. (80)

There is scarcely a glimmer of hope in these places and for people who find themselves under the thumb of such autocracies. The only way to outmode them is to follow Roland Barthes counsel: "to write about something [...][in order] to outmode it" (98). *The Repressed Expressed* is a map or guidebook indicating how people in such geographical prisons strive to transform—with things pure and clean—their agitation into a spiritual and political pathway that is free of pain and hurt from, and anger towards a dirty and corrupted world.

Oftentimes literary scholars and theorists have written about surveillance. Roland Barthes in his *A Lover's Discourse* questions what relation a writer can have with a system of power if he/she is neither its slave nor its accomplice nor its witness (89-90). The argument is that wherever a population is held back it must be watched constantly so that no one steps out of line. This is the purview of people such as Jeremy Bentham, George Orwell and Mikhail Bahktin who are of the opinion that by limiting privacy and stifling individuality people can be manipulated, coerced, and controlled. This must have been the drive behind Oscar Wilde's saying that "[t]he books that the world calls immoral are the books that show the world its own shame" (qtd. in Pat Scales 5). A book that does anything else does not cast an adequate reflection upon the structure it hopes to repudiate and dismantle.

Accordingly, scholars and specialists seize upon insecurity and uncertainty. There is surely turmoil that rolls and roils a society under attack from within. However, these are just symptoms of a government that does not work and has no genuine desire to work. Mikhail Bahktin, looking at a government's effectiveness, addresses issues related to spoken language. He states that, "[h]istories are like novels in that they set out to provide more or less comprehensive accounts of social systems" (qtd in Cruz 176). However, we are left to wonder whether they succeed as they are not written down in indelible ink. Are they accurate and truthfully imbedded within the culture? Unfortunately, the dialogic interaction of a society under duress is not always comprehensive, for the past is not always available and such gaps, breaks, or fissures yield all sorts of problems. The dictator or the autocrat, who rules with total power and not the peasant, controls the word, its context and the language it appears in. Within such a universe, characters/people are caught in the grip of physical challenges that push them to their psychological limits, which is why Eustace Palmer, talking of the African writer says: "naturally he will evolve new forms of expression" (x). Taking Palmer's claim a step further, Roland Bathes highlights that with "the power language [...writers] can do everything: even especially say nothing" (44). Most of the writers discussed in *The Repressed Expressed* deal with authority and its penchant for heaping abuse upon those they have caused to live in fear and the new forms of expression hinted at by Palmer. "The African novelists," Palmer contends, "have much to say to their society and to the world" (x). This statement is so true of any writer from any clime and time in which repression is the order of the day.

Even though repression would push people and writers alike to the fringes of madness, the writer who takes the arduous task of writing, going by Barthes, "… is not entirely mad: he is a faker" for "no praise of folly is possible" (91). Charles Dickens' treatment of the debtor's prison in Victorian England, in his 1857 novel *Little Dorritt*, emphasizes the specter of incarceration for those who cannot pay their bills. Their liberty is compromised when they have not been violent in any way. This is a terrifying way to harm and limit those who find themselves psychologically and financially conflicted in the Marshalsea prison. The very behavior of the mind and the interpersonal relations of all of the people in England changes and everyone walks meekly, gingerly and fearfully in an example of just how severely people's progress can be limited by the powers that be. To this effect, Dickens writes:

> I know nothing of philosophical philanthropy. But I know what I have seen, and what I have looked in the face in this world here, where I find myself. And I tell you this, my friend, that there are people (men and women both, unfortunately) who have no good in them—none. That there are people whom it is necessary to detest without compromise. That there are people who must be dealt with as enemies of the human race. That there are people who have no human heart, and who must be crushed like savage beasts and cleared out of the way. (155)

The obvious emphasis on "cleared out of the way" says more about the frame of mind of someone in a repressive environment than any language of even an outstanding novelist like Dickens. What does one do with people who fail to fall gently into line? All too often they are ignored, unwelcomed, deceived, and brutalized in the hope that they will, quite literally, fade away. Not only is it desired that the truth will disappear, but that they themselves will disappear with it. Such brutality is symptomatic of the deeply engrained irrationality of human nature. All of this is in reaction to a declarative opinion that neither refuses to be silenced nor accurately reported in a newspaper.

Through the various contributions of the writers in this collection, the "being" of individuals in the process of expressing the repressed in different cultures—in the globalizing world—is deconstructed in multiple ways. Furthermore, is it not the aim of writers to provide, through their narratives, an understanding of diversity and cultures in the current global dispensation? It is our hope, then, that this understanding will help promote "writing as a cultural and rhetorical act of communication" (Scholes, Comley and Peritz 2). By so doing, these essays hope to have captured and made known something about the kinds of work that writing does—or is expected to do—in our world (Scholes, Comley and Peritz 5). And, as such, it is structured to talk to the stead, situation, and plight of both writer and reader. The chapters find their strength in the force of unity upheld by the Havelian "embrace of a post-Babelian world in which there are wondrous varieties of human homes, identities, languages, particular possibilities… united perhaps only in its travail" (qtd. in Elshtain 8). In the present case, repression serves as the nucleus of the travail explored through its expression. Yet, like Patôckan and Havelian philosophy beginning from "the bottom" and from a "humbly respected boundary of the natural world," the authors in this volume have endeavored to delineate the natural boundary between repression and the expression of repression. Writing from various perspectives warrants the exploration of differing perceptions of repression and expression within different cultures and regions. Emphases laid situated and particular knowledge as emergent theories have resonance for broader theoretical insights.

This first chapter theorizes on transmodernity as a philosophy of liberation in Francis Nyamnjoh's *The Disillusioned African* (TDA). The chapter is made up of two sections. The first section recognizes the specific meaning and aspects of transmodernity as different from the prevailing shibboleths of Eurocentrism in postcolonial Africa and then argues that the result should be a critical pluriversal/transversal posture that understands Cameroonian/African identity lifeworlds as shards of a transmodern identity system which goes far beyond geographical and even geopolitical boundaries. The second section examines four elements of transmodernity – exteriorization, the women-men relation, the nature of cultural reproduction, and the fetishization of totalities – as elements of a philosophy of liberation and asserts that the transmodern project can contribute to the philosophy of liberation by achieving a co-realization of solidarity, which is syncretic or hybrid and which bonds center to periphery or so-called First World to Third World cultures. The chapter concludes by highlighting that transmodern liberation occurs not via negation, but via a subsumption from the viewpoint of an alterity that thinks of the postcolonial Cameroonian/African world as a transmodern organization characterized by plurality and diversity.

Aware, of the devastating effects of repression in an oppressed society like other writers in his predicament, Emmanuel Fru Doh sets out in Chapter 2 to expose this vexing practice and the art of circumventing it by skilled writers, literary guerillas as such, who are determined to inform, conscientize, and ultimately liberate their ideologically, politically, and economically shackled compatriots. He reveals that an oppressed society is like a volcano waiting to erupt because of the repressed ideas which need to be expressed and acted upon, diffusing the pressure within, so to say. This is the case with The Cameroons today, as Doh reveals through his study of four Cameroonian playwrights—Ba'bila Mutia, Victor Epie'Ngome, Bate Besong, and Bole Butake—who portray The Cameroons as a nation choking under the repressive grip of a disgusting autocrat heading an oligarchy masquerading as a government. Doh reveals that the consequences, according to these playwrights, is building tension and a potential explosion with time in the form of an uprising as clearly predicted by Butake. However, such an uprising is always heralded by a period of conscientization in the guise of a strong literary tradition, of which these playwrights are a part. Doh points out that as obvious as it is, The Cameroons is a disturbed and unstable nation today, and those in power are simply playing ostrich as they fail to acknowledge existing tensions and conflicts within the nation, hence the idea of repression. This is the status quo against which these writers are whistleblowers as such, as they do all to express the repressed ideas within society in an effort to build a better tomorrow for an oppressed and exploited lot vegetating in a stifling socio-political garden called The Cameroons.

The third chapter suggests that in addition to the more common, critical view of Bill F. Ndi's play as a protest play against political corruption, social manipulation, repression, and Francophone discrimination against English speakers in contemporary Cameroonian society, the specific problems faced by a young Anglophone student, Ngwa, at his local university have much wider implications for the academic world at large. Ndi's use of a classical (i.e. Aristotelian) plot structure for the play provokes reflection that corruption and pettiness of a provincial university setting is only a microcosm for academic, if not national setting, everywhere. The subject that is the focus of the drama is the sexual and political games of non-entities, but politically connected professors, forced upon a sincere, but naïve, local student who hopes to build a real-world career on the strength of his post-graduate studies. His hopes for a degree are thwarted by unfair treatment through the sexual harassment and bullying of his academic supervisor who is supported by her lover, the Head of Department, to whom the student must appeal for relief. The African setting and the playwright's background have pushed critics to see the play in African terms, but its message can easily be seen in cosmopolitan terms. Academe is no refuge from irrationality, corruption, pettiness, repression, and discrimination which are all universal human vices.

Chapter four explores Nyamnjoh's *Souls Forgotten* in which he places democracy and education in close proximity. The critic shows how the two are intertwined; they rise together and they fall together. This chapter also delineates the collapse of the educational system of The Cameroons in its six decades since independence and shows how intellectual inefficiency is encouraged at the expense of meritocracy. Furthermore, through a case study of an innocent boy's travel from his rural village, Abehema, to the city of Nyamandem, the chapter exposes the obliteration of an academic dream as a metaphor for the 1986 Lake Nyos disaster. Both are explosions, one chemical, the other intellectual. Further still, through the analysis of Nyamnjoh's narrative, The Cameroons is pictured as a nation experiencing a deterioration of its interior in more ways than one. The educational system is at risk and because of this, the national culture too. This yokes the education of the black man/woman in more than one way and on more than one continent.

The problem of the African and that of the African-American is remarkably similar and as such the accomplishments of Booker T. Washington in the United States seventy years before the life of fictional Emmanuel Kawanga articulates that both groups have their academic pursuit limited, confined, circumscribed and short-circuited. Both are similarly flawed systems in which the black person is the recipient of a mess created by others. Chapter Four illustrates how Francis Nyamnjoh's *Souls Forgotten* presents the ingredients for this traumatic recipe. The extent of the damage is examined and emphasized by the argument that this is a problem that can, and does, happen everywhere. Any student would surely want to know more about the worthy students receiving failing grades because the university—in "The Great City"—feels more comfortable acting like a corporation than an institution of higher learning. What's more, by extension, it harms Emmanuel Kawanga's village. This is a tragedy that travels, and no one can be counted upon to rein in the damage.

Chapter five juxtaposes rebellion and recollection; it attributes each to a specific period of human development as a way of drawing attention to two things: various periods when humans have to live by taking and executing orders from others, and when they have full autonomy to make critical appraisals of their youthful exuberance and/or apathy. Both exuberance and apathy are highlighted as manifestations of deeply rooted repressive socio-political and psychological traumas and their consequences. These, as the title, *Homeless Waters* indicates, lead to homelessness. As such, this chapter posits that every river—Nyamnjoh's metaphor for that which cannot be contained through repression—has a source, a bed, two banks, and a mouth to empty itself into the ocean or some other bigger body of water. A river that loses all or one of these—i.e. compelled by repressive forces to do so, would resist confinement and overflow its banks. The current unleashes an unfriendly and deadly force like that in whose grip Nyamnjoh's protagonist finds himself. Life could be well spiced if devoid of repression, yet the protagonist's turns out to be acerbic with the same said binary. The bearableness and unbearableness of belonging, of being in the chains of love and being free, underlie repression which pushes many an African in general and many an Anglophone-Cameroonian in particular to master the art of expressing the repressed. Consequently, *Homeless Waters* is the writer's guise to tell a bigger tale of tyranny rocking his people and their refusal to cave in to oppression. Such tyranny forces an overflow of expression from the masses—like a river out of its bed—seeking balance between calm and rage, solemnity and mischief. The chapter further draws similarity between the trajectory of a river overflowing its banks after a heavy downpour of rain and that of an over repressed population symbolized by the protagonist. It highlights the main elements of existence that the population has lost to becoming an unfriendly and deadly force. Above all, the travails and resilience of the protagonist hide a bigger, national or maybe an international tragedy. Through instances of repression—symbolic, rhetorical, personal, familial, societal—the potency of Nyamnjoh's figurative use of "waters" as the universal source of life, some kind of seminal fluids, in other words, is revealed and pushed to the height of vagrancy.

Chapter six explores how Bill F. Ndi's poetry, in a stark defense of Cameroon Anglophone Literature, enacts the tensions between the repressed poetic voice through the powers of figurative language, tone, and imagery to elaborate poignant denunciations of oppression and cultural reduction within these constraints. The chapter explores the condition of conflict as a predicament of human nature and economic necessity. It also puts forward how poetry such as Ndi's can assist in questioning human issues beyond competition for power and material resources. In collections such as *K'cracy, Trees in the Storm and other Poems* (2008), *Bleeding Red: Cameroon in Black and White* (2010), *Toil and Delivery* (2010), and *Waves of Anger* (2010) Ndi exorcises a national – if not pan-African or global – reality as despicable yet true through a number of harsh poems which seem, prima facie, to embrace "an-eye-for-an-eye" commandment. Often full of bleak imagery in his denunciations of violence and despair, Ndi's poems, nevertheless rise above their themes in order to offer hope – sometimes hinted at, sometimes tangible – to an increasingly wide readership. Beyond the expressed angst, the poet articulates a discourse which parallels a yearning for redemption and communal progress, applicable to The Cameroons and elsewhere. More recent poems, such as those in *Vestiges* (2013) or *Pride Aside and other Poems* (2016) seem to attune that angst and aim for a more reflective and introspective discourse which is, nevertheless, fully cogent with his previous efforts. The expression of repression in the case of Ndi's poems would not be only to take arms against injustice, but finding a way to articulate peace after conflict without giving up one's beliefs, ideas, and values.

The seventh chapter, "Yearning for a Distance: Prophetic Narrative in Zora Neale Hurston's *Jonah's Gourd Vine (1934)* examines Zora Neale Hurston's semi-autobiographical first novel and the ironic use of autobiography, ethnography and spirituality that lead the author to write about the people and places from which she tries to escape. Unwittingly, Hurston succeeds in being the implied prophet, occasional liar, and wayward father that she writes about in *Jonah's Gourd Vine*. Drawing on her interpretation of the biblical story of the prophet Jonah, Hurston uses the language of the South to provide a critical analysis of the contradictions of Southern religion. The gifted Pastor John Buddy Pearson (Jonah) both amazes and angers readers as he embodies the beautiful cadence of the poetic preacher with the philandering eyes of a cheating husband. Echoing the pattern that will follow Hurston's own life, he believes that distance is the cure for most diseases. Hurston's mother, who correlates to a quiet yet powerful figure by the same name in *Jonah's Gourd Vine*, gives the final diagnosis. Hurston's interpretation of this "female gospel" problematizes the comic nature by which she predicts her place in American literary history. *Jonah's Gourd Vine* illustrates that "yearning for a distance" only hides prophets, preachers, messengers, writers from the audiences who need them. Illustrating this pitfall, Hurston's autobiography *Dust Tracks on a Road (1942)* privileges Eatonville, Florida, as her mythical birthplace, while the fictional *Jonah's Gourd Vine* (1939) reveals her actual birthplace, Notasulga, Alabama. *Jonah's Gourd Vine* is the framework in which to access Hurston's vision of her family, religion and ultimately her own fate.

Chapter 8 delves into the exploration of Democracy whose very own definition requires the participation of all the people in a government of equality that regards the rights of each individual. Principally, the chapter underscores how in some democracies in Africa, the voices of one half of the population are clearly muffled in favor of masculine voices. In exploring Thomas Jing's 2008 novel, *The Tale of an African Woman*, the critic elucidates how the novelist recovers the voice of this lost half in a democracy. Through Jing's captivating narrative of a female protagonist, Yaya, the resistance of the repressed half in an imaginary traditional patriarchy is brought to the fore. Also, drawing from characterization, the chapter traces the lineage of bold and assertive women from which the protagonist hails. These women were not afforded the opportunity to express their talents and uniqueness. They refused to stay in their imposed lanes and acted independently of men who forced them to stay within the confines of traditional roles and under subjection to these men using domesticity or rape. It is a critical exploration of an atypical novel in which Jing, as an African male, breaks the mold of female writers giving voice to their voiceless sisters and boldly assigns major roles to female characters. This portrayal of women is a dramatic shift from the conventional wisdom of how African male writers create inauthentic female characters. Finally, the chapter critically examines how Jing transforms the negative impact of the earlier women whose rejection by society led some to mental breakdowns and even death, to create a modern version of woman who transcends opposition, thus liberating herself from traditions which impede progress. Her advocacies are changes—without which the society pays a costly price—to those traditions which constrain the intellectual, emotional, and psychological well-being of women and exclude them from places of power in African society.

Chapter 9 examines Emmanuel Fru Doh's take on the deterioration of the cultures of The Cameroons. Emmanuel Fru Doh's *Nomads* looks back in sadness at the terrible decision that led to the "union" of Southern Cameroons and *La République du Cameroun*. This chapter is about the haphazard way in which the "unified" nation has been and is being governed. *Nomads*, this chapter argues, is about cultural eradication through autocratic repression or domination and the attempts by the repressed to resist. This is not unique to The Cameroons, for this type of autocracy has proven to be a problem all over the world. Dictatorships have been a dilemma in nations too numerous to count. However, "Emmanuel Fru Doh's *Nomads: The Memoir of a Southern Cameroonian*: Censorship, Treachery, Instability, and the Emergence of a Nation," reveals the Anglophone-Cameroon identity and brings to light the collective patient struggles for sanity in a bifurcated land with two rules, two languages and two ways of doing business. Reading the text brings to the limelight the role of France and England in repressing this African nation from afar. And the big question is, how does Doh handle these issues differently from other authors in places of contention? His *Memoir* argues and advocates for an intellectual solution for the terror and chaos that emanates from a nation divided into Francophone and Anglophone regions. A spiritual approach is needed to swerve away from the immediate impulse to be violent. In other words, how does the human spirit trapped in a helpless circumstance like repression survive, react and think clearly? The chapter posits that a contemplative approach is what will get someone interested is the triumph of the mind. This is the best way to combat oppression, and literature, having a means of written expression, is the way to preserve the past for posterity.

The final chapter explores Francis B. Nyamnjoh's *A Nose for Money* to elucidate the *prison*, Land of Mimbo, in which nationals are trapped in a hapless condition that compels the writer to subvert language in rebellion against the crushing weight of oppression, and/or to reject the pain and sufferings brought about upon his people by the curtailing of basic freedoms in such a dictatorship. The chapter goes on to show how in the place of the voices and thoughts of his people, the writer, through the process of expressing the repressed, not only shapes his own identity as a committed writer but also shapes those of his fellow human beings who ask for nothing more than freedom from constraints of repression driving them to the verge of insanity. On another note, it examines how the writer takes up a fight that is another person's and questions the writer's effectiveness in the fight for a cause from which the only benefit he reaps is mental or psychological satisfaction. Besides, the chapter addresses how the repressed masses maintain their sanity. And finally, under scrutiny are the tools that Nyamnjoh uses to avoid falling prey to the repressive machine put in place by corrupt politicians and nitwitted leaders unwilling to hear any discussion focusing on their undemocratic practices. It is a sordid tableau of the land of Mimbo. Nyamnjoh's depicts an unsettling clime in which repression, oppression, and corruption are the order of the day. Such malpractices constitute the source of inspiration as well as the bricks with which are constructed the foundation and walls of Nyamnjoh's story, in which he gives free rein to his thoughts about what freedom of expression—devoid of repression—ought to be. These literary broadsides resound louder than the cannons used to muzzle any quest for freedom of expression in the worst imaginable dictatorship.

From the foregoing, the respective authors of the individual chapters in their exploration of repression and its expression, have through various theoretical considerations drawn attention to experiences and attitudes that highlight the literary, historical, sociological, philosophical and psychological ramifications of the trauma engendered by repression as well as the attempts to circumvent it. This collection of essays does not call for a general conclusion as the various chapters stem from different theoretical underpinnings. We have left the respective authors of the individual chapters to draw conclusions to their singular quest for crushing the overbearing weight of oppression and the pain and suffering it ignites. Anchoring on alterity, this book underscores that subsumption of repression, not its negation, as a combative weapon of choice. This explains why literary guerillas hone their art of circumventing repression which permeates societies without sparing even the academe. As such, repressed societies are pictured as nations experiencing an internal deterioration. In such cases, exuberance and apathy are manifestations of the deeply rooted repressive socio-political and psychological traumas and their consequences which writers exorcise as a despicable national – if not pan-African or global – reality to be met with an enthusiastic yearning for redemption and communal progress wherever repression shows its ugly head. In this vein, distance cannot be the cure for this ugly disease as has been demonstrated by the chapter exploring Zora Neale Hurston's endeavor to run away from her past. Instead, novelists must recover the voice of the oppressed in a dictatorship wherein autocratic repression or domination is equivalent to cultural eradication and must be opposed with vigorous resistance. Therefore *The Repressed Expressed* has been an attempt to shape and reshape both the writers' own identity as well as those of their fellow human beings in quest for nothing but freedom from constraints of repression which drives humans to the verge of insanity. All in all, *The Repressed Expressed* has used literary evidence to inform scholarship on opinions and beliefs relating to repression and expression through the critical assessment anchored in the eponym.

The Editors

Bill F. Ndi
Adaku T. Ankumah
Benjamin Hart Fishkin

Works Cited

Bahktin, Mikhail "The Dialogic Imagination: Four Essays." in Nigel Wood and David Lodge. *Modern Criticism and Theory.* Routledge, 2014.

Bahktin, Mikhail M. and Michael Holquist. *The Dialogic Imagination: Four Essays.* U of Texas P, 1981.

Barthes, Roland. *A Lover's Discourse.* Hill and Wang, 2010.

Buckler, William E. *Prose of the Victorian Period* Riverside, 1958.

Cruz, Glenn *Midnight's Orphans: Anglo-Indians in Post/colonial Literature,* Peter Lang, 2006.

Dickens, Charles. *Little Dorritt.* 1892. Classic Books, 2007.

Eagleton, Terry. *Literary Theory: An Introduction* U of Minnesota P 1983.

Elshtain, Jean Bethke. *Real Politics at the Center of Everyday Life.* John Hopkins UP, 1997.

Fishkin, Benjamin H. Adaku T. Ankumah, Festus Fru Ndeh and Bill F. Ndi *Outward Evil Inward Battle: Human Memory in Literature.* Langaa Research PCIG, 2013.

Larson, Charles R. *The Ordeal of the African Writer* Zed, 2001.

Milton, John. *Aeropagetica. The Essential Prose of John Milton,* edited by William Kerrigan, John Rumrich, and Stephen M. Fallon. Modern Library Classics, 2013.

Ngugi wa Thiong'o *Decolonising the Mind* James Currey/Heinemann, 1997.

——————. *Something Torn and New* Civitas, 2009.

Nyamnjoh, Francis, B. "Intimate Strangers: Connecting Fiction and Ethnography" in *Alternation* vol. 19, no.1, 2012, pp. 65-92.

Palmer, Eustace. *An Introduction to the African Novel.* APC, 1972.

Rousseau, Jean-Jacques. *The Social Contract.* Fitzhenry & Whiteside, 1978.

Scales, Pat. *Teaching Banned Books.* American Library, 2001.

Scholes, Robert, Nancy R. Comley, and Janice Peritz. *The Practice of Writing,* Bedford St. Martin's, 2001.

Shakespeare, William. *Julius Caesar. The Yale Shakespeare* (Complete Works), edited Wilbur S. Cross and Tucker Book Yale UP, 1993.

West, Mae. http://www.overlawyered.com/2015/09/are-you-showing-contempt-for-this-court-no-im-doing-my-best-to-hide-it/ Accessed 21 Nov. 2016.

Chapter 1

Francis Nyamnjoh's *The Disillusioned African:* a Philosophy of Liberation

Yosimbom Hassan Mbiydzenyuy

In his "Editor's Introduction" to Enrique Dussel (1996), Eduardo Mendieta argues that the central theses of Dussel's Liberation Philosophy highlight that "eurocentrism must be taken seriously as a *philosophical* problem" [because] "Dussel's [...] Liberation Philosophy de-centers itself in order to make a global or planetary claim [by ascending] from its particularity to globality" (xxvi). Dussel (1985) corroborates Mendieta's claims with this explanation that "Philosophy of liberation... functions in the name of the poor, the oppressed, the other, the one who, like a hostage within the system, testifies to the fetishism of its totalization and predicts its death in the liberating action of the dominated" (178). It involves the risk of death because it "emerges within the system, as a hostage and a witness to a new future order"; it "criticizes the system [and so] the system must criticize it, must persecute it" (179-80). As a magisterium that functions in the name of the poor/oppressed/other, liberation is an act that opens the breach, pierces the wall, and searches deeper into future exteriority. Liberation is the act by which the oppressed express/realize themselves. It incorporates a double moment in that it is "a denial of a denial in the system... a negation of a negation" (Dussel 62). Liberation holds that "[t]o deny what is denied by the system is to affirm the system in its foundation, for what is negated in the system does not cease to be an intrinsic moment in the system" (62).

In short, "Liberation is to leave the prison and affirm the history that was anterior and exterior to the prison" (62). Liberation Philosophy is inscribed within the popular traditions of the peripheral world and in the philosophical schools of Hamann, Schelling, Schleiermacher, Dilthey, Gadamer, Ricoeur, Levinas, Kierkegaard, Marx, and Bloch (Dussel 1998: 12). To Dussel, "[a]fter the fall of the Berlin Wall, Liberation Philosophy... developed a *positive* discourse from out of misery... and affirmed the real and necessary process of liberation of the great majority of humanity: trans-modernity as a future-oriented project" (14). By identifying *The Disillusioned African (TDA)* as a Nyamnjohian statement on the philosophy of liberation, this essay attempts to answer four Dusselian/transmodern(ist) questions: "Who is situated in the 'Exteriority' of The Cameroons/Mimboland system as the alienated and oppressed?" "What is the relation between women-men, the 'erotics'"? "What is the nature of cultural reproduction?" and "Which 'Totalities' have been fetishized in *TDA*?".

According to Magda (1989), Sardar (2004), Ghisi (1999, 2006 and 2008), Alcoff (2012), Ateljevic (2013) and Dussel (2004), the transmodern dream comprises "[a] future trans-modern culture [with] a rich pluriversity" and the practice of authentic intercultural dialogues that are conscious of "existing asymmetries [between] imperial-core or part of the semi-peripheral [and] central chorus like Europe... and peripheral world" (Dussel19). The transmodern project as a liberation intention involves dialogue and affirmation. *Affirmation* implies the self-valorization of one's own negated or devalued cultural moments (25). *Dialogue* is the intercourse between the critical cultural innovators that "is transmodern because the creative force does not come from the interior but rather from [the] exteriority or borderlands" (25) of modernity. Both affirmation and dialogue result in "the affirmation and development of the cultural alterity of postcolonial communities which subsumes within itself the best elements of Modernity" (26). The commingling of both should not develop "a cultural style that tends towards an undifferentiated or empty globalized unity, but rather a *trans*-modern pluriversality (with many universalities: Francophone, Anglophone, Lusophone, Hispanophone etc.), one which is multicultural, and engaged in a critical intercultural dialogue" (26). Ghisi, Sardar, Ateljevic, Alcoff and Dussel identify several engaging tenets of transmodernity. To them, transmodernity engenders an optimistic and democratic planetary vision. It supports a postpatriarchal rejection of domination; it acknowledges a post-secular rejection of religious divisions/dogmas; it promotes radical transdisciplinarity; it recognizes the right of each community to develop in ways that are uniquely suited to its culture and it articulates a critical cosmopolitanism. Transmodernity also encourages diversity of perspectives and pluriversal knowledge, and it is in constant dialogue with modernity and postmodernity. This essay further argues that *TDA* attests that transmodernity gives Cameroonians/Africans "the necessary political and epistemological position to transcend all (post)essentialist contradictions and treatments of race, gender, tradition, culture, economy, etc., and to create [a(n) Cameroonian/African] politics without inherent domination and superiority of one over another" (Ateljevic 46). Even though Cerutti-Guldberg (1989), Schutte (1993), and Castro-Gómez (1996 and 2008), have argued that Dussel's invocation of a "we"-subject among the poor returns us to a modernist meta-narrative, this essay is interested in the fact that Dussel's transmodernity is designed to retell the story of Europe itself. Further, it also incorporates the role of its other in its formation as a more accurate and more comprehensive and coherent account. It then proceeds to retelling the story of world history without a centered formation either in Europe or anywhere, in order that no one becomes the permanent center or persistent periphery (Dussel 1995: 33).

In the nations of what Dussel calls "peripheral capitalism" such as The Cameroons, the oppressed classes constitute the majority (1996: 8). In *TDA*, that majority is excluded from the "formal" democracies of Africa and are the manipulated by the leaders/elites. The Cameroonian/African leaders in *TDA* practice a "politicism" that does not understand the importance of the economical. As Keba points out in one of his letters to Moungo, the failure of the formal African democracies, shows that "democratic" politics without "economic" consciousness is a fictitious formality of false and reductive "rationality" (Dussel 8). This absence of economic consciousness is symbolically captured through an article entitled "Africa Forever," which examines Africa as a cow being milked by a black leader, under the strict supervision of a white businessman (Nyamnjoh 9). The milking of Africa is the milking of the African masses because in most African countries, peasants cultivate food and cash crops that enable the civil servants to excel in barren consumerism. The African concept of the taxpayer's money is different from that of Euro-America because the "only taxpayer in the economic sense of the word is the peasant who actually produces, who creates wealth" (Nyamnjoh 18) while the civil servants instead "squander the toil and bleeding sweat of the peasant" (18). In connivance with the *Ngomna* (the government) that specializes in "nicking from the blindfolded and the forsaken" (18), civil servants have failed to match their consumerism with creativity. When *Ngomnas* fail to make the peasants dance to their tunes, the foreign aid intended to relieve the peasants of famine and malnourishment is misappropriated by *Ngomna*-backed urban-center exploiters. Thus, the Cameroonian *Ngomna* fails to see The Cameroons as a community of communities. There is a larger community of a supra-national type, but whose particular communities – the ruler and the ruled, peasants and civil servants – can choose to have closer contact with other communities.

Ngomna's and the civil servants' politics of exploitation x-rays the nature and effects of the center-exteriority relationship as it affects the development of African economies which are lesser partners in the asymmetrical arrangements within the international economic system. The continuous milking of the exhausted African cow results in inequalities in the division of labor between the center and the periphery and low incomes in the urban centers. There is a trickledown effect. The weak industrial base of the periphery ensures that the relationship between Europe/interiority and Africa/exteriority is marked by great hope and even greater disappointment. Thus, Africa is a pyramid of three distinct classes: the toiling peasants who live in the rural areas, have no opportunity to steal either from others or the state and are only called upon to entertain their urban Lords/Masters either during National Day Celebrations, Revolution Anniversaries or at the visit of a foreign head of state (20-21). Also, there are the civil servants and literate or semi-literate urban dwellers who have the opportunity to steal from others, but who find it difficult to steal directly from the state because they are constantly under surveillance. This group is midway between the abject poverty and hardship of the village and the filthy riches and sumptuous plenty of the self-elected few (21-2). Finally, there are the African leaders who rule without legitimacy, have the exclusive opportunity to steal from the state; the self-elected watch dogs of the National Cake whose motto is get rich or perish: national political figures, their provincial and regional representatives, top civil servants and pseudo-intellectuals who forge panegyric poems and compose praise songs with the hope of being appointed directors of public institution (23).

This alienating/exteriorizing pyramidal structure reminds one that Bourdieu's concepts of economic capital, social capital and cultural capital are crucial to interiority-exteriority relations. *Social capital* is "the aggregate of the actual or potential resources linked to possession of a durable network of institutionalised [sic] relationships of mutual acquaintance and recognition"; and "membership in a group which provides members with the backing of the collectively-owned capital" (51). *Cultural capital* comprises three main subtypes: "institutionalised" [sic] cultural capital is formal education; "embodied" cultural capital are internalized cultural norms, and "objectified" cultural capital are objects with cultural value. *Economic capital* comprises objects that can be directly converted into money or "institutionalized in the form of property rights" (47). Bourdieu's three types of capital chart the dimensions in which social status and hierarchy can be described in Africa; with the peasants continuously being deprived of economic, social and cultural capital by the civil servants and African leaders. The pyramid establishes a praxis of domination that confirms Euro-North America as the center and Africa as the periphery. Within this praxis, the peasants/Africans are forced by the *Ngomna* of The Cameroons/Euro-North America to participate in the system that alienates them. They are compelled to perform actions contrary to their nature and historical essence and when they attempt to liberate themselves, the domination is transformed into repression, "the being that in practice reduces the other to non-being" (Dussel 54-56). This happens when Keba, Nyamnjoh's protagonist lands at the Kinshasa airport. His landing coincides with the return of an exiled opposition leader from Belgium. Like his Cameroonian/African counterpart(s), Mobutu unleashes his dogs of war, and the airport is invaded with bullets, grenades, and tear gas (147) and Keba is seriously wounded in one arm that would eventually be amputated at the Laquintini Hospital upon Keba's return to The Cameroons.

When the Yondo Black (Douala Ten) political crisis happens, Keba tries to accomplish the liberation ambitions he nurtured during his sojourn in England. Unfortunately, Yondo Black and his fellow "subversives" are tried and sentenced by a Military Tribunal in Yaoundé. This is followed by the launching of the Social Democratic Front (SDF) party against the wishes of a government that is determined to frustrate genuine change (148). Yondo Black, his friends, the SDF and its militants are considered by *Ngomna* as the other who has a history/culture of exteriority, and so cannot be respected. The social, economic and cultural capital centers of Bourdieu's postulation have refused to let the other be other. Government-backed institutions like the Military Tribunal in Yaoundé have continued to incorporate the Yondo Black and SDF other into a strange/foreign totality "to totalize exteriority, to systematize alterity [and] alienation" (Dussel 1985: 53). The alienation of SDF militants such as Keba, forces them "to lose their Being by incorporating them as a moment, an aspect, an instrument of another's Being [thereby displacing them] from their own center and [making them] to revolve around the center of a totality alien to them" (Dussel 53). This totalization of exteriority is further captured through three documents that reveal the white man's biases towards Africans: Barley's *The Innocent Anthropologist* in which the author relies on the limited/limiting experiences of the Dowayos of Northern Cameroons to conclude that "Africa is home to the most astonishing physiques" and "unromantic and brutish" sexual encounters (110); Dr Vancroft's fieldwork memoirs in which Vancroft fails to distinguish between the Grassfield Region of The Cameroons, Cameroon, Africa and the Third World (111); and the Belgian Minister of Colonies, Belquin's 1920 speech ("The Duties of Missionaries in Our Colony") commissioning missionaries leaving for Belgian Congo to "consider all blacks as little children whom [they] must continue to deceive and manipulate even long after independence" (119). Barley's, Vancroft's and Benquin's generalizations are Eurocentrism at their best. But, when Barley declares that "[e]very tribe had someone to despise" (110), he unwittingly acknowledges, from the point of view of transmodern relative advantage and superiority, that every race, every nation, and perhaps, every anthropologist has someone to despise. The launching of the SDF is an attempt to create a centerless center and Black's, Keba's and the SDF's attempts to bring genuine change confirm that "liberation of the oppressed is put into effect by the oppressed, but through the mediation of the critical mentality of the teacher, the leader, the organic intellectual" (Dussel 93). Yondo Black and Keba are prototypical organic intellectuals because they do not live in an ivory tower – they live and work "in and with the people, as an 'organ' in the body politic – with and within the people" (93).

Contrary to Dussel's argument that "the cultural revolution by liberation must start and must be put into effect by the people and from within its popular culture" (1985: 93), the SDF adopted the slogan "Power to the People." The slogan's surrender of power to the people establishes the SDF as part of a popular culture; the nucleus of resistance to oppressors. This is not a suggestion that the SDF and other forms of popular culture come to life spontaneously. The Cameroonian people alone cannot liberate themselves; the critical mentality of organic intellectuals (such as Keba, Moungo, and Monique) and of critical communities or political parties (such as the SDF), are "indispensable so that a people... discern the worst that it has in itself (introjected imperialist culture) and the best that it has from antiquity (cultural exteriority)"(Dussel 94). Both the organic intellectual and the critical community must be aware of the atrocities of "culture of the center" that always looks to dominate in the present order. In the world of *TDA*, the imperialist culture is the refined culture of Euro-North American/African/Cameroonian elites. Echoing Fanon (1967), Dussel asserts that these African elites, alienated minorities in their own nations, are scorned by the creators of the culture of the center thereby making them outcasts of history. They ignore their national culture, despise their skin color, pretend to be white, speak English or French with Oxbridgean and Parisian accents respectively. They dress, eat, and live as if they were in the center (Dussel 91-2). In *TDA,* Moungo tells us that African leaders suffer from "a delusion of superiority and a bizarre nose for red herrings" (26). They are childishly elated to "have houses in Europe or America where they can afford to live better than the middle class white that stubbornly claims to be superior to them" (26). During every Bank Holiday, African presidents' and ministers' wives jostle with middle class housewives in giant supermarkets in Oxford Street where they have their hair retouched. These leaders buy designers' rights for particular dresses in order to stop other women from dressing like their wives/mistresses who boast of a thousand pairs of shoes, rings of ruby, diamond and sapphire. African leaders know nothing about their countries' problems, but they know American, English, French, and Western histories. They excel in Elizabethan Literature, uphold Victorian values, recite Shakespeare, chuckle at Chaucer's tongue-in-cheek humor, praise Dickens' plume, criticize Racine's sentimentalism, and agree with Corneille's fanatical commitment to "La Patrie" (27). The colonial schools taught them to make passing or footnote reference to their people or ethnicity. In transmodern terms, the African leaders/elites know what they do not need and need what they do not know. At the same time, economically, they encourage the production of what they do not consume and consume what they do not produce.

Despite the leaders' socio-economic and political aberrations and the resultant pessimism that permeates Nyamnjoh's analysis of the Cameroonian masses'/Africans' victimhood, the fighting spirit of transmodernity pervades the world of *TDA*. Especially in the final dream-letter from Keba to Moungo's wife, Keba predicts "the signs of a crumbling system" (134). The crumbling system in *TDA* demonstrates that there is transmodern politics when the boundary separating those who claim to have been born for politics from those whom the system claims were born for the "bare" life of economic and social necessity is put into question. The commingling of the "downtrodden and forgotten bulk of the Darkened continent" (150) is a transmodernist statement that genuine political or artistic activities always involve forms of innovation that tear bodies from their assigned places. The disruption that the Keba-Moungo epistolary exchanges effect is not simply a reordering of the relations of power between existing groups. As a *dissensus* (Ranciere 2010 and 2011), the violence and bloodshed that has made the tyrants desperate is an activity that cuts across all forms of cultural identity. Both the novel and its transmodernist activities have to do with reorienting general perceptual space and disrupting forms of belonging/becoming.

The Waterloo of African tyranny—a transmodern project that is a corealization of solidarity and which bonds center to periphery, woman to man, race to race, and occidental to Third World cultures – can only be assured by a liberating politician who is the prototype of the statesman. We are not referring to antiheroes of African leadership/elitism but to the Kebas, the Moungos and the Moniques who provide provocative insights into The Cameroons'/Africa's complex web of despair. Their transmodern struggles negate the negation of the oppressed and affirm their non-exteriority; they are prophets of life; founders of freedom, not its assassins (Dussel 77). These are the real heroes who know that the potential relativism of transmodern pluriversality can and should be avoided. These can be realized by developing provisional—African/Cameroonian/Francophone/Anglophone—metanarratives of global history that can illuminate local conditions. Yondo Black's trials and the launching of the SDF party are examples of these conditions. Provisional metanarratives such as the SDF contingently ensure a move away from vertical authority toward "flatter," more "horizontal," organizations. They also nurture an uninformed view as "global reconciliation" within the global vision of connected humanity. This recognizes that each community or region needs to be free to develop in ways that are uniquely suited to its culture. They have the potential to articulate a critical cosmopolitanism and to produce knowledge beyond Third World and Eurocentric fundamentalisms by fostering a decolonial approach that would search for universal knowledge as pluriversal knowledge based on horizontal dialogues among different traditions of thought.

The second transmodern practical horizon in *TDA* is the relationship between women and men. In Dusselian terms, the other of the machist totality is the woman. In the world of *TDA*, the masculine comprises the subject, the activity and the possession of the phallus and the feminine constitutes the object and passivity. The women-men relation contributes to transmodern liberational categories that need to be de- and re-constructed through an examination of how phallocracy becomes conquest, plutocracy, and social domination; the machist culture of hypocrisy and the mystification of women's domination (Dussel 1985: 9). That is, political action consists in showing as political what was viewed as "social," "economic," or "domestic" (Rancière 2011: 4); blurring the feminine and masculine boundaries. It is what happens whenever "domestic" agents such as women reconfigure their quarrel as one concerning the common, concerning what place belongs or does not belong to them and who is able or unable to make enunciations and demonstrations about the common (4). There is transmodern politics when there is a disagreement about what is the relation between women and men, when the boundary separating the machist political from the feminine social or the public from the domestic is put into question. Erotics, to some degree, is a way of re-partitioning the political from the non-political. That is why, in *TDA*, it seems to occur "out of place," in places not supposed to be political (4).

In *TDA*, the relationship between women and men is problematic, often referred to with epistemic caution. The relationship is understood without being rigidly defined – much like the concept of "cultural area" whose contours are blurred, but whose effects are clear. This women-men relationship is a perspective – that of African leaders – and implies a specific tradition in the sense of a living transmission that takes various forms of marginalization. That relationship is patriarchal because it is built on power relations in which the African women's (wives/mistresses of African leaders and the female masses) interests are subordinated to those of the African leaders. These power relations take on many forms, from the sexual division of labor and the social organization of procreation to the internalized norms of femininity by which the leaders live. In The Cameroons/Africa of *TDA*, power rests on social meaning given to biological sexual difference because African leaders preach African Socialism, yet find nothing wrong with European consumerism, purchasing a £40,000 bedroom in London for a voluptuous concubine. Again, they stop every other woman from bearing the same designer name with their wives (24). These leaders equally purchase superfluous pairs of shoes, rings of ruby, diamond and sapphire for their wives and mistresses and encourage them to be impulsive squandermaniacs, globetrotting in search of economy-crippling body creams and make-ups (26).

The above points each carry shibboleths of a Cameroonian androcentrism that focuses on what Mazrui refers to as the distortions of "urbanization without industrialization"; "verbal education without productive training"; "secularization without scientification"; and "capitalist greed without capitalist discipline" (5, 6). The term, androcentrism, coined by Gilman in 1911 denotes a system of thought centered exclusively on male identity and values.

In *TDA*, the female constitutes a deviation from a norm. The novel depicts a perfect example of how the belief that man is the "superior" sex affects the organization of social institutions to the extent that an androcentric system automatically rewards the "superior" gender. Socio-economic and political thought revolves around the "man/woman" dualism, but that is not an equitable relationship because it connotes a master/slave dichotomy. The superiority of the male half of the equation is predicated upon the subordination of the female half. The latter half is thus exiled from the value paradigm and only surfaces when the African leaders wish to exercise aspects of kleptomania. Even though both the wives and mistresses of these leaders enjoy a certain degree of superiority over other women and men in The Cameroons/Africa, these male leaders consider their wives/mistresses *personae non gratae* when it comes to socio-economic and political issues that matter because their wives/mistresses are simply there to satisfy their risible insatiable appetites.

However, Keba and Moungo are already making attempts to tear down the walls of androcentrism in The Cameroons. In their virulent condemnation of the powers that be, they choose Moungo's wife, Monique, as their partner in struggle. Their alliance indicates that transmodernism is amongst other fundamental concerns of the politics of "othering," marginalization and the construction of a "subaltern" subjectivity by colonialism. Moungo, Keba and Monique are out to dismantle naturalized assumptions about gender through a denial of the centrality of imperialist or patriarchal culture (abrogation) and a seizure and reconstitution of imperial culture and/or discourse (appropriation). These strategies through which patriarchal and/or imperial norms are rejected and/or subverted from a transmodernist standpoint have culminated in Keba's decision to settle in Menchum Division where he is actively teaching "the peasants how to make political and economic capital out of their sweat and toil" (150). Keba's lessons to the peasants constitute a two-dimensional scream (Holloway 12): a demonstration of peasant rage that arises from present experience and carries within itself a hope and a projection of possible otherness. Keba's scream implies a tension between androcentrism that exists in The Cameroons and the apparent equality of gender which exists. The scream from Keba, the critical mentality, the teacher, the leader, the organic intellectual, is a scream of horror and hope. Transmodernity emphasizes that "horror arises from the bitterness of history, but if there is no transcendence of that bitterness, the one-dimensional horror leads only to political depression and theoretical closure"; and that, "if the hope is not grounded firmly in that same bitterness of history, it becomes just a one-dimensional and silly expression of optimism" (Holloway 14).

Another practical horizon of transmodernity as a philosophy of liberation is that of the African/Cameroonian people as the *subject of culture*; the question of cultural reproduction. The pedagogy of liberation is a cultural revolution, and in the Africa of *TDA*, it is a revolution of popular culture in which neither folklorism nor Eurocentric rationalism, as Dussel would have it, is the

> liberating reason, which discovers a new 'objectivity', has as its function to unify the historical 'tradition' of a people with the necessary technological and scientific development according to the real exigencies of the nation, and not simply imitating foreign models. (11)

Unfortunately, there seems to be no cultural reproduction in *TDA* because the "imperialist culture" of Euro-North American elites, the culture that all other cultures are measured against, is dominant. In Dusselian terms, "[t]he Mona Lisa critiques all other paintings; Beethoven's Fifth Symphony catalogs all other musical compositions; Notre Dame is the proto-type of all churches" (1985: 91). This culture is partially refracted in the oligarchical culture of dominant groups within Africa/The Cameroons. It is the culture that the African ruling class admire and ape because they are fascinated by the "progress" of the center. In *TDA*, these elites, alienated minorities in The Cameroons, like elsewhere in Africa, are scorned by the creators of the culture of the center viz. that of the Queendom. Thus, the universe of *TDA* resembles Fishkin's postulation that in *Mind Searching*: "[t]he culture gravitates with gratification [and] [p]eople have a sense of entitlement to luxuries and material possessions on an individual basis and are reckless when it comes to using power and natural resources for posterity" (qtd. in Benjamin Fishkin, Adaku Ankumah and Bill Ndi 181). Such undependable leadership is key to tracing the geo-politics of knowing/sensing/believing as well as body-politics of knowing/sensing/understanding the predicament faced by the African masses. When Fanon closes his exploration with this supplication, "[o]h my body, make of me always a man who questions!" (181), he is expressing, in a single sentence, the basic categories of transmodernist epistemology: "the biographical sensing of the Black body in the Third World, anchoring a politics of knowledge that is both ingrained in the body and in local histories" (Dussel 132).

In *TDA*, the culture of the oppressed is the culture of the masses. Keba, Moungo and Monique assert that it is the reproduction *ad nauseam*, the kitschiest vulgarization of imperialist culture refracted by the leaders' oligarchical culture and passed on for consumption by magazines, schools and national day celebrations. Keba recalls how in primary school, he and Moungo were taught to sing "London's Burning" and read readers written to suit the needs of English pupils. The Francophones amongst them paid religious attention to Tintin. They were treated to a school leaving examination set in Cambridge and Paris by examiners who knew absolutely nothing about The Cameroons. In secondary school, they were told that history, geography and literature are exclusively Western, and they learnt to recite the rise and fall of the English Pitts, Walpoles, Disraelis, Gladstones, Palmerstones, Chamberlains, and Pretenders. They crammed everything ever written by Frederick the Great of Prussia, Catherine the Great of Russia, Joseph II and Maria Theresa; Prince Metternich of Austria; Louis the Sun King; Napoleon, the warring soldier of France; Bismarck, the Iron Chancellor of Germany; Churchill, the witty Premier of war-time Britain; etc. Geographically, they knew about ship building in (Tyne, Tees, Clyde) and the agrarian and industrial revolutions in England; more about the Rhine-Ruhr industrial complex in Germany and more French vineyards than their own villages (98). This entire process of cultural alienation is profoundly ideological inasmuch as it expresses supposedly universal knowledge or ideas and hides the domination that oppressed countries and classes suffer. Through alienation of the masses from their real culture, ideology propagates imperialist enterprises and produces a market for its products. To Dussel,

[c]ultural domination is thus an element of political and economic alienation; ideological cultural imperialism today surpasses all other types of anterior cultural influx. [It is supported by the sciences and] those whom Chomsky calls 'intellectual warriors', the elite formed at Harvard or Yale. (1985:92)

TDA portrays these elites, viewing the real culture of the masses simply as folklore fit only for performances, such as traditional dances during national celebrations and visits of their Western dignitaries. In *TDA*, the task of liberating and reproducing the indigenous culture(s) of The Cameroons rests in the hands of Keba, Moungo and Monique who are consistently aware that beyond the oligarchical culture of the dominating elites can be found a diluted national culture. The critical nuances of the Keba-Moungo epistolary exchanges constitute the affirmation of national culture; a liberating confrontation with imperialist culture, which is a necessary first step on the road of the Cultural Revolution of Menchum Division.

The Cultural Revolution starts from within their popular culture and is put into effect by the people of Menchum. In order to reproduce an/a indigenous/popular culture that possesses the symbols and the traditions of accumulated wisdom, Keba demonstrates a memory of historical commitments and knowledge of its enemies as he abandons the treasures of city life in the Queendom and Douala to return to Menchum Division where he "live[s] and work[s] with the resettled but forgotten victims of the 1986 Lake Nyos disaster" (149). To authenticate that popular culture, far from being a minor culture, is relatively the least contaminated nucleus of resistance to oppressors, the peasants of Menchum assume their transmodernity/transmodernization as messengers of change as the narrator make of him "the only hope for a better and caring Africa" (149). These messengers not only engender dialogues between the critics of the metropolitan-core and the critics of the cultural-periphery but engineer dialogues between the critics of the periphery. They start as intercultural South-South dialogues then gradually become South-North dialogues. The dialogues will bring about transversal and mutual cross-fertilization among the critical thinkers of the periphery and those from border spaces of Menchum.

The ethos of such pedagogical and cultural reproduction demands that the Kebas know how to listen with respect to the people because "[o]nly the genuine teacher who has become a patient and enthusiastic disciple can attain to an adequate discernment of the reality in which a people finds itself" (95). Such patience and enthusiasm engender a lifestyle that fosters humility and service as well as "dedicates a critical awareness to affirming the values inherent in the young and in the people" (95). Keba fits squarely into this role because he has "lost faith completely in the modern power elite" and believes that "[a] new sort of leader [has] to be moulded[sic] for Africa, and as far as he [is] concerned, the peasants [offer] the best hope in that connection" (149). Keba manifests a collaboration that unifies, mobilizes, organizes, and creates an anti-ideological veracity as a fundamental pedagogical attitude as "[Keba] is revolutionising[sic] the peasants with his ideas" (149). He is teaching them to speak out for themselves by asking questions that embarrass the rich and powerful. Keba's postmodernist aim is ensuring that the Cameroonian/African elitist model of democracy, freedom, justice and power meets its Waterloo (149). He teaches the masses that from liberating revolutionary culture will spring forth a new world culture, an alternative much richer than imperialist/oligarchical culture, viz. transmodernist culture.

Fetishization of totalities accounts for another transmodern perspective as Liberation Philosophy affirms "the political as in the empires or the state; as historical manifestations of the divinity [...] because ruling ideology is a historical manifestation of the divine, such as the 'Western and Christian civilization' or the *American way of life*" (Dussel 11). The concept of fetishism is central to Karl Marx's critique of capitalist society because with capitalism there is an inversion of the relation between people and things, between subject and object (Holloway 2002/2005: 81). Fetishism implies that "there is an objectification of the subject and a subjectification of the object: things become the subjects of society, people become the objects" (82). Fetishism does not only bring physical misery, it sanctions the inversion of things and people. Thus, Marx condemns capitalism for the fetishization of social relations. But, from the popular cultures of Africa, the transmodernist can, however, affirm the absolute only in the case that it would ground, justify, or give hope to the oppressed in their process of liberation. By leaving Douala for "Menchum Division where he plans to live and work with the forgotten victims of the 1986 Lake Nyos Disaster" (149), Keba affirms that absolute. This move is a negation of divinification; it teaches peasants to know and assume their responsibility as "messengers of change" (149). The negation of the divinification of every totality, as negation of the negation of the human person, is the negative and correlative moment of its affirmation. *TDA* draws attention to collective transmodern hermeneutical task to discern in these fetishisms their regressive elements and to empower the creative moments of human affirmation of justice, autonomy, and freedom (Dussel 11).

In *TDA*, the milking of Africa, capitalism, consumerism, the fate of African peasants, the pyramidal structure of African society, the African leaders' false sense of pride, the biased nature of Western research, tribalism, elections, democracy, monopartyism, multypartyism, neocolonialism, the African's acquisition of wrong/misguided education, imperial culture, patriarchy, etc. are totalized and fetishized. The Western trained oppressive African leaders/elites have instrumentally reified them without considering their utility and the exigencies on the part of historical subjects, their interests, and the thematic objects. Their fetishization is also motivated by the leaders' craving to create a fake consensus hegemony (Dussel 1985). Viewed from the perspective of the excluded, the historical record of the above fetishisms is full of institutionalized dissimulations that result in numerous socio-economic and political aberrancy: Africa's pyramidal structure; the institutionalization of monopartyism; the Yondo Black affair; illegal plundering of African natural resources; assimilation of Eurocentric epistemologies; the forgotten victims of the 1986 Lake Nyos disaster; and compulsive consumption of Western commodities. By criticizing these fetishizations, the transmodern ambition in this essay proposes a rearguard criticism based on the experiences of large, marginalized African minorities and majorities that struggle against unjustly imposed marginality and inferiority, with the purpose of strengthening their resistance (Santos vii). This transmodern yearning acknowledges that there is a certain malleability to the language of transmodernity that prepares transmodern grounds for both valorizing non-fetishization conceptions of liberation and for proposing counterhegemonic understandings and uses of fetishized concepts, such as human rights and democracy (ix).

Reading *TDA* as transmodernist philosopher of liberation, the image that keeps coming to mind is a nightmarish one like that painted by Holloway (8-9). Africans are all in a room with four walls, a floor, a ceiling and no windows or door. It is a bleak room that reminds one of Fishkin's description of Nyamnjoh's universe as a prison in which both warden and prisoner share identical fate in varying degrees, "a mix up, an untidy mess or confusion in which people do not know what they are doing or why they are doing it… a tale of upheaval" (185). The room is furnished and African leaders are sitting comfortably, while the masses are not. The walls are advancing steadily inwards, threatening to crush Africans to death. There are discussions within the room, but they are mostly about how to arrange the furniture. Africans leaders do not seem to see the walls advancing. From time to time, there are elections about how to place the furniture. These elections are not insignificant: they make African leaders more comfortable, the masses less so; they may even affect the speed at which the walls are moving, but they do nothing to stop their relentless advance. As the walls grow closer, Africans react in different ways. The leaders absolutely refuse to see the advance of the walls, shutting themselves tightly into a world of Disney and defending with determination the chairs on which they are sitting. Some (like the militants of the SDF) see and denounce the movement of the walls, build a party with a radical program and look forward to a day in the future when there will be no walls. Others (Keba, Moungo and Monique) run to the walls and try desperately to find cracks, or faults beneath the surface, or to create cracks by banging the walls. Looking for and creating cracks is a transmodern activity which involves throwing ourselves against the walls and then standing back to try and see cracks or faults in the surface.

The two activities are complementary: transmodernity as a philosophy of liberation makes little sense unless it is understood as part of the desperate effort to find a way out, to create cracks that defy the apparently unstoppable advance of capital, of the walls that are pushing Africa to her destruction. Nyamnjoh captures this defiant act of creation of cracks by structuring the plot of *TDA* around the indefatigable attempts by Keba, Moungo and Monique to sensitize the Cameroonian/African masses and the Cameroonian/African leaders/elites. From the point of view of the leaders who defend their armchairs and discuss the arrangement of the furniture in the run-up to the next election, Africans are undoubtedly mad – the Kebas, the Moungos and the Moniques who run about seeing cracks that are invisible to the eyes of the African leaders sitting in the armchairs. The aggravating thing is that they may be right; perhaps we are mad, perhaps there is no way out, perhaps the cracks we see exist only in our fantasy. The old revolutionary certainty can no longer stand. There is absolutely no guarantee of a happy ending. The opening of cracks is a transmodern deconstruction/opening of an African world that presents itself as closed. It is the opening of categories that on the surface negate the power of human doing, in order to discover at their core, the doing that they deny and incarcerate. This *ad hominem* critique attempts to break through the appearances of a world of things and uncontrollable forces in order to understand the world in terms of the power of human doing. It is the recognition that irreducibly multiple and heterogeneous forms of power flow in every direction within the social fabric, offering multiple points of resistance and garnering an epistemological insurrection. The method of the transmodern cracks is dialectical, not in the sense of presenting a neat flow of thesis, antithesis and synthesis, but in the sense of a negative dialectics, a dialectic of the African masses' misfitting. Transmodernity as a philosophy of liberation thinks of the African world from the perspective of the masses' misfitting. African transmodernists want to understand the force of the masses' misfitting. They want to know how banging their heads against the wall over and over again will bring the wall crumbling down.

Thus, this essay has proposed a double cultural disarmament, both horizontal and vertical for transmodernity as a philosophy of liberation. This kind of liberation is akin to what Emmanuel Fru Doh endorses by considering Anglophone Cameroon Literature as a weapon/battle against the marginalization of Anglophones (13). Horizontally, Cameroonians/Africans must de-absolutize their respective transmodern cultures. They must relativize them by recognizing that they do represent for each of them their anchoring point. They are neither the symbolic reference point of their dialogues nor a point of subsumption from the viewpoint of an alterity assuming postcolonial Cameroonian/African world(s) as a transmodern organization characterized by plurality and diversity. Cameroonians/Africans must ensure that the aspirations of transmodernity are not defined starting from the categories/presuppositions of one culture – Anglophone Francophone, Cameroon, Lusophone, Hispanophone, African, Western etc. – but "starting from all cultures which are present" (Vachon 40 qtd. in Eberhard 19). This implies that Africans need to reflect on the intercultural foundations of transmodern liberation by turning their attention not only to Africa's diversity but also to the epistemological, anthropological and cosmological foundations that exist in the diverse intercontinental traditions. An intercultural approach to transmodern liberation will take Africans further by accepting the process of the transmodern dialogue to abandon both obnoxious African and Western references and to accept other frames of reference (Eberhard 19). Such liberation also accepts that in the liberation process, new frameworks as the SDF party and Keba's education of the masses of Menchum are invented and that they do not necessarily need to have or claim any kind of universal validity or assume the status of a totality and eventually become fetishized. Vertically, transmodern cultural disarmament will consist in "liberating [African] life from the exclusive grip of a single culture of [transmodernity] or of the sum of cultures of [transmodernity], but by going through them" (Vachon 1995b: 40-41 qtd. in Eherhard 19). In this regard, Nyamnjoh's transmodern liberation is neither only about preserving Cameroonian traditional cultures, nor about accepting the different Cameroonian ways of living, "of co-existing in a mutual indifference or in a resignated tolerance" (Eberhard 19). It requires a common horizon and a new vision symbolized in *TDA* by Keba's willful descent from the stand of an "advantaged" elite to that of a "disadvantaged" leader of the masses or Fanon's "amputated" humanity within the restricted categories of epidermalization (Nyamnjoh 112). This new vision would be a continuous journey of both divergence/redivergence and discovery/rediscovery.

In the first part of this essay, I attempted an insight into the tenets of transmodernist liberational philosophy. In the second, I used explications of characters such as Keba, Moungo, Monique, the militants of the SDF party, the victims of the Lake Nyos Disaster and the African leaders/elites to assert that *TDA* subscribes to a transmodern philosophy of liberation by drawing the readers' attention to the distinction between "epistemic locations" and "social locations" (6). In line with *TDA*'s transmodernist liberational inclinations, I have argued that African leaders/elites are socially located in the oppressed side of First World/Third World power relations does not automatically mean that they are thinking from a subaltern epistemic location. It has been proven that transmodern/subaltern epistemic perspectives are knowledge/action coming from below, and that produces a critical perspective of hegemonic knowledge in the center/periphery power relations involved. However, the essay does not claim a transmodern populism where counteraction/knowledge produced from below against hegemonic domination is automatically a transmodern subaltern move/episteme. The contention has been that Keba must fulfill the conditions of an organic intellectual to be able to qualify to lead the victims of the Lake Nyos Disaster and other subalternized groups. The essay recommends "a horizontal dialogue as opposed to the vertical monologue of the West/[African leaders, requiring] a transformation in global power structures" (27). Cameroonians/Africans "cannot assume a Habermasian consensus or an equal horizontal relationship among cultures and peoples globally divided in the two poles of the colonial difference" (27). Cameroonians/Africans need to start imagining alternative transmodern worlds beyond Eurocentrism and Anglophone/Francophone/Lusophone/Hispanophone fundamentalism. As opposed to Habermas'/African leaders' "project that what needs to be done is to fulfill the incomplete and unfinished project of modernity" (27), Nyamnjoh's is a call on Cameroonians/Africans to fulfill The Cameroons'/Africa's 21st century unfinished and incomplete mutating project of decolonization. Instead of a single modernity centered in Euro-North America and imposed as a global design to the rest of the world, *TDA* "argues for a multiplicity of decolonial critical responses to eurocentered modernity from the subaltern cultures and epistemic location of colonized people around the world" (27). Again, Nyamnjoh's is "equivalent to 'diversality as a universal project' which is a result of 'critical border thinking,' or 'critical thinking from the margins' as an epistemic intervention from the diverse subaltern locations" (27) of The Cameroons/Africa. To borrow from Holloway (2010), *TDA* asserts that it is time for Africans to travel with crude transmodern maps (36). Between transmodernity as a philosophy of liberation and action, there may be correspondence, but there is no sequence. Africans may not necessarily reach the same transmodern place, and many of them may not even reach any recognizable transmodern place, but *TDA* attests that they share the same starting point of disillusionment, and that is enough inspiration.

Works Cited

Alcoff, Linda. "Enrique Dussel's Transmodernism." *Transmodernity*, vol.1 no. 3, 2012, pp. 60-68.

Ateljevic, Irena. "Visions of Transmodernity: A New Renaissance of our Human History?" *Integral Review*, vol. 9, no. 2, June 2013.

Ateljevic, Irena. "Transmodernity: Integrating Perspectives on Societal Evolution" *Futures,* vol. 47, 2013.

Bourdieu, Pierre. "The forms of Capital." In: *Handbook of Theory and Research for Sociology of Education.* Edited by J. G. Richardson. Greenwood,1986.

Castro-Gómez, Santiago. *Crítica de la razón latinoamericana.* Barcelona: Puvill Libros, 1996.

———. "(Post)Coloniality for Dummies: Latin American Perspectives on Modernity, Coloniality, and the Geo-Politics of Knowledge," edited by Mabel Moraña, Enrique Dussel, and Carlos Jáuregui *Coloniality at Large: Latin America and the PostcolonialDebate*. Duke UP, 2008.

Cerutti-Guldberg, Horacio. "Actual Situation and Perspectives of Latin American Philosophy of Liberation." Translated by Ofelia Schutte. *Philosophical Forum* vol. 20, no. 1-2 Fall-Winter 1988-1989, pp. 43-61.

Doh, Emmanuel. *Anglophone Cameroon Literature: An Introduction*. Lexington Books, 2014.

Dussel, Enrique. *Philosophy of Liberation.* Translated by Aquilina Martinez and Christine Morkovsky. Orbis Books, 1985.

―――――. *The Invention of the Americas: Eclipse of "the Other" and the Myth of Modernity*. Translated by Michael Barber. Continuum, 1995.

―――――. *The Underside of Modernity: Apel, Ricoeur, Rorty, Taylor, and the Philosophy of Liberation*. Translated and edited by Eduardo Mendieta. Humanities, 1996.

―――――. "World-system and Trans-modernity." *Nepantla: Views from South* vol. 3, no 2, 2002, pp. 221-44.

―――――. "Transmodernity and Interculturality: An Interpretation from the Perspective of Philosophy of Liberation." (2004) www.enriquedussel.org/text/transmodernityandinterculturality.pdf ACCESSED 24 Jan. 2016

―――――. "Philosophy of Liberation, the Postmodern Debate, and Latin American Studies." In *Coloniality at Large: Latin America and the Postcolonial Debate*. Edited by Mabel Moraña, Enrique Dussel, and Carlos Jáuregui. Translated by Rosalia Bermúdez. Duke UP, 2008a.

―――――. *Twenty Theses on Politics*. Translated by George Ciccariello-Maher. Duke UP, 2008b.

Eberhard, Christoph. "Opening up Spaces for Peace: A Dialogical and Transmodern Approach". (Pour la rencontre scientifique de l'Institut International de Sociologie Juridique à Oñati, 3 et 4 Avril 2000.

Fanon, Frantz. *Black Skin, White Masks*. Grove Press, 1967.

Fishkin, Benjamin. "A Costly Gift to the Receiver: Francis B. Nyamnjoh and the Alienation of the African" in *Fears, Doubts and Joys of Not Belonging*. Eds. Benjamin Fishkin, Adaku Ankumah and Bill Ndi. Langaa RPCIG, 2014.

Foucault, Michel. *History of Sexuality Vol. 1: An Introduction*. Translated by Robert Hurley, Pantheon Books, 1978.

―――――. *Society Must Be Defended*. Picador, 2003.

Ghisi, M. L. "The transmodern hypothesis: Toward a dialogue of cultures." *Futures*, 1999, vol 31, no 9-10, 1999, pp. 879-1016.

―――――. "Transmodernity and Transmodern Tourism", in: Keynote presented at the 15th Nordic Symposium in Tourism and Hospitality Research: Visions of Modern and Transmodern Tourism, 19–22 October, 2006, Savonlinna, Finland.

Ghisi, M. L. *The Knowledge Society: A Break through Towards Genuine Sustainability*. Arunachala, 2008.

Gilman, Charlotte. *The Man-made World; or, Androcentric Culture.* Charlton, 1911.

Grosfoguel, Ramón. "Decolonizing Post-Colonial Studies and Paradigms of Political-Economy: Transmodernity, Decolonial Thinking, and Global Coloniality". *Transmodernity,* vol 1, no 1, 2011, pp. 2-38.

Holloway, John. *Change the World without taking Power.* Pluto, 2005.

_____. *Crack Capitalism.* Pluto, 2010.

Mazrui, Ali. *Cultural Forces in World Politics.* James Currey, 1990.

Mignolo, Walter. "Geopolitics of sensing and knowing: On (de)coloniality, border thinking, and epistemic disobedience." *Confero* vol. 1, no. 1, 2013, pp. 129-150.

Nyamnjoh, Francis. *The Disillusioned African.* Nooremac Press, 1995.

Rancière, Jacques. *DISSENSUS: On Politics and Aesthetics.* Edited and Translated by Steven Corcoran, Continuum, 2010.

_____. "The Thinking of Dissensus: Politics and Aesthetics." In *Reading Ranciere.* Edited by Paul Bowman and Richard Stamp. Continuum, 2011.

Santos, Boaventura de Sousa. *Epistemologies of the South: Justice Against Epistemicide.* Paradigm, 2014.

Sardar, Ziauddin. "Islam and the West in a Transmodern World", 2004. Online article, available from Islam Online - Contemporary Issues: www.islamonline.net/servlet/Satellite?c=Article_C&pagename =Zone-English Living_Shariah/LSELayout&cid=1158658505216. August 18, 2004. Accessed 8 Jan. 2016

Schutte, Ofelia. *Cultural Identity and Social Liberation in Latin American Thought.* Suny UP, 1993.

Chapter 2

The Playwright as Whistleblower: Drama and the Expressing of the Repressed in The Cameroons.

Emmanuel Fru Doh

Owing to the political climate in most countries south of the Sahara, nations that were given birth to by exploitative and equally repressive colonial strategies, it is not surprising that the luxury of writing for art's sake is rare. Writers from such nations find themselves steeped in socio-politically turbulent surroundings engendered by corrupt dictators cum colonial puppets whose idea of a nation's welfare is maintaining themselves in office at all cost. Their methods are repressive and, more often than not, they enjoy the patronage of leaders of former colonial nations which tend to benefit from such plagued societies, in spite of the lot of the local citizenry. Accordingly, such writers transmute into literary guerillas with their pens and ideas for weapons since they are usually writing against the trends of these corrupt and repressive regimes. George Ngwane is of the same view for he writes of Anglophone-Cameroon writers:

> The writer must be in the pull of action. To arouse his Anglophone Cameroonian constituency from the apathy and despair into which they have sunk, the writer's métier must, be transformed into hand grenades in his literary arsenal for venting his crusading spirit. (35)

Hence, Ngugi wa Thiong'o's claim that "Drama has [its] origins in human struggles with nature and with others" (36) for, when people are oppressed their society is that of repressed feelings and aspirations that must be let loose. In other words, such are societies in which people are anxious to vocalize their feelings but are held hostage by the forces of authoritarianism often concretized by an existing Gestapo. The outcome in such societies is a slow and painstakingly groomed revolution, the eruption of which is always preceded by a period of sensitization. In some cases, political pamphlets are used to quickly educate the oppressed, and more often, a strong literary tradition is given birth to, to express the repressed concerns of the oppressed. The goal of these writers then is always to call the oppressors to order, sensitize the oppressed and help them find a way out of their quandary; hence my idea of the playwright as a whistleblower in The Cameroons.

Of African nations and their acquisition of independence, Osita Okagbue has aptly posited, just as earlier observed in this venture, that "The condition of African independence was ... created by and during colonialism, and exists neo-colonially today as a way of ensuring that the colonizer surreptitiously maintains a continued dominance and interference in the lives of the colonized" (52). In this light, The Cameroons stand out because of the contorted, unique, and arguably criminal manner of her emergence into nationhood, coupled with the agonizing character of ongoing corruption and apathy in the nation. Even then, the vampires, according to Bole Butake, sucking dry the nation's lifeblood refuse to address these pertinent issues thinking that by repressing them the vexing status quo will continue thriving with the powerful and privileged flourishing at the expense of the exploited and humiliated "wretches" of society—the proletariat. Yet, every Cameroonian aware of the intricacies involved in *La République du Cameroun's* effort towards her acquisition of her pseudo-independence along with administrative practices under her first president, Ahmadou Ahidjo, and the sitting octogenarian, Paul Biya, will swear not all is well. Despite this, nothing is ever discussed in an effort to address the knotted status quo with a parliament peopled mostly by hand clappers and grateful misfits in their role as representatives of their largely uninformed masses. The incumbent president himself displayed this lack of patriotic love by declaring it *"sans objet"*—pointless—when an opportunity to visit the nation's grievances presented itself in the early nineties with the Anglophone population calling for a sovereign national conference. Face it, the Francophones are as upset as the Anglophones even if for different reasons, which all later culminate in the debauched political status and waning standard of living in The Cameroons today. A quick excursion through The Cameroons' emergence as a nation will expose the tortuous and tenuous path to independence, the repressive administrative tactics of the post-independence regimes, and, consequently, the whistle blowing role of select Cameroonian playwrights and their drama which express repressed facts about the nation.

The Portuguese were first on the shores of The Cameroons and ended up naming the territory *Rio dos Cameroes* because of the large quantities of prawns they found up the Wouri River. Then came the Germans as a colonizing authority in 1884, and called the country, Kamerun. Alas, Germany's colonial romance with the territory was cut short by Germany's defeat in World War I, leading to the loss of her colonies to the allied forces. Owing to a June 28, 1919 League of Nations' mandate, *Kamerun* was partitioned into two unequal parts, without consultations with the indigenes. The bigger geographical portion was given to France that had far less colonial turf compared to Britain, which, as a result, received a much smaller section of The Cameroons. The embarrassing claim, on the part of these western nations, has been that these factions were to be schooled in effective self-governance, democracy in other words, before being returned to the citizens. It is today common knowledge, however, that the idea of "schooling" these factions in western democracy was only a front as the supposed supervising nations immediately started exploring and making away with natural resources from these League of Nations (and later United Nations—UN) trust territories in their charge.

Decades after, when these territories felt it was time for their independence, it took a bloody conflict marked by barbaric techniques on the part of the colonialists for them to get a semblance. The French were especially ferocious as they were determined to design the nature of the independence they were willing to accord their section of the trust territories, which had now become Francophone. The French language had been imposed on the people as the official language over German. France's illegal methods led to the creation of a militant wing by members of the dreaded *Union des Populations du Cameroun* (UPC) party, which had gone underground after the French outlawed it in 1955. Cameroonian patriots, mainly from the hard working and equally foresighted Bamileke and Bassa ethnic groups, were then accused of terrorism and slaughtered by the French, using both French and Cameroonian troops in executing these dastardly deeds on East Cameroonian soil. Of this French goal and tactic, Richard Joseph has observed: "There is a clear pattern to the use France has been willing to make of its military presence to control and determine local political arrangements" (25). Yet, until date, this is a part of The Cameroons' history that remains anathema as nothing has ever been officially said about it, either because of the shameful atrocities visited on the people by France, or because some Cameroonian "traitors" who were involved are still alive and in positions of power in the nation's government, or else it is for both reasons. Mathieu Njassep, who was Ernest Ouandie's [1] aide de camp, confirms this by his declaration, which is part of a documentary on The Cameroons' pseudo-independence: "*Notre pays a beaucoup souffert, et on le cache; on le cache.*" "Our nation has suffered a lot, and they are hiding it; they are hiding it" (my translation, "Africanheritagevideo").

It is about this same time, 1961, that the English speaking part of today's The Cameroons succeeded in twisting the arms of Britain and the United Nations into granting them their own independence, an equally intricate and conniving process which denied the territory independence on its own merit and instead gave the people a devil's alternative for an independence option: join the Federal Republic of Nigeria or *La République du Cameroun*. They joined the latter and emerged with The Federal Republic of Cameroon. Unfortunately, contrary to the provisions of the Federal constitution intended to guide and uphold the union, domineering and predominantly Francophone regimes have continually manipulated this structure until the country has lost its federal status and is now being called *La République du Cameroun*, the name of former French speaking Cameroun before the union with the English speaking part of the country. One of the implications of this political gimmick, and that is the one favored by the government, is that Francophone Cameroun has succeeded in annexing Anglophone Cameroon, a scenario the latter has refused to accept. To the Anglophones, instead, Francophone Cameroun has voluntarily opted out of the union but is using its military to illegally occupy the territory of the English speaking Cameroons. It is mainly for this reason that Anglophones were calling for a sovereign national conference in the early nineties, but the dictator Paul Biya said it was pointless.

The truth remains though that The Cameroons, as a nation, has been burdened by two different regimes, that of Ahmadou Ahidjo, 1960 – 1982, and that of Paul Biya 1982 to present. The former was a repressive regime such that even a spouse could not trust a partner for fear he or she might be an agent or informant of the brutal secret police in place at the time. Of the tortuous and repressive structure Ahidjo put in place, J. F. Bayart has observed:

> One of Ahidjo's primary tasks during the early years of his regime was to snuff out all competing sources of autonomy and legitimacy: the demotion of the traditional chiefs, the disruption of personalist and ethnic "machines," the neutralization of West Cameroon particularism, etc. (77)

Elsewhere, the effectiveness of Ahidjo's repressiveness is properly captured by Mongo Beti: "The regime of Ahmadu Ahidjo has succeeded in enveloping the country in a cloak of silence whose completeness the revolutionaries had not expected and for which the Cameroonian President is indebted, without doubt, to the prestigious protector who reigned in Paris...." (97)

Biya's regime, meanwhile, has been a national disaster without a progressive national agenda other than his determination to latch onto power at all cost, even as the nation is pathetically disfigured by mismanagement, corruption, and the lack of accountability. True, the kind of oppressive torture used by Ahidjo to anchor the ship of state has gone underground somewhat, thus emboldening recklessness and ineptitude to a degree even dreams could not capture during Ahidjo's tenure. Consequently, The Cameroons under Biya is like a pirate-commandeered ship in a stormy sea without a captain, and so the pirates rival each other, and even the hostages, at pilfering their own loot and property while masking the disarray with the excess supply of liquor aboard even as it keeps them from contemplating their united plight and that of the ship.

Briefly then, since a more in-depth treatment of the subject is beyond this paper, this is The Cameroons' tormented history that has culminated in a mismanaged, corrupted, disgruntled, and divided nation. A truly patriotic head of state would have addressed these issues, given apologies where due, and restructured the constitution as deemed appropriate by the people in an effort towards building a united nation. Alas, even with all the signs of a sick nation, its contamination stemming back from the dawn of its attempts at nationhood, those in power are denying the truth by suppressing the nation's bloody and chequered past while brandishing a superficial and hopeless sense of wellbeing to whomever wishes to buy their tale and political theatrics. It is about this sophisticated scenario of repressed facts that The Cameroons' playwrights are whistle blowing. Their goal is to educate and conscientize the young, uninformed, and even the informed but frightened or lethargic as to what happened at the dawn of nationhood and that which is going on in the nation today that has succeeded in transforming a once upon a time national haven into a socio-economic and political backwater, and what needs to be done to salvage the situation. Hence our appraisal of Ba'bila Mutia's *Before This Time, Yesterday* (1993), Victor Epie'Ngome's *What God Has Put Asunder (1992)*, Bate Besong's *Beasts of No Nation* (1990), and Bole Butake's *The Dance of the Vampires (1999)* as plays expressing the repressed in The Cameroons.

It is my conviction that in life one must look back from time to time to see how far one has come in order to determine which way and how far one still has to go. The repressed brutality at the dawn of The Cameroons' independence, when the French and their Cameroonian lackeys slaughtered and razed to the ground villages of Cameroonians against post-independence French presence in *La République du Cameroun*, is the focus of Ba'bila Mutia's *Before This Time, Yesterday*. This play was premiered at the Goethe Institute in Yaoundé, Cameroon, in 1993, confirming Praise Zenenga's observation that "…critical historical moments often necessitate the birth of new theatrical forms and practices" (14), and consequently, Herbert Grabes opinion that literature "is a cultural construct" (2). Nevertheless, Mutia could not have broached on such a sensitive topic in a straightforward manner without risking torture or lengthy periods of incarceration even in the seemingly, and comparatively speaking, less oppressive Biya era.[2] This is the brutal, shameful, and so forbidden part of The Cameroons' history, intentionally neglected by the authorities and so scholars dared not approach it for fear of their lives. Only a few like Abel Eyinga and Albert Mukong could dare refer to this phase of The Cameroons' history in public as they had themselves been guests of honor at secret police torture "luncheons" in underground cells, and, like Eyinga, had gone overseas on exile from where he wrote.[3] Mukong, on his part, no longer cared about his life, which he had long sacrificed in the fight for The Cameroons' independence and the socio-political integrity of the Anglophone-Cameroonian in particular and so remained in The Cameroons even when freed from detention.

Accordingly, Mutia's entire setting is the dream world and his subject of concern a psychoanalytical hiccup recurring in sporadic spasms when his protagonist, Sango, goes to sleep. Sango is so badly agitated in his dreams such that his wife, Chantal, gets worried, especially by the escalating nature of the dream and Sango's behavior during these dreams. After confirming his agitation as a consequence of the same dream, which he then qualifies a nightmare, Chantal suggests they find out the cause and meaning behind it, especially as Sango's screams during recent episodes are getting to the kids.

Sango's tormented id can immediately be seen as representative of a guilt ridden national conscience from which informed but unpatriotic leaders are running away instead of facing it as Sango is about to do. Because Sango cannot remember the content of his dreams, which seems to stem from some trauma beyond the physical, Chantal suggests they visit Dr. Vesso, a psychiatrist at New Deal Clinic. The doctor confirms the need to unravel the mystery behind the dreams before Sango's subconscious is overburdened and his dream theatrics spill over into his consciousness and he goes about raving mad. The preparatory phase for the hypnotic session begins revealing interesting questions about Sango's past, such as how his parents died and why his uncle Abassa went to prison and hates talking about the past. Uncle Abassa warns Dr. Vesso about the secrets he is trying to unearth. The hypnotic session reveals a raid in a village in which Sango's parents are killed by invading white soldiers, with one of them holding a blue, white, and red flag, and strangely Tonton Onana aka Commandant Sikamba and chief of military operations of the resistance, is fighting on their side instead. It dawns on one then that these must be French soldiers, with their blue, white, and red national colors and Commandant Sikamba for a national traitor not only showing them the way but fighting alongside the French as they attack, kill villagers, and raze down villages belonging to sympathizers of the UPC militants who had gone underground. How very reminiscent of the betrayal and death of Um Nyobe, the charismatic leader of the UPC party, for Martin Atangana has written about Um Nyobè's death: "The decision to kill Um Nyobè was made by Prime Minister Ahmadou Ahidjo and was approved by French authorities who could have opposed it" (92). He goes into details shortly after:

> Abel Eyinga reported that Charles Okala, who was a minister in the Ahidjo Cabinet, confessed to him that before making his decision, Prime Minister Ahmadou Ahidjo consulted three members of his government including Charles Okala himself and Charles Assalé. Okala refused to reveal the name of the third person. After the decision was taken to physically eliminate the secretary-general of the UPC, the order was given to the army. On the morning of September 13, 1958, a small army unit highly equipped and guided by their informer, Luc Makon ma Bikat, opened fire on unarmed people, killing Um Nyobè, his mother-in-law Ruth, Pierre Yem Mback, and Jean Marc Poha. Some of Um Nyobè's companions were able to hide and then run away. (92)

Mutia's play then is not a tale nor is his message an accident. He is urging the nation to confront the past as a way of healing and yielding forth a better today and tomorrow, for Sango's reaction upon uncovering the treacherous role of his uncle and now boss and Minister of State, Tonton Onana, is to challenge him. He does, and efforts at bribing Sango with a position as director in the ministry fails as Sango is determined to expose Onana as a traitor. A struggle ensues during which Onana, who had whipped out a pistol, inadvertently, shoots himself in the chest.

By revisiting the very sensitive yet repressed phase of The Cameroons' history, Mutia is daring to walk a mined path. He has voiced what consciously, or otherwise, nobody wanted to voice, even though they think about it all the time. Those in powerful offices with things to hide about their involvement in the bloody affairs of this phase of The Cameroons' history must have gone to lengths to keep this phase of The Cameroons' history buried; they must have believed Mutia's play, even with significant props like the color of the French flag mentioned, to be about an ordinary dream. Through this venture, therefore, Mutia succeeds in asking questions about a chapter in The Cameroons' history which has remained suppressed for decades. He triumphs in pointing out that there were traitors in the house that needed to be brought to justice in one way or the other. It is not for nothing, nor is it by accident that Dr. Vesso's clinic is called New Deal Clinic, the name Paul Biya accorded his government when he came into power: the new Deal Government. Were Biya a true patriot, Mutia is saying, then he would have turned The Cameroons into a cleansing and healing scenario like the New Deal Clinic, and like Dr. Vesso and his New Deal Clinic trying to resolve Sango's predicament with his dreams, Biya should have gone into the roots of The Cameroons' existing political tensions and tried resolving them. This was something he could do, but he chose to look the other way while pretending all is fine even as he is almost taken out of office by a coup d'état barely two years after. Mutia also succeeds in pointing out, even if the government will not acknowledge it, that there are disgruntled Cameroonians still incensed by the role French and Cameroonian traitors, at best ignoramuses, played in the obliteration of Cameroonian villages. Mutia's point is that this was wrong, and so there is the need for such victim territories and their citizens to be given due apology by the government of *La République du Cameroun*, at the very least, for peace to reign while a true sense of national unity is reborn; hence, Mutia's role as a playwright and whistleblower expressing the repressed in society.

On his part, Victor Epie'Ngome's *What God Has Put Asunder* confirms the searing and fragmented nature of The Cameroons state entity due to existing grudges within. Whereas Mutia's play, somewhat, bridges both Anglophones and Francophones and their struggle for independence, since members from both sections of society were part of the outlawed UPC (Union of the Peoples of Cameroon/*Union des Populations du Cameroun*) party, Epie'Ngome is essentially concerned with the Anglophone predicament within the union of Anglophone and Francophone Cameroons formed at the dawn of both sections' independence, and correctly referred to at the beginning as the Federal Republic of The Cameroons. Epie'Ngome's concern, therefore, is with the state of the union between the Anglophones and the Francophones, at large, and not just mainly the tensions within the Francophone section exhumed by Mutia's play.

On the surface, Epie'Ngome's play is about a marriage gone wrong, but, at the allegorical level, the marriage signifies the union of English and French speaking Cameroons. Weka, a well-behaved orphan girl grows up in an orphanage and is, without her opinion, given out in marriage to a certain Garba by the rector of the orphanage, Reverend Gordon, despite Emeka's presence as an alternative suitor. It is not surprising then that Emeka interrupts the wedding ceremony on the basis that he is a better suitor to Weka given that both of them grew up in the same orphanage; a point which is dismissed by Reverend Gordon since, to him, they were just childhood friends. The ceremony is brought to its logical conclusion, even with Weka arguing that she does not know Garba well enough to be his wife. Emeka's warning of the truth coming out some day, however, leaves an awkward premonition looming over the observance. Mindful of the irregularities surrounding the ceremony, with the bride arguing against the groom and the groom taking exceptions to parts of the wedding vows, Reverend Unor, the supervising official, establishes the union but declares it probational. The couple will live together for ten years to get to know each other well. If after the probation period they want to remain as husband and wife, then they would exchange wedding rings. Notwithstanding, the couple is pronounced husband and wife.

In the end, Weka's conditional husband, Garba, and head of the emerging Cooperative union, turns out to be a cheat as he is having an affair with his driver's wife, Fatou, who is also his secretary. Garba's financial recklessness, as he squanders the Cooperative's money as if it is his private allowance, shocks even his paramour, Fatou. Ironically, Weka is also having her own affair with Garba's chauffeur, Sanni. In the end, both cheating couples discover themselves. Weka leaves Garba's house for her parental estate, which she had long abandoned. In the meantime, Weka meets Emeka whose undying hopes of starting a relationship with her she squashes. Reverend Gordon also makes known his regrets at having let Weka off the way he did because he believed Weka's family's estate was economically worthless; a mistake. Garba's attempt to get back his wife culminates in a scuffle, during which he is thrown out by Weka's children. They end up in court, where those responsible for are able to witness to the circumstances around the union, convincing the presiding judge of its probationary basis. In the end, Weka has her freedom from Garba since the conditions presented by the court make it possible for Weka to nullify the union.

As earlier observed, Epie'Ngome's play is seemingly just about an ordinary marriage, but this allegory is really about the history of The Cameroons and the consequential predicament within The Cameroons today. By his technique, Epie'Ngome has been able to express government repressed Anglophone feelings about their union with their Francophone counterparts, a union into which the Anglophones considered themselves maneuvered by the Francophones and the overseeing authorities of this former UN Trust territory, only for them to find themselves reduced to second class citizens in a union with corruption at a level they had never experienced before. Allegorically then, Epie'Ngome's protagonist, Weka, the young orphan girl who is coaxed into an undesirable union with Garba, who represents the northerner, Ahmadou Ahidjo, at the head of government of the former East, is, in fact, West Cameroon. This was the term of reference used for Anglophone-Cameroon during the federation phase of the blighted union. In this light, the orphanage stands for the United Nations whose orphan, Southern Cameroons, was as a Trust Territory, but the name segued into West Cameroon (Weka), upon the formation of the federal union with Francophone-Cameroon which became East Cameroon.[4] Reverend Gordon then is the United Kingdom administering this trust territory, the orphanage in allegorical terms. Emeka, given the Igbo roots of his name, is Weka's other suitor, representing the Federal Republic of Nigeria, the other choice given Southern Cameroons as her ticket to independence. Jim Ricon, meanwhile, epitomizes the newcomer in the acquisition of colonies along with her role in today's power struggle: the Unites States of America. As I have observed elsewhere,

> With these main characters thus identified, the allegorical dimension of Epie'Ngome's play becomes obvious. Weka's stay at the orphanage, her rape by Rev. Gordon the rector, her

marriage to Garba under phoney circumstances, Garba's violation of the terms of marriage and the problems between him and his wife make the analogy between Weka's plight and that of Southern Cameroons today obvious. (110)

Furthermore, we see Southern Cameroonians today, very much like Weka and Garba in the court scene, struggling to gain the attention of the United Nations in order to have their union with *La République du Cameroun* revisited so as to emerge with a permanent solution to this travesty. Britain's role in governing Southern Cameroons, the orphan, and the UN being the orphanage, confirms Rev. Gordon, the Rector of the orphanage, who brings up Weka but not without sporadic carnal sprees with her, the personification of Britain which did benefit from Southern Cameroons' territory that served as a source for raw materials. It is not surprising then that it is Rev. Gordon and the authorities of the Orphanage who give Weka away in a marriage that is as dubious as the transactions that led to Southern Cameroons' union with *La République du Cameroun* and in which exercise Britain and the UN played an equally embarrassing supervisory role. Therefore, the case presented by The Southern Cameroons National Council (SCNC) to the UN is really Epie'Ngome's court scene involving Garba and Weka. This seems to be Epie'Ngome's predication, a repressed idea, of the potential final outcome of this union: it will take the UN to finally resolve the discrepancies in the union between Anglophone and Francophone Cameroons; after all, they are the magicians who conjured this monstrosity into existence.

This is the issue with The Cameroons' union today, yet it is being repressed by the incumbent regime, like the preceding one, as all its operatives deny to acknowledge publicly the fact that there is a problem with the union, which needs to be addressed, hence Epie'Ngome's expressing of the repressed in *What God Has Put Asunder*. As if to confirm the corrupt practices that led to its emergence, the union has distinguished itself as a most corrupt sociopolitical entity, yet the government is not only in denial but is repressing the truth about the decadent state of affairs even though it is public knowledge already. It is not surprising then that Bate

Besong's *Beasts of No Nation* paints a disgusting picture of the union and the plight of the citizens within, especially the Anglophone's.

Accordingly, Besong's *Beasts of No Nation* is an unforgiving play out to expose the mess the nation is. Set in a fictional African municipality, with a name, Ednouay, which is an anagram of The Cameroons' political capital city, Yaoundé, and in the tradition of the absurd, the play moves from section to section identified by subtitles. The opening section is "Parabasis" which is followed by "Beasts of No Nation," then "Aadingingin and the Nightsoil-men," and finally, an "Aftermath."

The play opens with a grimly revealing scene with the Narrator engaged by the Nightsoil-men who are asking for their freedom even as they complain about the degrading nature of their workplace—the lavatory with the pervading smell of shit; a fact about Anglophones in The Cameroons documented by Piet Konings and Francis B. Nyamnjoh in real life:

> In the political domain, Anglophones complain of Anglophone exclusion from the key government and party positions and of their inferior role in the decision-making councils and organs.... A general complaint among Anglophones is that they are assumed to be only fit to play 'deputy' or 'assistant' to Francophones, even when they have clear superior expertise. (67)

It would seem then that the Anglophones are the night-soil-men in Ednuoay. Besong is alluding to Anglophones' feelings about being outsiders in their own nation, along with the disgusting second-class jobs reserved for them by the oppressive system as pointed out by Konings and Nyamnjoh. In the section "Beasts of No Nation," a burlesque with the Blindman playing Aadingingin and the Cripple, Otshama, reveals further the expositions made by Narrator and the Nightsoil-men in section one: without their identity cards they cannot be considered fully integrated into the municipality and this would lead to the writing of petitions. One, however, does not fail to realize the frustrating disposition of the government in all that the Nightsoil-men are trying to achieve. They are either asked to make their complaints through the proper channels or asked to pay exorbitantly in the form of expensive fiscal stamps. For example, they are told through Otshama (Cripple) in section two, by Aadingingin playing Blindman, "…to put in an application, and attach on it: fiscal stamps to the tune of one million c.f.a per application" (24). Section three of the play "Aadingingin and the Nightsoil-men" reveals Cripple, the Blindman and the Nightsoil-men caricaturing the treacherous habits of the municipality's irresponsible gentry. Scene four, easily the most disgusting of the play, reveals the fetid nature of the Nightsoil-men's occupation, along with the collapse of the social order in Ednouay due to corruption. Otshama then exposes his ineptitude at dealing with the requirements of the Nightsoil-men by telling his Eminence lies about the state of affairs within the Municipality. Aadingingin also displays the woeful nature of his mayoralty over Ednouay in the manner in which he allocates his budget:

> …You know the crisis budget I have
> to work with. [..] A mere c.f.a. 500 million.
> Now, I have already spent c.f.a.
> 350 million for tissue. [..] c.f.a. 100
> million for izal, disinfectants … (50)

This unhealthy financial predicament is made worse by the Nightsoil-men's demands. Their rebelliousness exposes to Aadingingin his own administrative inefficiency such that one can only conclude he has a rebellion brewing when he kills Otshama, and the Nitghtsoil-men escape.

Beast of No Nation, then, is a playwright's way of expressing that which he cannot seem to declare openly in a repressed system. Consequently, the state of The Cameroons is miniaturized into a mere microcosm, a municipality, along with the attendant officials who display the pathetic level of chaos and corruption reigning in the nation as county workers. Then, there is the primary grievance of the Anglophones as second-class citizens in their own country, which is here exposed by the Nightsoil-men. Hence the playwright considers the Nightsoil-men and their work place a lavatory. A citizen's predicament could not be more disgusting in his own fatherland Besong seems to be saying by accenting a repressed fact through a play that stinks of filth, corruption, and the mismanagement of the nation's resources.

Another playwright disgusted by the repressed state of affairs in The Cameroons today is Bole Butake as evidenced by his graphic play, *Dance of the Vampires (Vampires)*. The play opens with a First Movement with its horrifying setting along with predominantly, seemingly meaningless and equally fruitless exchanges between the villain, Psaul Roi, and his aides: Song, Chief of Protocol, and Town Crier. One is immediately struck by the villain's implicit name: Psaul Roi. The biblical Paul and Saul meshed into "Psaul," along with "Roi" which is French for king. At once, one's mind goes to The Cameroons' incumbent leader and his sovereign status as head of state. In these exchanges between Psaul Roi and his assistants, Psaul Roi reveals that he does not know his officials nor has he met them before, just like Paul Biya of The Cameroons, of whom it is said appoints and dismisses some state ministers without ever having met them in person.

Occasionally, Psaul Roi betrays his desire to possess absolute power. As if to buy security and the trust of another individual, he shows Town Crier and later on Song, his Chief of Protocol, envelopes stuffed with money and asks them to help themselves. Unlike Town Crier, who caves under Psaul Roi's pressure and stuffs envelopes into his pockets, Song confines himself to one envelope only. Even then, Song has to leave as he has to preside at a meeting. Psaul Roi fears his fate is about to be decided at the meeting and so decides to join Song even though Song makes it clear he has not been initiated. Psaul Roi dismisses this need and points out that should Song go along with the former's plan to gatecrash the meeting, then by the next day, "there will be only two vamps" (153) in the kingdom, they (Psaul Roi and Song) will have all the money to themselves.

The second Movement, with its eerie setting, reveals Psaul Roi disguised as Song and taking part in the four pillars' deliberations about His Royal Majesty who demands initiation. Psaul Roi holds the pillars hostage and demands he be initiated since there is a rule that anyone who stumbles on their meeting must be initiated. It is made clear that this will cost the people too much, and according to masked figure, South: "Blood, fire and destruction shall henceforth be constant visitations in this land" (155). It becomes obvious that the pillars had no, or little, integrity for no sooner is the decision to initiate Psaul Roi arrived at when we see them scrambling for their own share of the booty. Psaul Roi promises them money and he is given absolute power in exchange.

Third Movement amounts to a display of the total absurdity of Psaul Roi's leadership. The setting is such that one thinks he is about to deliver a moving speech to his people only for him to display his ineptitude at such a task, especially a speech by rote. Accordingly, Song, his Chief of Protocol, begs him, in vain, to stick to the written speech. And then he begins rambling from one concern to another. Unique is the double-edged nature of his uneasiness, for it reveals how the people and Psaul Roi relate to the issues raised. Whereas the public's apprehension is authentic in that it shows how society is affected by Psaul Roi's inefficiency, given that he is totally out of touch with reality, just like his real life Cameroonian *alter ego*, Paul Biya, it matters to Psaul Roi, on the other hand, only because he feels it misrepresents his royal image: he has absolute power. As he rambles, he, inadvertently, exposes further the evils of his regime. The abuse of power is a major flaw. He addresses his citizens in the presence of heavily armed guards, and on one occasion, he threatens a member of the audience with being seized and taken away by the soldiers if the speaker's response is not loud enough. Beyond this threat to the speaker, he exposes the manner in which he uses the military by declaring thus:

> What? I permitted you to speak; didn't I? Now you sit down and learn from me because I know better or the soldier will take you out and I don't care what he does to you. (157 – 158)

Another major flaw exposed by Psaul Roi's rambling, typical of The Cameroons today, is the concentration of power and wealth in the hands of his cronies. One man is Chief Commander of the Royal Armed Forces, Town Crier, Chief of Protocol, and Chief Counselor. One would think one is dealing with a society that is lacking in population at the very least, and qualified citizens at best, but this is not the case, given the crowd present to listen to this leader; it is simply a question of concentrating power in the hands of a few friends through favoritism. Beyond subservience to an absurd degree,

Song has not displayed any other remarkable quality that warrants his person to be the meeting point of several high level functions. Anyone in the crowd could easily serve in any of the capacities heaped on Song; alas, the crowd is populated by Psaul Roi's critics and not his servile cronies.

Psaul Roi's rambling also reveals a leader who listens to rumors circulating amongst his citizens. Whereas the citizenry listens to rumors because of a regime that denies them information, one can only wonder why Psaul Roi, on his part, chooses to listen to rumors. In the process, he reveals the complicated nature of his sexuality as society holds he is not sexually virile; how very much like stories surrounding the incumbent in The Cameroons, at least as of the time of Butake's writing. The result is that he exposes how he has eliminated the women in his life for trying to smuggle more virile young men into the palace to help with their special needs:

> Aren't women curious beings? I have seen men who have given up their manhood in order to be wealthy. Others, like me gave it up for power. But no matter how much wealth you put at the feet of a woman she will never be satisfied until you can make her tick. And they tried to escape with my wealth since they could not get their he-goats into the palace to service them. So I had them snuffed out. (159)

It is with this same nonchalance that Psaul Roi receives tragic information about parts of his nation. When he learns of an earthquake in the mountain, with two thousand dead, he feels no remorse for his people. This earthquake brings to mind the 1986 disaster at Nyos, a hilly location in the Bamenda Grassfields of The Cameroons, where after thousands of human beings and cattle were found dead in their stride, villagers confessed of having heard a loud sound, "boom," from the direction of Lake Nyos. In a most childish and ridiculous manner, Psaul Roi blames the victims for not having heeded his recommendation when he asked them to leave the mountains and settle in the valleys. One cannot help wondering how a simpleton like this became leader of his people. But then, one remembers the corruption that reigned in Second Movement, culminating in his acquisition of absolute power. To him, the casualties of the earthquake are vandals and he is grateful for the whole tragedy as it has left him with 2000 less vandals. The result is that he is challenged by a member of his audience and accused of being without sympathy. For this audacity à la John the Baptist in the Bible, Psaul Roi, like Herod, immediately sentences his challenger to death by decapitation: "Soldier, I command you to bring that vandal's head to the palace. Take him out now and his stubborn head shall henceforth decorate our royal and sacred altar" (159). What sovereign power, much akin to the real life situation in The Cameroons where the head of state once told a TV editor in chief, for example, that he could get him out of his post by simply gesturing with his head. If human life means nothing to this despot, of what use then is the national treasury if not to serve his whiles. He instructs his new Town Crier and Chief Commander to inform neighboring kingdoms of the tragedy that has befallen his kingdom and to request aid, preferably in cash, which he can go on to swindle as was the alleged situation with the aid arriving The Cameroons for the Lake Nyos victims:

> Dramatize the situation as best as you can. Tell them we have lost five thousand dead in an earthquake and volcanic eruption and that half the kingdom has been destroyed. More than twenty thousand wounded and shelterless and foodless. We are desperately in need of aid … no… financial assistance to begin the painful and very difficult task of rebuilding our broken kingdom. (159)

In the manner of such corrupt leaders, he instructs that soldiers go to the scene of the calamity and recover anything of value left, for the royal purse. Just then, news arrives that "all the important markets in the low-lying regions of the land have been razed to the ground by fires" (159), a potential riot. Psaul Roi's response is to order troops in to salvage the goods for the palace. Again, he is challenged from the crowd and called "mad." Psaul Roi orders the soldiers "to shoot to kill" at his own citizens, a command that brings to mind Bamenda, Cameroon, in the early nineties just before the state of emergency was declared. Psaul Roi ends up running "for dear life" (160) at Song's behest, realizing the soldiers cannot contain the irate crowd.

Fourth Movement reveals Psaul Roi in another macabre setting akin to some occult priest drinking and playing cards while anticipating news that the rebellion, which brings Third Movement to an end, has been crushed. The tragic quality of Psaul Roi as a leader emerges at once as he is anxious to hear the number of citizens that have been killed in the process of suppressing the rebellion. Killing his rebellious citizens is to him a better option to wasting money on detention camps. As a result of all the slaughtering that has taken place, "The survivors have all fled the land …" (161). This Movement is simply overwhelming in how it expresses the repressed and displays scenes so powerfully evocative of recent history in Butake's The Cameroons. The hopelessness of the leaders comes out in the fact that because of the self-exile option chosen by his endangered citizens, he is a "ruler without the ruled" (161) and this does not bother him. In real life, one can only imagine the number of Cameroonians who have left The Cameroons during Biya's tenure because of its socio-political purposelessness. Hence, Psaul Roi declares:

> The best for the ruler. No headaches with vandals and no need to distribute the meagre resources. Get the soldiers to build incinerators and sizzle the bodies in them. Or dump them in the rivers and lakes. Anything, so long as the stench does not contaminate the palace (161).

True to his agents provocateur, again reminiscent of Butake's The Cameroons, we encounter a treacherous armed forces that for cash rewards, would obliterate the citizenry their profession demands they protect even at the cost of their own lives. Anne Reef witnesses about such a system:

> In order to prevent resistance to the empire that is partly real but is also the product of state paranoia, troops must defend the borders, while within the country, a special apparatus of the empire detains, interrogates, tortures, and kills its subjects rendering its judicial system an impotent travesty, precipitating emigration, and sowing the seeds of its own ideological and physical destruction. (338)

What an apt representation of the predicament Butake has exposed in *Vampires*.

The Movement goes on to reveal how trite and corrupt Psaul Roi's system is: everything and seemingly everyone has a price. Deserted by the delegations to foreign kingdoms, he hopes, along with Song, more money will come in to aid abate the deteriorating status of his kingdom. And then he is not happy he is receiving aid in kind instead of cash. He is so desperate for cash that when he hears an Albinian emissary has interesting proposals with relations to cash, he immediately contradicts himself and receives the emissary whom he had sworn not to meet.

The Albinian emissary's country is willing to do business with Psaul Roi's kingdom but regrets its being without citizens who should provide the labor while also functioning as the consumers – the market. Psaul Roi's royal ego, even in the face of desperation, causes Albino to lose his patience with Psaul Roi; he threatens to abandon Psaul Roi and his predicament. Psaul Roi's meaningless approach to governance is then expressed when his pointless self-praise and the sycophancy on Song's part is met with a damning and revealing declaration by Albino: "Can I go now? I am a business man. Time is money. Where I come from, we don't have time for aimless words" (165). Through Albino's subsequent observation, Butake is able to pass judgment on typical deals struck by western leaders and their emissaries on the one hand, and mostly unqualified, desperate, and mostly idiotic African leaders. Albino points out plainly the stupid and meaningless deals they are about to make and the need for him to be trusted: "Your Excellency the Most Royal, there is no business without trust, without goals. Your goal is your throne, power. Mine is gain. Shall we seal with a handshake? (*as they shake hands*) Done!" (165).

Fifth Movement discloses exactly Butake's opinion of his nation's military: one motivated by financial remunerations primarily and without a sense of commitment to the fatherland. Nformi's words betray not only an unproductive but also a virtually mercenary unit masquerading as a national force. Nformi confesses that because of Albino's directives, they of the armed forces are being made to work harder than they had ever worked before. And then he declares in a most embarrassing manner with regards to their "services to their nation: "We are predators not vultures" (166). Albino's response makes the embarrassing declaration and Butake's thoughts about his nation's military poignant:

> What wonderful predators you are! Preying on your own kind. Don't you see the consequences of your own folly? I have had to bring in specialists from Albinia to build the incinerators and to fell trees for wood and transport it to the various locations. And here you are asking me for more compensation. (166)

A military that prides itself with wiping out its own people; this is their only work, and when asked to do something worthwhile and productive, they want more pay. Indeed, before Boko Haram, one had been forced, from time to time, to wonder the role played by the armed forces of The Cameroons beyond saluting the flag, marching on 20th May[5], and harassing citizens on behalf of an inept and unpopular head of state, in the name of national security. Through Albino's words, Butake is able to declare the military of The Cameroons unproductive. The only time they have had to pull the trigger like real soldiers, one would have thought would be at some war, but no, it is when they "shoot to kill" their own citizens during an uprising against a sterile regime. Butake goes on to damn an armed forces with reversed priorities. Their approach to rebellions had always displayed the Cameroonian security forces mere puppets in the hands of unpatriotic political puppeteers. For a nation that has a whole army protecting the president, Albino's declaration is a lesson in national security as opposed to Song's sycophantic stance in the following exchange:

> Nformi: There is no money for our rewards?
> Albino: Exactly! The great monarch is broke and Albinia has sent me to rescue the land.
> Song: The monarch! To rescue the monarch!
> Albino: In Albinia, we do not think individuals, we think people.
> Nformi: I like that. (166)

The security forces of The Cameroons should confess like Nformi: "... Here we think only His Most Royal Majesty because we are frightened of his royal edicts, instruments and proclamations. Now I have discovered his real strength and I am ashamed to be making the discovery only now" (166).

It is equally significant that the regime in The Cameroons is headed by a Paul whose name is not far removed from Butake's Psaul. Even in this nomenclatural display, Butake's choice amounts to a scathing insinuation. Butake's use of sound effects in this damning declaration is effective. The "P" in "Psaul" is definitely silent confirming Paul's regression to [P]saul. By such an audacious and equally ambitious stylistic technique, Butake is able to express the repressed in the mind of the vast majority of his compatriots. Had this leader, Paul, been a repentant, true, and devoted leader, then his name Paul would have been appropriate like his biblical namesake who went from a murderous persecutor, Saul, to a repentant protector of Christians and a preacher of the truth, Paul. The Cameroons' Paul is regressing instead, hence he goes from Paul, a name he does not deserve, looking at his record as a leader, to Saul the persecutor of his own citizen; a combination of both portraits yields the tragic identity, Psaul. And since like his real life alter ego, who once declared he had twenty more years to live when his disgruntled citizens wished him dead, he is accorded the last name Roi, the French word for "king"; a disposition idiotic African leaders love to nurse of themselves. Remember a once upon a time Bokassa of Central African Republic, and a Mobutu Sesse Seko of once upon a time Zaire? They were all oppressors, in the fashion of Shelley's "Ozymandias," besides whose worthless historical royal and despotic portraits stands nothing but humiliating facts about their disastrous reigns.

Albino goes on to expose and damn Psaul Roi's system further when he accuses them: "Too many words. That is the problem with you people" (166). He then contrasts a better administrative set-up when he warns against Song's potential behavior:

> ... Song you will kindly tell his royal majesty that I have received his request for cash and that it is receiving the very serious attention it deserves. However, the final decision rests on

the ruling council of Albania. So don't come back here tomorrow, or the next day, or next week or the week after to ask for money. You may now return to your monarch. (166-167)

Albino here reveals an organized government with a system such that decisions are arrived at through the deliberations of a ruling council, unlike those spontaneous declarations and pronouncements by a power drunk monarch like Psaul Roi. How often has the National Assembly of The Cameroons been ridiculed for its disservice to Cameroonians given its rubberstamp role with relations to decisions taken by Paul Biya, seemingly, Butake's "Psaul" in *Vampires*?

Song leaves Albino's presence, realizing that all else depends on the Albinian council coming up with the cash Psaul Roi needs even as he warns Nformi not to let Albino fool him. His warning is a harbinger of what follows. Albino educates Nformi, the military general, into seeing how intelligent men like him have permitted an alcoholic despot to manipulate and exploit them. When Nformi reveals the power-politics behind the scene with families taking turns to rule the kingdom, Albino thrusts his game-changing idea: "Has your family taken its turn?" (168). That Butake has The Cameroons at heart is clearly communicated by Nformi's declaration "...And now his royal majesty is reigning over the forests, sands, and the grassfields" (168), geographical features representative of the national and specifically, regional landscapes of The Cameroons. Albino's question to Nformi is a clear insinuation of what needs to be done, and Nformi does not miss the cue—the need for a coup d'état—for he points out the huge task awaiting Psaul Roi's successor. Even the army is aware of the recession into which the nation has been thrust. Albino, in the manner of Western regimes who use and dispose of dim-witted African leaders on the whim, promises Nformi help. This is a frightening and audacious call by Butake: we need help to get Paul out of there. Nformi thinks death is too good for Psaul Roi given the destruction he has visited upon the kingdom. Nevertheless, he is ready to go on with the coup d'état with support from Albino. He warns Albino, however, that he will not take over to become an Albinian stooge; there will have to be some changes. Albino likes Nformi's frankness and agrees to do "business" with him.

Sixth Movement begins with Psaul Roi irate over Song's report about his encounter with Albino. He is convinced Albino has turned the royal armed forces against him. The tragic reversal in Butake's play takes place just now: Albino visits the palace to report that in line with his mission as an emissary to explore business opportunities with the kingdom, he has seen that opportunities abound but Psaul Roi's approach to governance has sent his citizens into exile making the kingdom indisposed to business ventures. The coup d'état is underway as Nformi arrives and calls Psaul Roi by name instead of using all his characteristic fatuous and meaningless titles; he even threatens to smash his way in if they will not let him into the palace. The direction of the coup is different from what the brain behind it—Albino—expected. The coup is a total cleansing bent on eliminating Albinians and their thieving interests in the kingdom as well as despotic kleptocrats like Psaul Roi and Song.

It is then obviously Butake's convictions that Africans need to oust the West from their land while the likes of Paul Biya are made to account for all they have done wrong to the citizens. One cannot be wrong then in asserting that Butake's work and the strategy sustaining its development amount to a concretization of Reef's conviction that "Art, both visual and verbal is often used as a form of political and social expression"(332). Hence, Bole Butake's *Dance of the Vampires* is a virulent summation and final indictment of Paul Biya's worthless and treacherous decades as president of The Cameroons. Butake's message is long overdue, repressed by a despotic system he has thus finally exposed.

This study of four Cameroonian playwrights and their concerns reveal their world as one tormented by so many ills they can no longer stomach: ills repressed for long by dictatorial whims that have transformed the citizenry into a frightened lot and their nation into joke. It is not surprising then that in the end, even with the risk to their own lives, it is these playwrights' decision to express pent-up practices that have, from the onset, only worked towards the alienation of sections of the citizenry—divide and rule in other words—and the destruction of the socio-political structure of an endowed nation. From the treacherous founding efforts towards nation building as revealed by Mutia, through the betrayal and hijacking of Anglophones and their identity by scheming Francophone regimes as expressed by Ngome, the ensuing dictatorship, corruption, and exploitation of the masses revealed by Besong, to the total collapse of the Cameroon nation through the prevalent and domineering activities of sects, secret societies, and the blatant mismanagement of the nation by the Biya regime revealed by Butake, it is not surprising then that while the forces of evil were at work, they inadvertently transformed the society into pressurized cauldron until these playwrights used their craft as a means of venting.

It is without doubt that under Ahidjo and Biya, Cameroonians have been an oppressed bunch, and while only a few could express the repressed during Ahidjo's era, a lot more are engaged in this role currently. Notwithstanding, it is only a front for those the secret service is sure about what they are saying, end up paying a visit to their underground "chapels" designed for political witch hunting. These playwrights success at exposing treachery, corruption, negligence, and the outright violation of the laws of the land simply because those in power think they can do whatever they like with a rudderless ship of state, is, to say the least, commendable given the odds. Through their efforts then, it becomes obvious that where human beings exist in groups, repression, to a certain extent, will exist, but the spirit of the oppressed will continue to fight back in any way possible. Using literature, drama in particular, as one way of fighting back by sensitizing the oppressed through theatrical renditions of oppressed facts has been a largely successful approach towards freedom.

Although writing about theater and political repression in Uganda, another country south of the Sahara, Rose Mbowa's words sound true of these Cameroonian playwrights. Their works are "… responses to the horrors unleashed by political repression" (87) on their people and they deem it their responsibility to fulfill their role as writers by joining, if not leading, in the yet to be militant struggle to liberate their people and install freedom. For freedom to the oppressed is their right being denied them; it is therefore a destination to which they must arrive, sooner or later, by one of two paths: the sound of their voices or that of the gun. The choice is largely in the hands of the oppressor. But since most oppressors are usually so stupidly selfish they always lead an innocent people through a bloody war only to return to the table, a choice they had been given at the onset. It is my hope that through these brave efforts at expressing the repressed by Cameroonian playwrights, The Cameroons' leadership will be patriotic enough as to listen to the oppressed lot, look within, and then engage in honest dialogue. Such an approach to nation-building will lead to a truly peaceful country peopled by hardworking, purposeful patriots dedicated to their homeland and its wellbeing, instead of irresponsibly masquerading a gulag held in place by Orwell's dogs, both foreign and domestic, in the name of a nation. Hence the idea of the playwright as a whistleblower who uses drama to express the repressed in The Cameroons.

NOTES

[1]The now legendary Ernest Ouandié was born in 1924 in Ndumla, Bana district in Haut-Nkam; a Bamileke man in other words. Ouandié is a household name in The Cameroons today because of his leadership role in the Union of the Peoples of Cameroon (*Union des Populations du Cameroun* – UPC), a left-wing pro-independence political party and their struggle for French speaking Cameroon's independence in the 1950s. Even after independence was accorded French Cameroon in January of 1960, Ouandié continued to resist the French-backed government of President Ahmadou Ahidjo. Accordingly, he was captured in 1970, tried and found guilty of plotting to assassinate Ahidjo. Ouandié was publicly executed on 15 January 1971 in Bafoussam.

[2]The seemingly less oppressive atmosphere in Biya's era was just a front. Bate Besong a firebrand scholar and playwright was detained when agents of the regime were finally able to understand some of his plays.

[3]Abel Eyinga and Albert Mukong were major political figures in The Cameroons: the former along Francophone lines and the latter Anglophone. Both were vehement critics of the Ahidjo and Biya regimes. Mukong, especially, remained a political prisoner under Ahidjo for most of his life. Because of his book *Prisoner Without a Crime*, he is also known to many by that title.

[4]The "K" in Weka, instead of a "C" mindful of the claim that "Weka" stands for West Cameroon, is an intentional allusion to German presence and influence

in the affairs of The Cameroons. Under German colonial influence, Cameroon was known as Kamerun; hence the "K" in "Weka."

[5] There is the need to understand that The Cameroons, in reality, has two national days—January 1, 1960 when La République du Cameroun gained her independence from France, and October 1, 1961 When Southern Cameroon became independent and joined La République du Cameroun to emerged with a federation of the two independent Cameroons: The Federal Republic of Cameroon. In a rather arbitrary, at best dubious, manner Ahmadou Ahidjo, albeit claims of a referendum, then president of Cameroon decided that May 20th will become the country's national day because on this day in 1972, according to Ahidjo, the nation voted against the federation to emerge with a Unitary system which was administered from Yaoundé solely. Hindsight, it was one successful step in the direction of eliminating the federal image of the country in a bid to finally eradicate the Southern Cameroon character of the nation as is seemingly the case today with the once-upon-a-time Federal Republic of Cameroon, which was made up of two Cameroons, now appearing as one nation with the appellation of one of the partners only: La République du Cameroun. This remains a national controversy as the former Southern Cameroons is questioning this new appellation which, obviously, does not represent her citizens. Hence the meaninglessness of this so-called national holiday to most Cameroonians, especially those of former Southern Cameroon.

Works Cited

Africanheritagevideo. *Cameroun: Autopsie D'une Pseudo Independence. You Tube.* Africanheritagevideo, 13 July 2013. www.youtube.com/watch?v=AB69vkTeBTA, 30 June 2016.

Atangana, Martin. *The End of French Rule in Cameroon.* UP of America, 2010.

Bayart, J. F. "The Structure of Political Power in Gaullist Africa." *Gaullist Africa: Cameroon Under Ahmadu Ahidjo.* Ed. Richard Joseph. Fourth Dimension, 1978. 66-81.

Besong, Bate. *Beasts of No Nation.* Nooremac, 1990.

Beti, Mongo. "The Hidden Truth About Cameroon." *Gaullist Africa: Cameroon Under Ahmadu Ahidjo.* Edited by Richard Joseph. Fourth Dimension, 1978, pp. 93-99.

Butake, Bole. "Dance of the Vampires." 1999. *Lake God and Other Plays*. CLE, 1999. 143-73.

Doh, Emmanuel Fru. *Anglophone-Cameroon Literature: An Introduction*. Lexington, 2015.

Epie'Ngome, Victor. *What God Has Put Asunder*. Pitcher, 1992.

Grabes, Herbert. "Literature in Society/Society and Its Literature." in *Literature in Society*. Edited by Regina Rudaityte, Cambridge Scholars, 2012, pp. 1-17.

Joseph, Richard (ed.). "The Gaullist Legacy." *Gaullist Africa: Cameroon Under Ahmadu Ahidjo*. Fourth Dimension, 1978. pp. 12-27.

Konings, Piet, and Francis B. Nyamnjoh. *Negotiating an Anglophone Identity: A Study of the Politics of Recognition and Representation in Cameroon*. Brill, 2003.

Mbowa, Rose. "Theater and Political Repression in Uganda." *Research in African Literatures* vol. 27, no. 3, 1996, pp. 87-97.

Mutia, Ba'bila. *Before This Time, Yesterday*. Silex/Nouvelles du Sud, n.d.

Ngugi, wa Thiongo. *Decolonising the Mind: The Politics of Language in African Literature*. James Currey, 1986.

Ngwane, George. *Bate Besong (Or the Symbol of Anglophone Hope)*. Nooremac, 1993.

Okagbue, Osita. "Dreams Deferred: National Theatres and National Development in Africa." *Performance Inter-Actions in African Theatre 3: Making Space, Rethinking Drama and Theatre in Africa*. Edited by Kene Igweonu and Osita Okagbue. Cambridge Scholars, 2013, pp. 51-71.

Reef, Anne. "The Art of Darkness: Repression and Its Expression in J. M. Coetzee's Waiting for the Barbarians, Athol Fugard's Tsotsi and Sue Coe and Holly Metz's How to Commit Suicide in South Africa." *IJOCA* Spring. vol. 1, 2007, pp. 332-52.

Zenenga, Praise. "Hit-and-Run Theatre: The Rise of a New Dramatic Form in Zimbabwe." *African and African American Theatre Past and Present*. Edited by Rhona Justice-Malloy. U of Alabama P, pp. 14-20, 2010, vol. 30 of *Theatre History Studies 2010*.

Chapter 3

Bill F. Ndi's *Gods in the Ivory Towers*: An Expression of Universal Academic Tragedy

Richard Evans

Gods in the Ivory Towers is a one-act, academic play, set in a post-colonial, developing country in Africa. We understand immediately that we are in Africa from the names of the places and characters, but a definite geographic location is left purposely vague as the action of the play takes place in dream space or imagination as we are informed specifically by the playwright in the Foreword: "Purely from the realm of imagination and experiences lived in dreams, the passage from the real to the hereafter; any coincidences in names of places or persons spring from imaginative nomenclature..."(*Gods in the Ivory Towers* 3). This curious disclaimer hints at a society fraught with issues of freedom of speech and expression, and with potential tragic consequences. Since the author, Bill F. Ndi, is Cameroonian, the critic and scholar Peter Vakunta, in his 2010 review of the play for the Langaa Research an Publishing Group, presumes that the center of the action of the drama, the village college in Ngoa, is a microcosm of the tense, often corrupt, academic and national politics in contemporary The Cameroons itself: "[i]n no uncertain terms, this play satirizes pseudo-intellectualism in the playwright's country of origin" (Web). With The Cameroons as an assumed backdrop, political, social and linguistic tensions dramatized in this play have been explored carefully by Africanists Emmanuel Fru Doh and Aduku T. Ankumah in her recent book, *Nomenclatural Poetization and Globalization* (Chapters Eight and Nine).

As a drama protesting academic corruption against the often unseemly political antics of a developing nation with a burdensome colonial legacy, *Gods in the Ivory Towers* has immediate appeal for audience and for critics searching to anchor the play in the actual life experiences of its Cameroonian author. Post-colonial literary theory, too, offers instant grist for a critic's mill and certainly a legitimate framework for socio-literary analysis of this play and its author's role as a critic of his own society through drama. Radical, African theorist Frantz Fanon reminds us of the significance of artist and thinker in the struggle for African development when he quotes the words of Sékou Touré at the beginning of his essay, "On National Culture": "There is no place outside that fight [against colonial oppression] for the artist or the intellectual....." (266). Although the words of the play's Foreword are meant perhaps only as a political cover for the author, they also provide a broader, interpretive direction for understanding the drama in academe overall beyond the African setting of the work itself since solely Cameroonian politics or locale unnecessarily limits appreciating the cosmopolitan implications of any text or play, like the one under study, which expands into the academic macrocosm. Universal concerns about the intellectual integrity of the individual scholar, bureaucratic corruption of academic freedom and its relation to the pressures of political forces outside the university are played out in a local context but extend beyond it. Indeed, aspects of *Gods in the Ivory Towers* could as easily be a factual report on academic malfeasance in the United States, found almost every month in *the Chronicle of Higher Education,* as much as they are the center of this fictional play, satirizing dysfunctional educational practices in linguistically divided The Cameroons.

The following critique will focus on the universal aspects of the play that, although occurring in an African setting, transcend African politics or geography. First, the plot will be summarized and reviewed briefly to provide a basic orientation to the play for those who may not be familiar with the content; next, the events of the plot will be analyzed carefully to bring out its cosmopolitan features in contrast to its particular local characteristics. The tragic arc of the plot will show a classical, Aristotelian movement that contributes to universalizing the rise and fall of the protagonist and supports a cosmopolitan message beyond merely a Cameroonian setting. Thus the play operates on two levels, both as a protest against specific abuses of Francophone higher education in The Cameroons and as a general admonition against misuse of the values academic meritocracy wherever such abuses happen in world of academe.

While Doh, Ankumah and Vakunta, cited above, read *Gods in the Ivory Towers* against the topical socio-political background of The

Cameroons, stressing prevalent and continuing issues of post-colonial corruption, political factionalism, linguistic disunities and specific African nomenclatural symbolism, the play also invites broader considerations of the fiction of academic meritocracy and or mediocrity which arise in many academic settings beyond The Cameroons or Africa. Honest academic ambition, thwarted by sexual and political harassment, the major subject of the play, is an all too common issue in academe beyond the borders of a developing nation. Moreover, the title of the play with its plural *Towers* points to issues in many academic settings beyond Africa. It is all too obvious to anyone who has been subject to a dissertation or tenure review committee that professors, department heads, and deans are, indeed, even without capricious abuse, "gods" in their own realm. Thus, these "gods" pose a challenge to their advisees who would love to express their disagreements and or repressed thoughts and feelings but through the power rituals of academe are reduced to mere conformity, stripped of realistic, oppositional response and left only what James C. Scott considers to be a "public transcripts" which are generally "performances" acceptable to the controlling group (1-16; 43-69).

The action of the one-act *Gods in the Ivory Towers* involves five characters, three students, Ojong, Mballa and the protagonist Ngwa; two academicians from the University of Ngoa, Lecturer Nnomo and the Head of Department, Professor Guignol. The names of these academicians as suggested by Doh and Ankumah echoes the expression of the repressed. Ankumah especially writing about the Head of Department points out, "Thus he is a pawn of the government, controlled by others who are more powerful but giving the appearance that he is in charge." And of the lecturer she says, "[h]er name, Nnomo, which appears like a homophone of "no more" may be Ngwa's way of resisting the frustration…" (qtd. in *Nomenclatural Poetization and Globalization* 163-165).

Also, standing outside the action of the play itself, there is, an unnamed Narrator, the town crier and seer, who introduces the setting, intrudes several times during the course of the action to control the time line within the plot, and after the conclusion of the dramatic action gives a final comment on the fate of Ngwa, projected into the future, years after the play has ended. Given the importance of names in the play, and especially the name of the protagonist, the Narrator's lack of a name raises immediate questions. How does the absence of a name limit the Narrator's power to intervene in the action of the play? He seems to control the time frame of the plot, but nothing else. Does the Narrator's position as a reporter, a non-actor in the drama, open up space for the expression of typically repressed words and actions? The Narrator's invisibility, in spite of his highly significant role in the scheme of plot structuring of the play, challenges one to questioning whether in Bill F. Ndi's dramatic universe, characters such as his protagonist and Narrator—with such important role—must be reduced to nothing. Again, could it be as Ankumah holds, "a form of resistance to the status quo"? It clear that this act of resistance to naming is the playwrights way of casting the Narrator in a position of defiance to any form of ethnic identification—the tool generally used by the powers that be to repress the common man (165). Anonymity has its price but also its power: While the nameless Narrator is repressed out of the dramatic action, the repressed ugliness of ethnic and linguistic discrimination is expressed fully.

Before the action of the play opens, the Narrator sets the stage. He informs the audience that the protagonist has a name of destiny, that of the village hill, Ngoa. His father has so named Ngwa to give him the same strength as the hill, Ngoa, that formidable obstacle that all in the village must overcome and on which stands the village college, the academic climb through which will be the subject of the coming short play. The name and setting all bring to mind the idea of an imposition as well as challenges heaped upon a people. It echoes the idea of the all too common cliché "uphill task". And the destiny child is intended to fight the overbearing repression.

The action itself of the drama commences with a short scene, a conversation between Ngwa and his fellow student Mballa about Ngwa's name of destiny, his academic ambition and his (over)confidence in achieving his academic goals. Ngwa confirms the power his name and destiny against the doubts of Mballa:

> MBALLA (Stands up from his sitting position. Scratches his forehead) I just don't know how to put it. But I will be plain and

direct. Do you think your father did justice in choosing your name?

NGWA (Still laughing) Look at.... (pauses) Look at ....my friend, I laugh not because I am stupid. Maybe because I am blind to seeing the plagues around us and have for eyes just the mind. And far beyond the ordinary, and maybe the naming! (Toning higher) My name! Yes, it was justice! I mean justice done! done to me and entire people of Ngoa! (6-7)

Here the protagonist displays some overconfidence that the ancient Greeks called *hybris*. We can recall, for example, the positive mood of Oedipus in the open scene of *Oedipus, the King*, as he is entreated by his subjects to save them from the plague in their city as he has already saved them from the Sphinx. The form of the entreaty is, in fact, the form of a prayer, an entreaty to a god, which Oedipus accepts without demure. Perhaps overconfidence is Ngwa's tragic flaw as it was for Oedipus.

Then, very quickly, the Narrator advances the time frame to the next scene where he locates Ngwa already having arrived on campus in his intellectual prime. We find Ngwa on campus, again in conversation with another student, Ojong, who is depressed and discouraged about the problems of discrimination he has encountered as a student. Ngwa exudes his previously displayed (over)confidence to Mballa in his comments to Ojong during their discussion: "Just don't stop believing in the ultimate victory and in yourself"(20). Immediately after this confident affirmation, in which Ngwa encourages Ojong to move upward and onward in the face of discouraging odds, poignantly, Ngwa knocks at the office door of his soon-to-be degree supervisor, where the significant complication in the plot begins to unfold and Ngwa's overconfidence is put to the test.

The dramatic arc has risen deliberately and gently to this point but the dramatic crisis is looming for Ngwa with his middle-aged, female supervisor, Nnomo, who wants sexual favors in return for academic support. When he refuses to give into to her explicit inappropriate advances, Ngwa suffers a sharp reversal of his academic fortune. He is accused of sexual harassment by his supervisor in a Potiphar's wife ploy and expelled from the university through her influence with the department head, Professor Guignol who himself has a sexual relationship with Nnomo. Furthermore, Ngwa is exiled from the village because the department head employs his political connections to the village king. Thus, Ngwa's ambitions for advancement in the village are defeated temporarily through both academic and political corruption. It is no doubt Doh underlines the fact that Bill F. Ndi's consideration of, "the HOD a sex puppet is a damning verdict on the powers that be in the nation, village, or university campus called Ngoa." (Qtd. *in* Ankumah 181)

The compact simplicity of the plot, carried forward by Ngwa's conversations with thinly developed characters, turns the locus of critical interest of the play in two directions, to its African political issues, which have been the subject of previously noted critical commentary and toward the structure of its plot. The importance of the latter will be analyzed in detail here below.

First, however, on the point of character development in the play, the Africanist critic, Peter Wuteh Vakunta, in the previously cited, 2010 review of *Gods in the Ivory Towers*, notes that the play neglects, in general, building fully formed characters and further suggests this lack of development as flaw of hasty composition: "One shortcoming of the play is its skeletal characterization. There are no round characters in the play."(Web.) If we agree with Vakunta that the characters are, in fact, psychologically sketchy or flat, then perhaps they are meant to work more as motivators and directors of action in the plot than as highly developed, psychological character studies in themselves. Although Bill F. Ndi's play does not present characters as mere abstractions, such as those in a morality play like the late Medieval *Everyman*, the power of the drama definitely lies in its action, the development of professorial collusion and injustice, rather than in the characterization. The critic must wonder if this "skeletal characterization," pointed out by Vakunta, could be a deliberate authorial strategy to focus on the action itself, based, in fact, on Aristotle's original definition that tragedy: "in its essence is an imitation, not of men as such, but of action and life, but of happiness and misery (*On the Art of Poetry*, trans. Cooper, 24). Here a student of drama might suggest an apt comparison between character development in Sophocles' *Oedipus, The King* and that of Euripides'

Medea. Whereas *Oedipus* relies on the reversal of fortune and precipitous fall of the protagonist as its central focus, *Medea,* although offering no true tragic hero of the Aristotelian type, does present several well-rounded characters beyond the protagonist, the philosophizing nurse, the caddish Jason and a subtle chorus as the core of its entertainment interest. The audience can hardly see the lack of full psychological development in the subordinate characters of *Oedipus, The King* as a literary flaw. In fact, Aristotle has argued to good effect that it is the action in drama which is central, not necessarily the characters:

> In a play, consequently, the agents do not perform for the sake of representing their individual dispositions, rather, the display of moral character is included as subsidiary to the things that are done. So that the incidents of the action, and the structural ordering of these incidents, constitute the end and purpose of the tragedy. (*Aristotle* 24)

This principle, applied to *Gods in the Ivory Towers,* could suggest a deliberate move by Bill F. Ndi to de-stress character development and would contribute to emphasizing the universality of the action over the particularity of character psychology in the play. There would be, then, no need for a critic to speculate, as Vakunta does, about hasty composition on the part of the playwright as the source of some deficiency in character development within the drama. Contrast, for example, those characters in Euripides' *Medea* and Sophocles' *Oedipus, the King.* In the *Medea,* even minor figures such as the nurse and tutor get full-blown, sharply defined personalities. Jason and Medea are highly realistic figures with carefully drawn psychologies since the psychology of revenge is the focus of the play. In the *Oedipus,* on the other hand, characters like shepherds and even major figures such as Creon and Jocasta serve more as backdrops to the universal philosophical problems of the fate of Oedipus, the god's justice and human freewill. Sophocles' play emphasizes philosophical issues whereas Euripides' play stresses the intricacies of personality; both are forceful plays but the development of characters is totally different.

If they are not highly refined through personal psychology, then the characters' names, uniquely African, do function as important signs for the direction and movement of the plot as well as clues to potential, Cameroonian political commentary. The significant role of onomastics in the play has been discussed in Adaku T. Ankmah's remarks, "All in a Name: Nomenclature in Francis B. Nyamnjoh's *The Travail of Dieudonne'* and Bill F. Ndi's *Gods in the Ivory Towers*" in *Nomenclatural Poetization and Globalization*, Chapter Eight. First to speak, actually before the action of the play itself begins, is the significantly nameless Narrator. Emphasizing the importance of names in the play, Ankumah sees this namelessness as a political statement by the author: "Remaining nameless can also be a form of resistance to the status quo." But beyond "cry[ing] for the wasted youth" (*Gods in the Ivory Towers* 4) and protesting the societal status quo, the Narrator provides essential framing role before and after actual drama. He offers information about the protagonist's name and fate before the drama actually starts, controls the time within the play by intruding into the action and changing the scenes throughout, and after the drama ends, predicts the future. Although the Narrator is essential for framing the drama, he is not really a character in the play; he has no existence in the action itself and thus, no name. From the superior position of a seer, outside of the action, he controls time; after the play ends, he authoritatively pronounces from that superior knowledge Ngwa's ultimate triumph in a somewhere distant future:

> Months have passed and well as years! Guess what happened to Ngwa! [...]. Ngwa now views his people looking up for him to drop them his bread crumbs. (53)

The Narrator is the non-time bound spokesman, unlike all the other characters, who allows the audience to see beyond the temporary tragedy of Ngwa's immediate misfortune within the scope of the play itself. He sees into the future, outside of the drama, where Ngwa has fulfilled his name. Thus, protagonist's name, Ngwa, marks the play with a distinctive African color but also translates that name beyond mere quotidian political issues into the realm of universal symbol. Ngwa has the same name of the local hill, Ngoa, as the unnamed Narrator states in the introduction:

> Nevertheless, Pa Mbeh, a lunatic...thought in naming his son after the hill, he was imbuing this child with the strength which will permit him to untie the fate the gods have tied and dropped in front of his fellow villagers....Taking cognizance of this fact, the son is goaded to fulfill his father's dream.... (*Gods in the Ivory Towers* 4)

Casting the protagonist's father, Pa Mbeh as a lunatic is in and of itself a subtle statement from the author, pointing out the overbearing repression that the people of Ngoa are subjected to on a daily basis. It has left everyone on the verge of lunacy and only a madman would dare to take to challenging the status quo. Besides a madman who gives a destiny name to his child cannot be held liable for the becoming of his child. Again, Bill F. Ndi draws attention to the fact that his is a universe in which repression has peaked the height of ridicule that the lone visionary is a madman who has the wisdom to vest his hopes and aspirations in his son's name.

The playwright himself provides insight into the way Cameroonian writers use name symbolism to create literary characters in "The Global Reader and Names in Literary Works by Peter W. Vakunta, Bill F. Ndi and Emmanuel Fru Doh":

> The name thus transcends its primary role/function as a character identity marker to become an embodiment of the character's wellbeing or malaise; in short, his or her entire existence. (Qtd. in Ankumah, *Nomenclatural Poetization and Globalization* 125)

This name of destiny, pronounced by the Narrator/seer before the action of play commences, relates Ngwa both to African as well as to world literary tradition. Ngwa's fate is linked powerfully by his name to the characteristics of the village hill, Ngoa, high standing as well as an obstacle to be overcome by all who need to climb it. Ngwa is set on the trajectory of climbing by the destiny of his name, and his journey is universalized through that mythical symbolism evoked by climbing the mountain, the mountaintop experience. The fateful name initiates the dramatic arc of *Gods in the Ivory Towers* as the fateful name, Oedipus, resolves the dramatic arc in Sophocles' *Oedipus, The King* when the shepherd messenger definitively reveals the identity of Oedipus: "So you were named, from this (mis)fortune, who you are" (*Oedipus Rex* 1036, my translation). The name of Oedipus, revealing his self-identification as the murderer of his own father, serves as the linchpin in the unraveling of his life, the reversal of his previous good fortune, at the very moment of his personal epiphany in the play *Oedipus, The King*. In *Gods in the Ivory Towers*, Ngwa's name forecasts a successful outcome to Ngwa and the audience. Ngwa's tragedy, his fall, evolves from defeat of his personal self-assessment and immediate expectations, and only the seer unbound by time or ethnic identity can ameliorate Ngwa's tragedy for the audience by revealing the future successes beyond the play itself.

The protagonist realizes the significance of his own name from the very outset and the destiny it foreordains at the beginning of the drama. In the first interaction of the play, a conversation between Mballa and Ngwa, Mballa asks Ngwa what he thinks about his name: "Do you think your father did justice in choosing your name?" (6) Ngwa confidently answers the query with an almost messianic enthusiasm: "Yes! My name! Yes, it was justice! I mean justice done. Done to me and to the entire people of Ngoa" (7). Mballa is not on stage to reveal the psychology of his own character but to showcase Ngwa's name of destiny and the confidence Ngwa has in the power of that name to direct the future of his successes.

At the end of this first scene, after the dialogue on destiny between Ngwa and his friend Mballa, collapsing time, the Narrator intrudes and directs the audience out of the action in order to comment on Ngwa's progress up the hill of academic success:

> Time has passed. With astute ease, Ngwa has been successful in climbing the ladder up to the summit of Ngoa; well developed muscles, well read, he finds himself at the village center, the very peak of Ngoa! (11)

Ngwa is now a post-graduate student at the village university. His symbolic climb up the hill of attainment reveals a young man in his prime, ready to develop academic prowess and translate that success into some kind of political or social power. While he is searching for an academic supervisor for his post-graduate project in sociology, Ngwa expresses his philosophy of complete positivity in a dialogue with a skeptical and depressed fellow student Ojong: "Just don't stop believing in the ultimate victory and in yourself" (*Gods in Ivory Towers* 22)! Right here Ngwa begins his trajectory to defeat as he, relying on his overconfident philosophy of positive thinking, with youthful exuberance and naiveté, encounters the corrupt, linguistic and sexual politics of his university. He convinces a thirty-something year old female lecturer to take him on as a research student, despite the fact that he is not a native speaker of French, a significant political disadvantage in a pro-French university, where Francophones hold the positions of administrative power and discriminate against Anglophone bilinguals as Vakunta notes in his review that: "Professor Guignol is openly spiteful of Anglophone students" (Web) and he cites the play text where the professor rhetorically derides English speakers: "These English speakers...! Do you think it is for nothing that we label them in our tongue, I mean French as 'les gauchers'?" (40)... In fact, the uneasy co-existence between these two linguistic communities is captured in the following remark from Professor Guignol: "You know... Em! Em! Don't you think that you would find it a bit difficult pursuing your studies in a language so foreign to Anglophones?" (23)

But far worse for Ngwa than linguistic discrimination, which apparently he has overcome in his first interview with the Head of Department, is his relationship with his female supervisor Nnomo. Her role in the play to provide a focus for sexual corruption, which most typically in Western academe comes in the form of male-on-female harassment. But for Ngwa, the reverse is true and this unexpected reversal of gender harassment creates a seemingly more perverse, topsy-turvy world for the protagonist. After many attempts to arrange an advisory meeting, Ngwa finally visits Nnomo's house one morning for long-awaited, academic supervision. There he is greeted by a blatant attempt at seduction:

    NNOMO   The living room is not conducive for me! Come and let's discuss your work here. One's got to be relaxed...!
    NGWA   (*Hesitantly makes for the room. Disbelieving his eyes. Screams!*) OOO Oh! Good God!

NNOMO (*Stark naked seating on her bed with legs well spread out. Threatening with a finger place on her mouth.*) Sh... shut it up! Make no scandal! Or else you shall... (35)

Even in the face of such forceful sexual aggression, which Ngwa finds intensely distasteful, he wants to argue logically and naively asserts that his business is academics only: "I came here to talk academics, no more, no less" (36). Ngwa frantically runs out of the house, leaving Nnomo naked and frustrated on the bed. Her role in the above scene is far from feminist critic, Nfar-Abbenyi's; she posits that African women are "portrayed as passive, as always prepared to do the bidding of their husbands and family, as having no status of their own and therefore completely dependent on their husbands" (4). Bill F. Ndi's casting of Nnomo in this light heavily contradicts what most feminist critics have often chastised as male tradition in African writing for attributing roles of powerlessness, haplessness, subservience, passivity, etc. Nnomo is a "career academic", asserting her powers and influence in an effort to reverse the roles in a male dominated society. She is in position of power and does all she can to prove she is in control. Bill F. Ndi seem to suggest a self-determined character—be him male or be her female—with agency like Nnomo would oppress those with lesser influence. With this representation, Nnomo does not fit Deidre LaPin's "classic and inescapable image of wife-mother at the core of the feminine literary persona" (qtd. *in* Nfar-Abbenyi 4).

Almost immediately, upon leaving Nnomo's residence, indignant Ngwa heads for the office of the Head of Department to lodge a formal complaint for sexual harassment against his supervisor. But before he can get to Professor Guignol, Nnomo has anticipated his move, got there first and prejudiced the air. She must reclaim whatever power her position as a university lecturer grants her, even if that entails slandering an innocent student whose only crime is that of rejecting her sexual advances. She engages the professor in a dialogue.

NNOMO (*Takes in a deep breath*) Professor, you remember that small rascal....
HOD The one under your supervision?

NNOMO Yes! That Anglophone! He has begun fomenting trouble.... (39-40)

Until this point, Ngwa has suffered persistent difficulties getting an appointment with his supervisor and a blatant inappropriate sexual advance. Yet at this stage, he seems to have no idea of the bigger picture of corruption, the illicit pact between his supervisor and the Head of Department that will cost him his academic career. With his accustomed naiveté and bravado, Ngwa boldly goes forward with his complaint to Professor Guignol: "I have a formal complaint to make! I came here for that!" (41).

What occurs now, however, is much worse for Ngwa than suffering a lecturer's inappropriate sexual advance. Professor Guignol and Lecturer Nnomo have colluded to expel Ngwa from the university because their own personal interests and prejudices, Nnomo because she has been jilted and Guignol because he is jealous of Ngwa's youthfulness and further dislikes his Anglophone background. This collusion, seemingly unanticipated by Ngwa, between his superiors in the academic hierarchy represents a betrayal of any semblance of fairness or impartiality, a complete violation of the academic principle of judgment on the basis of merit. Yet Ngwa, holding on to naive idealism, his tragic flaw of overconfidence, remains incredulous about his situation to the very end. The reversal of his status from student to expelled student and his recognition of that reversal occur in the same moment while he still argues and struggles as he is cast down from the summit of Ngoa:

HOD *(Pounces on Ngwa. Grabs him by the throat. To Nnomo.)* Get hold of him by the legs! We have to throw his down the abyss.

NGWA *(wrestling with HOD. Stern)* If this is a joke, then it has become like a hand shake that's gone beyond the elbow! So stop it.

(HOD and Nnomo continue jostling him: struggling to put him down. They finally get to putting him down.)....

NGWA *(Laughing)* This is the greatest blunder that both of you are committing; thinking power means madness and greatness, constant rise. No...! *(As they let him fall.)* This is not the way to repay an honest citizen and son of a taxpayer. We shall meet again when I shall rise to face Ngoa anew! (45)

In an almost non-existent denouement, Ngwa is not shown suffering as, for example, Oedipus the final section of *Oedipus, The King*. In fact, the final lines of the play show Nnomo and Guignol off to nightclub or restaurant to celebrate crassly their mutual victory, gloating over the expulsion of Ngwa who has all along believed in the merits of hard work, integrity, and dignity:

HOD   He is now gone! Let's go and feast over this victory! Where can we go to?
NNOMO   The nightclub! Or a decent restaurant downtown! (46)

The place of choice to celebrate this insipid victory is in and of itself a statement to lambast the reduction of genuine intellectual pursuit to the mediocrity of belly politics or carnal pursuit. For, from every indication, neither is a restaurant nor a nightclub any place comparable to the Salons of the French Revolutionary era wherein the philosophes could meet, reflect, recollect and discuss seriously on a variety of issues plaguing the society. Could the levity of the choice for a setting to celebrate Ngwa's expulsion and fall be read as a desire, from the playwright, to highlight how oblivious these oppressors, dubbed *Gods* are in treating lightly the misery they visit upon the oppressed?

The above discussed slap-stick expulsion scene, with Ngwa being quite literally thrown out and the comical victory exit of Guignol and Nnomo, lend some support to Vakunta's question of how to classify *Gods in the Ivory Towers* in terms of genre: tragedy, tragicomedy or comedy. Tragedy, however, would appear the best answer, despite the satirical elements in the play. The plot structure that reveals Ngwa's change of states from academic achievement to expulsion does follow Aristotle's conception of the involved plot. He underscores that:

An involved action is one in which the change of fortune is attended by such Reversal [*As Aristotle explains, a change from one state to its exact opposite*] or by such Discovery [*recognition of a heretofore unknown factor*], or by both and each of these two incidents should arise from the structure of the plot itself; that is, each should be the necessary or probable result of the incidents that have gone before, and not merely following them in point of time-for in the sequence of events there is a vast difference between *post hoc* and *propter hoc*. (Aristotle, *Art of Poetry* 34)

Ngwa who has expected success all along; on the issue of sexual harassment, goes to the office of the HOD in full expectation that Professor Guignol will receive his complaint seriously. Then, in the same moment, he discovers the truth of corruption and collusion in his university as he is expelled physically by the offending supervisor and the authority to whom he is appealing his case. Ngwa goes from student in good standing to expelled *persona non grata* in a flash of time. Regardless of the comedic expulsion scene and the final, satirical victory celebration of Nnomo and Guignol, the audience realizes that Ngwa is truly a miserable, tragic figure at the end of the drama. And his tragedy seems not to differ from that of those in the post-colonial setting of the play. His state is confirmed explicitly by the commentary of the Narrator, who speaking from outside the dramatic action of the play, summarizes Ngwa's final status:

> NARRATOR (*Enter. Miserable.*) God forbid bad things. I will never show up here again to tell that which was not fair to any sane mind, Just three days after Ngwa has fallen and heavily, too. That was not sufficient. The King ordered Ngwa's banishment from the village. (46)

This key commentary tells of the playwright's desire to address the too often discarded unfairness to any sane mind as the Narrator states. He further strikes a note of hope with promises by the Narrator to make this his last appearance to show or tell that which is repressed in this dramatic universe. The audience can only hope were the Narrator to reappear, he would be bringing them good tidings. Ngwa's troubles have continued to multiply from academic expulsion to political banishment as his position deteriorates even farther away from that earlier, expected success predicted by his name of destiny.

The tragic arc concludes rapidly with *peripeteia* and *anagnorisis*, but does Ngwa's fate excite in the audience emotions of pity and fear that Aristotle's theory of tragedy expect? Perhaps, if the audience is one in the developing world where educational options are few and public universities are closely linked to the dominant political regime. A U.S. or European audience might react with more indignation at the injustice and mockery of merit, but that attitude grows out of the knowledge that in such a situation students in more democratic systems have many options, legal and personal. If conforming to a corrupt *status quo* or being thrown out of the university were the only real choices facing an audience in a repressive economic and political situation, Ngwa's fall, no doubt, would provoke fear and pity, particularly since the Narrator confirms that the play has ended in tragedy for Ngwa despite those elements of comic lampoon, satire, and exaggeration in the final scene.

The Narrator, however, is not finished yet. After a brief moment off stage, he comes back for a last report on Ngwa, years in the future:

> Hey folks! I really have to come back though I promised not to. You really have to know! Months have passed, as well as years! ... Ngwa now views his people looking up for him to drop them his bread crumbs.... And now I see those who ejected him longing they were with him. (47)

Ngwa has achieved success beyond the framework of the play; he has arrived at the top of another height—Gerinah Heights—but the audience does not get the particulars. He has fulfilled the destiny of his name in a somewhat unspecified manner but clearly not through justice at the college of Ngoa from which he was ejected by a corrupt and vindictive collusion of the professors under whose authority his academic life was directed and subsequently deleted.

What message does *Gods in the Ivory Towers* reveal? Vakunta and Doh see primarily a critique of Cameroonian politics; a political protest, played out in the microcosm of a university setting. This reading is, no doubt, compelling and realistic, yet looking beyond the politics of a specific nation, we can visualize events and attitudes that move us beyond specific political scenario of one nation to academe in general. At the end, through the Narrator, who exists above the time frame of play itself, we hear of the ultimate triumph of the tragic protagonist who has clearly been defeated within the temporal limits of the play itself. The Narrator, standing outside the action, narrates a prophetic and comprehensive diegesis that reports the position of Ngwa at the beginning of the action and his final disposition of ultimate triumph: "Now I see those who ejected him longing they were with him" (47). Those professors who appeared as gods to an abused student now are shown to be the petty, provincial functionaries that have always been, toying with the ambitions of their students who believe that they are gods. The god-like status of the corrupt professors is resisted by Ngwa, resulting in his dismissal from the university. Attaining power through certified knowledge in a corrupt bureaucratic system is shown to have its limits. A degree from The University of Ngoa is not the only route to power. In the end, the professors see their own lower positions in the political pecking order. The Narrator reveals that the roles of Ngwa and those who cast him down have been reversed completely: "Ngwa now views his people looking up for him to drop them his bread crumbs" (47). Again, the note of longing expressed by those who ejected Ngwa points to the fact that his success has been met at a more auspicious clime that attracts the envy of those who wanted him down in the first place. Ngwa's has transcended the defeats of his tragic past and victory is complete.

From the foregone analysis, the dominant message of *Gods in the Ivory Towers* is monitory, suggesting that academicians have less power than one might be lulled into conceiving that they have. Through Ngwa's tragedy, Bill F. Ndi exposes a bigger social, national and even universal tragedy. As much as the play reveals the petit corruption of Anglophone and Francophone politics in the Cameroonian education system (Vakunta), the play underscores the need for professors in whatever setting to be more philosophical, supporting academic values of open enquiry and honest research where they can be true philosopher kings, rather than acting as tin-pot dictators in a microcosm that is ultimately subordinate to broader, cosmopolitan forces.

Works Cited

Ankumah, Aduku T. "All in a Name: Nomenclature in Francis B. Nyamnjoh's *The Travail of Dieudonné* and Bill F. Ndi's *Gods in the Ivory Towers.*" In *Nomenclatural Poetization and Globalization*. Edited by Adaku T. Ankumah, Langaa RPCIG, 2014, pp. 145-168.

Aristotle. *On the Art of Poetry*. Translated by Lane Cooper. Rev. (ed.), Cornell UP, 1947.

Doh, Emmanuel Fru. "Names and Nomenclatural Distortions as Dramatic Technique in Anglo-phone-Cameroonian Literature." In *Nomenclatural Poetization and Globalization*. Edited by Adaku T. Ankumah, Langaa RPCIG, 2014, pp. 169-193.

Fanon, Frantz. "On National Culture." In *Everyday Theory: A Contemporary Reader*. Edited by Becky McLaughlin and Bob Coleman. Pearson, 2005.

Ndi, Bill F. *Gods in the Ivory Tower: A Play*. Authorhouse, 2008.

_____. "The Global Reader and Names in Literary Works by Peter W. Vakunta, Bill F. Ndi and Emmanuel Fru Doh." In *Nomenclatural Poetization and Globalization*. Edited by Adaku T. Ankumah, Langaa RPCIG, 2014, pp. 133-144.

Nfar-Abbenyi, J.M. *Gender in African Women's Writing: Identity, Sexuality, and Difference*. Indiana U.P. 1997.

Scott, James C. *Domination and the Arts of Resistance: Hidden Transcripts*, Yale U.P. 1990.

Sophocles. *Oedipus Tyrannus. Sophoclis Fabulae*. Edited by A.C. Pearson, Oxford UP, 1924.

Vakunta, Peter W. "Book Review: Bill F. Ndi, *Gods in the Ivory Towers: A Play*." Langaa Research and Publishing Initiative Group. www.langaa-rpcig.net/+Book-Review-Bill-F-Ndi-Gods-in-the+.html Accessed 4 March, 2016.

Chapter 4

Francis Nyamnjoh's *Soul's Forgotten*: A Rejection of Poor Education and Failing Democracy

Benjamin Hart Fishkin

No, I'm talking about the way universities operate, every day, more and more like corporations. As Benjamin Ginsberg details in his 2011 book, "The Fall of the Faculty: The Rise of the All Administrative University and Why It Matters," a constantly expanding layer of university administrative jobs now exists at an increasing remove from the actual academic enterprise. It's not unheard of for colleges now to employ more senior administrators than professors. There are, of course, essential functions that many university administrators perform, but such an imbalance is absurd — try imagining a high school with more vice principals than teachers. This legion of bureaucrats enables a world of pitiless surveillance; no segment of campus life, no matter how small, does not have some administrator who worries about it. Piece by piece, every corner of the average campus is being slowly made congruent with a single, totalizing vision. The rise of endless brushed metal and glass buildings at Purdue represents the aesthetic dimension of this ideology. Bent into place by a small army of apparatchiks, the contemporary American college is slowly becoming as meticulously art directed and branded as a J. Crew catalog. Like Nike town or Disneyworld, your average college campus now leaves the distinct impression of a one party state.

--Fredrik deBoer, "Why We Should Fear University, Inc.: Against the Corporate Taming of the American College", *The New York Times*, September 9, 2015

A democracy is only as coherent as its public institutions. Institutions need people and those people must be cooperative with one another. Frederik deBoer's reference to academic jobs that exist "at an increasing remove from the actual academic enterprise" represents a sharp and purposeful break in the structure of the modern university. A broader social view of the subject means that for children to develop properly they must be well educated and well schooled. This, on a wide and international scale, is not happening. The young must trust in their surroundings and believe in the democracy that they are allegedly a part of. This is also not happening and it is because the system of education is not conducive to how education should work.

Nowhere is this truer than in the literature of Francis B. Nyamnjoh, who goes out of his way to portray how the poor education of his protagonist is indeed a cause for all of us to panic. To begin such a study with a long quotation such as this one, published less than four months ago in *The New York Times*, is necessary and relevant because functional democracy so relies upon education and the political will to extend it to everyone—even those who cannot afford to pay for it. The poor education of Emmanuel Kwanga, Nyamnjoh's protagonist, is widespread throughout the world. The author presents this narrative as a way for him to reject as unacceptable a system that does nothing at all other than prepare those imprisoned within it for failure. *Souls Forgotten* describes a situation in which the poor education conferred on Emmanuel Kwanga is an image in a mirror. It is the author's hope that everyone who gazes into the pier glass will take notice and change what appears on the wall space between the windows.

Almost seven decades ago Jean-Paul Sartre told everyone about the need for the writer to make sense of the world that surrounds him or her. The writer exists to actively and provocatively point out problems while removing the wool that has been pulled (often by ourselves and our loved ones) over our eyes. The purpose is to free, to liberate, to educate and change the readers' thought process. "I am given this world with its injustices, it is not so that I might contemplate them coldly, but that I might animate them with my indignation" (Sartre 62). Sartre looks at authorship as the most effective way to present displeasure to society. Nyamnjoh does the same thing, but in *Souls Forgotten* there is so much more shit to shovel (Sartre 62). The abnormal impairments of Africa are even more intricate and more insidious than those of Sartre's Paris. *Souls Forgotten* is a dystopian novel, giving George Orwell, Aldous Huxley and

Margaret Atwood a run for their money in the present without having to dream up a nightmarish future.

A coroner or pathologist who looks at Mimboland with deliberation finds an Africa which must reshape itself. It is a locale enmeshed in the throes of a spiritual deficit and the viewer has no time for lamentation. This is the subject of Nyamnjoh's *Souls Forgotten*. He is pinpointing for all of us that the forward progress of the African is what is repressed. He denounces the system, but he does not do it directly; instead choosing a series of illustrations to expose the ugly face of society that permeates and pervades each and every one of its crevices. If Sartre exists to ask what literature is then Nyamnjoh is here to answer that it is a conduit of discontent, an intentionally placed burr under the saddle that is placed upon each of our backs.

Nyamnjoh's protagonist hopes along the line of American philosopher John Dewey; fervent advocate of the power of democracy. According to Dewey, there is a direct link between education and democracy. The relationship between the two can be beneficial or it can be harmful. Unfortunately, in the real world, as Emmanuel Kawanga will soon realize, many of these hopes and aspirations are silly, of no purpose and smack of false fantasy. His experiences and relationships with the outside world are fraught with problems and his attempts to learn, study and reason at the university are blocked and without the slightest possibility of success. The reality he experiences is that all the lessons he is taught coming up are wrong. He needs a new philosophy and this desperate, fervent and feverish journey to battle something unpleasant that cannot be changed is encapsulated in the text of *Souls Forgotten*. The novel is Kawanga's way of searching to figure out the ineffectiveness of the world around him. These delusions that he discovers have kept Cameroonians rudderless, without utterance and easily neglected. Instead of the absence of hereditary or arbitrary class distinctions that a philosopher and educator like John Dewey championed a century ago, Kawanga gets surveillance. The students are not encouraged to be informed and engaged. One of his professors appears "…still in his robes as academic hangman" (12). As an academic, Dewey wants ideas to flow unimpeded; like a stream to a river and then a river to an ocean. Regrettably, the water of which I speak is all too often tainted with pollutants, without fish, and undrinkable. There is a sense of noxious academic ruin that pervades the academies that have been created in Mimboland.

Every step that a person takes through the university campus ceases to enlighten. The human mind is encouraged to be inefficient. The intellectual is depleted. Thus begins Emmanuel Kawanga's journey into an adulthood of diminishing returns. His future at the University of Nyandem is equivalent to that of a prison. Instead of having a new student's bright optimism Emmanuel journeys to town with the expectation of being "circumcised afresh" (Nyamnjoh 7). He couldn't be more unprepared and ill equipped for the nineteenth century literary realism that Nyamnjoh purposely thrusts him into well after that time period ceases to be. He does not understand the breaks of the game nor even that he is enmeshed in one. He has no money. He has never seen electricity. He is precisely the opposite of the romantic hero enjoyed by the westerners who frequently visit his nation. He is not Oliver, in *Oliver Twist*, or Pip, in *Great Expectations*, or Sissy Jupe, in *Hard Times*, or Donald Farfrae, in *The Mayor of Casterbridge*, or Pendennis in Thackeray's work of the same name. Instead of being a male Cinderella or a cartoon character from a Norman Rockwell drawing, Emmanuel is a boy with obstacles rather than greatness thrust before him. He is so negative in his surroundings that Dickensian is positive by comparison.

As a social scientist, Francis B. Nyamnjoh presents a modern Africa deficient of feeling. Yet everyone still plods along aimlessly. In an interview published in the French weekly newspaper *L'Express* in May 1957 with psychoanalyst Jacques Lacan he states "...to be an obsessional means to find oneself caught in a mechanism, in a trap increasingly demanding and endless" (*L'Express,* May 1957). Is this not the plight of the modern African? Yes, there is humor in the novel, but one can't help realize that *Souls Forgotten* is a tract which exists to call out and shame those at the top who claim democracy but practice treachery, autocracy and dictatorship all the while removing any semblance of life from those beneath them. The searcher or seeker who is trying to unravel this tangled mess is dropped into a bottomless pit of ceaseless anxiety. Once he does come to the conclusion that something is very wrong

...he suffers the torturing need to verify it, but he doesn't dare because he fears he will appear as a crazy man, because at the same time he knows well he did accomplish it; this commits him to greater and greater cycles of verification, precaution, justification. Taken in this way by an inner whirlwind, it is impossible for him to find a state of tranquility, of satisfaction (Published in *L'Express* in May 1957).

This is the discontent, according to Nyamnjoh, that is literature. It exists to point out why the students at the University of Asieyam are left listless and lifeless. It is no wonder that Emmanuel suffers from food poisoning upon returning to his home village which is devastated by an incredible disaster. Education and democracy are lacking and this spiritual bankruptcy yields volcanic consequences. An explosion on August 21, 1986 killed nearly every living creature in that portion of The Cameroons. This cataclysmic burst mirrors the nation's collective psychosis. Everyone seems to be caught in some sort of fog. Jacques Lacan even goes so far to state that identity is based not on reality but on an illusion (McLaughlin and Coleman 543). Emmanuel calls this discordance a "chemical reaction" which produces hallucinations, distortions and delusions (96). Is this not the atmospheric quality that now characterizes the governments of so many African nations formed in the early nineteen sixties—an illness that Lacan refers to as a devastating and hurtful neurosis resulting in "...inversion, isolation, reduplication, cancellation and displacement" (Lacan's "The Mirror Stage as Formative of the Function of the I as Reveled in Psychoanalytic Experience" as qtd. in McLaughlin and Coleman 551)?

The storm outside mirrors the storm inside in a modern Shakespearean tragedy which creates chaos out of order. Both disorient. Medically speaking this may be a form of paranoia, schizophrenia, grandiose delusions or hallucinations. That is debatable. What is not debatable is that his dreams foretell a terrible poisonous gas emission. The University of Asieyam is every bit as bamboozled and out of sorts as the African villages in the northwestern portion of the nation. Cha, Nyos and Wum were devastated. Like the December 1984 leak of gas in Bhopal, India in which metyl isocynate leaked and killed more than 20,000 victims, here in Africa Carbon Dioxide explodes from under a lake. Why did such a toxin exude from the lake near the Nigerian border killing, birds, snakes cattle and approximately 1,800 people? Was this an actual accident or an intentional international disaster with the pieces left for someone else to retrieve and reconstruct? The calamity, one of the worst possible afflictions, is of unknown origin and it is this panic and this plague worthy of the Old Testament that Emmanuel encounters when he returns from the big city. Nyamnjoh calls this the "Great City" (Nyamnjoh 10). Frantz Fanon calls this incredible discomfort and cold disappointment "cognitive dissonance" in *Black Skin, White Mask* (Fanon qtd. in Hussein Abdilahi Bulhan, *Frantz Fanon and the Psychology of Oppression 4, 61, 191*). Terrible harm is inflicted on the psyche, Fanon argues in *Black Skin, White Masks*, when there is a fierce collision between the way we would like things to be and the way things are. The result is neurosis and Kawanga's suffering is a violation and disfigurement of irreparable proportions. Tellingly, he eats a rancid avocado and lands in the hospital; a victim of what infests the region. A victim of colonization which steps in and acts as a wedge between himself and the values which existed before the arrival of the white man. In Mimboland, Nyamnjoh says "...few fights make sense, without co-optation of supernatural powers with the help of personal witchcraft, witchdoctors, cult members and magic" (Nyamnjoh 302). The spiritual antecedents of Nyamnjoh's African are further away then ever before.

As a boy Emmanuel could eat fruits from any tree without suffering the same effects. There was once a time when Africa, just like the stoics of classical Athens, had no dilemmas. No one was restive. No one was upset. Life had a balance. There were no illusions. The philosophy is that "...our brother's burden is our burden. We have always stood firm that society can stand together when one person's child is only in the womb" (Nyamnjoh 310). Phrases like this tap into the temperament that brings people together. *Souls Forgotten* takes this consistency, folklore, voodoo and black magic and turns it on its head to reveal a society that has lost its way. Not only that, outsiders have manipulated this change in position. The spirits, with human prodding, have had a change of heart. In haste, and without forethought, the people of Mimboland have been influenced by greed and have lost the message of protection. The consequence of this loss is a trauma one can never get over.

Souls Forgotten, an ominous title when you think of it, is a cultural autopsy. It is a dissection, or an inspection, by an eyewitness whose analysis looks back not with anger, but with bashful sadness at humanity's excesses while concluding that hypocrisy is universal and spills over into the classroom. Everyone cries, but students cry even louder. One reason for these tears of rage is that the democracy Dewey once pinned all his hopes on is promised, anticipated, hoped for, but never delivered. The vote, like formal education, changes nothing. A half-century of such behavior has produced a society that repeats the same bent, subordinate and maladjusted posture. Democracy should be about finding a mechanism to keep the best of Africa's past alive while simultaneously having that vote count as a mechanism of change. It is about preserving national culture that existed centuries ago. Here, in Abuja, Luanda, Yamoussoukro, Tunis, Cairo, Yaoundé and Algiers, democracy has failed, but that is not what concerns the author the most. Francis B. Nyamnjoh wants to know *how* it has failed and *why* this failure has been so spectacular and so pervasive. Then he wants to know how this failure has been masked behind a facade of competency. This is tantamount to representing that Mimboland's dictator is superficially projecting an image of the togetherness he lacks. He wants to know how a dictatorship can trample on people's dreams, young people's dreams, and do so with oppressive intimacy, all the while dispensing trivialities and vague platitudes.

In the United States, perhaps seventy years before Emmanuel learns the limits and shortcomings of education in a nation that does not truly want it, Booker T. Washington notices a very similar problem. Both the African and the African-American have their academic training limited, confined, circumscribed and short-circuited even before it truly begins. This is a spiritual crisis. If the gospel song made famous by Mahalia Jackson reads, "…our souls look back and wonder how we got over" (she sang it under the Washington Monument in August of 1963 during the March on Washington) the question(s) in light of these terribly similar developments in both The Cameroons and Alabama is why did it take so long? Why were there so much opposition and resistance to inculcating a formal education and democracy to the international black man? Why have the universities, instead of nurturing the people who need them the most, stood in the way of true academic and economic progress in the modern world? In African myth, the Sankofar bird looks backwards to determine how it must move forward. Nyamnjoh's looking backwards means towards a communal and interdependent life. Jackson's looking backwards means towards salvation. Washingon's looking backwards, at the nation's history as a bondsman, means that a pragmatic solution more powerful than the other two put together is needed; he needs the marketplace. No one can take full advantage of the marketplace without an education.

When Emmanuel leaves for the University of Nyandem he is expected to ultimately be an aid to his people. He owes the people of the village that reared him. Like Washington's message far across the ocean there is a financial incentive for his education. His exposure to corruption on campus prevents this and Emmanuel is quickly and clearly on his own, with very few resources just like the students at Tuskegee Institute. Booker T. Washington is the first to mention the notion of the African-American entrepreneur. Emmanuel has no alternative but to be that entrepreneur. Up until that point in history, in both countries respectfully, this type of training was lacking. Dewey's dream of a land of education and democracy, while admirable, was elusive. The black man, regardless of location, however well intentioned, was hindered by problems that were "baked in" to the schooling system that existed in name, but not in practice or authenticity. Economic development of the population, African or African-American, is thwarted while all the while the individual is given public messages of encouragement which belie the fact that he is an unwelcome guest.

The African-American, like the African in *Souls Forgotten*, had been the victim of a disaster (Nyamnjoh 306). Emmanuel's village of Abehema had been damaged in particular (Nyamnjoh 306). The black man, no one would argue, was the recipient of someone else's mess. The dirty, cluttered, confused and untidy conflicts and differences come from the west and, in the case of The Cameroons, reach back to the nineteenth century. Literary theorists argue, and I would agree, that postcolonialism has forgotten (if it ever understood it in the first place) that each human being is of unique worth and that worth cannot be measured in hard currency. This was noticeable since the first German trading post in Douala was formed in 1868 and Kamerun became a German colony in 1884. *Soul's Forgotten* shows that despite the best intentions of the best of them, Europeans introduced more problems to Africa then they solved. The nightmare of the dystopian novel presented here in the form of *Souls Forgotten* is that the need for control tends to dominate the need for independent thought. Under such a system the African finds himself or herself upon a treadmill. According to Francis B. Nyamnjoh "...the more one dug the more there seemed to dig" (Nyamnjoh 311). Instead of prosperity one gets class divide. This is the leap Kwanga is trying to make. Instead of scientific modernity one gets cultural amnesia. Most troubling of all is that this unequal ebb and flow that introduces wealth and a new value system, might make the African more like white people.

This was not the only problem. The university system in Africa, largely imported from the west, could not decide on the true definition or direction of a "Genuine Intellectual" (Nyamnjoh 4). In Mimboland the very tongue of the academic world swerves chaotically between Muzugulandish and Tougalish (English and French). The students cannot easily read the language they are tested on since as children they are taught the other. *The Bible*, the economy and the academy are being disrespected by a system that rewards administrative mediocrity while fearing clarity and meritocracy. Booker T. Washington, Emmett J. Scott and Lyman Beecher Stowe argue in *Booker T. Washington: Builder of a Civilization*, never forgot for a moment that he was living "...in a world of unpleasant facts, where those unpleasant facts have to be faced..." (Scott and Stowe Preface). So is the African under the yoke of postcolonialism. This was universal and it permeated all geographical borders. Academic thought can be controlled by force. This was an exercise in sheer cruelty in the pursuit of power. "When two years are spent doing a single programme of Orthodox Law, then something somewhere is basically wrong. Why can't something be done right for me in this bloody university? Just what is my crime?" (Nyamnjoh 2). Emmanuel's crime is that he is competing himself into the ground at a university which Benjamin Ginsberg argues is functioning more and more like a corporation. Would Socrates, Plato, Xenophon or

Aristotle ever be described as...

> ...[lecturer's] driven, by jealousy and lack of self-confidence, to frustrate students whom they see as rivals in all domains, academic in particular. It all stems from the dubious idea of the scarce cake my folks call *Kwang* – the good life which, as you know, is so enticing that whoever tastes of it is no longer in a hurry to give others a chance. We are quite aware of the abyss of discord down which such satanic greed can plunge our society. Imagine what would happen if we all started struggling and biting the ears off one another's head, either because they've sliced off far too much for themselves, or because others have dared to ask us for a piece too! Where two brothers fight over the *gari* their mother left them, the ants are sure to rejoice over what is bound to spill. Unfortunately in our case, any fight is likely to be so bloody that even the ants would be poisoned by the bad blood running in all our veins!" (Nyamnjoh 120 – 121)

Part of this unpleasantness is that something that in theory should be wonderful, like the opportunity to learn, can in reality be just the opposite. A brainy intellectual tossed out of school, like Emmanuel, has no income. He lives off his live in girlfriend, aptly named Patience, who quite reasonably wants her boyfriend to get a job. In the professional sense there is nowhere for him to go and he has handled his business correctly; studying hard and doing everything right to ensure that he has a future when, all the while, it is predetermined that he has no chance. Many of his peers in The Cameroons also suffer. Emmanuel sees them in bars drinking Manawa ("Brainwasher") beer not after work but *instead* of work. This is a big problem. Are the Irish in a James Joyce novel not doing the very same thing under the influence of the British? This is a topic people would rather not talk about. This is the silent, corrupt system that throws obstacles and obstructions before the progress of the young (often forcing them to leave and seek a living elsewhere). Emmanuel Kwanga's ties to the old ways leave him without money, influence, power or even means to pay the rent. Look at how different this is from Francis Nyamnjoh's articulation of the inherent African philosophy that a person's child is only in the womb

(Nyamnjoh 9 - 10). The commercial and financial development of the African was, in reality the corruption of the African by the corrosive Muzungulander. African society, at one time, had no such problems but it has them now. Patience's home village of Camp-Kupeh is situated along the coast "...and as such has been more exposed to the storms of superiority that blew across the Atlantic" (Nyamnjoh 135). These discordant winds of imperialism wreak and they are sent intentionally, harming the African in many places at the very same time.

The education of the colonized African, just like Washington's concerns about the education for the African-American, also had more than its share of problems. Everything is not as advertised. Our young antihero, Kwanga, is not happy or does not remain happy for very long. The campus that enamored him upon his arrival as a boy, at some point after a few years of study, begins to lose its luster. When the bright starry lights had gone, "...I began to see the Great City in its true colors" (Nyamnjoh 11). It is quickly revealed that "In a wink my idea of Nyamanden had changed, from a garden of blooms to a jungle where the able preached one thing and did quite another..." (Nyamnjoh 12). The artificial world that is discovered throws him into an emotional tailspin. Francis Nyamnjoh calls the university town a "passing illusion" (Nyamnjoh 12). It is like a dream formed by aesthetics, focused only on outward appearances. If the working world had to change for the African a two year delay was going to expose him only to false hope and empty promises.

Look at how different this is from the upbringing of the African—before the introduction of Western style university education. In an African village like the one that produced Kwanga everyone is supported. Nothing is surreptitious. The past is valued and, when it comes to religion, Mimboland has a divine healer. Such a person mediates between the living and the dead in a world where not even the deceased are outsiders. There is no skepticism or bitter derision. This taught and tense social dynamic in sub-Saharan Africa indicates that society is changing. Students like Emmanuel are not ready for what they find in the Great City. The theme of illusion, of being had, of being betrayed or being sold down the river by your own people appears again and again. *Souls Forgotten* looks back wistfully to an era where children valued their parents. It was not unheard of to stay with them—they were the best teachers. The novel challenges a deviation from this old system. New views about capitalism, wealth, poverty, learning and spending were not the steps that Nyamnjoh feels are needed to make a discussion on this topic very essential and probative.

Whenever education anywhere stumbles society everywhere falls to the ground. These universal flaws, be them in America right now, as Benjamin Ginsberg indicates, or in the Africa of the 1960's, as Francis B. Nyamnjoh indicates, become essential ingredients of our collective literature. Virtue is punished and evildoing is rewarded. This is the exact opposite of the classic storybook we instinctively expect. There is a deep crisis within the universities because genuine democratic culture remains on the periphery of such institutions. An ethnographic study and systematic recording of human culture is not supposed to produce such negative results. But it does produce such negative results; so much so that The Cameroons in 2005 and 2006 was rife with student protests, strikes, and violence. This novel of what should be a rite of passage is contrastingly an unflinching, and at times funny, realistic portrayal of the nightmare of how children are introduced to modern society.

In 1848 the Indian born British satirist William Makepeace Thackeray wrote a coming of age story. *The History of Pendennis: His Fortunes and Misfortunes, His Friends and His Greatest Enemy*, just like *Souls Forgotten*, is the opposite of a Horatio Alger story. The principal male is not a poor boy who had nothing, but rather a child who grows up within earshot of everything. His father, in today's lexicon, would be a pharmacist. His mother would be a parent piloting a "helicopter" even though the rotorcraft would be a contraption that would not exist for nearly one hundred years. Pen, if not born to genuine wealth, is privileged enough to attend the equivalent of the Cambridge University. Like so many before him, such as Charles Dickens' Phillip Pirrip, and after him, such as Thomas Hardy's Jude Fawley, he is a baby born in the country who sets out to make his way in the city.

Like any boy of the era--England under Queen Victoria practically invented the modern term of Empire--he had no lack of confidence as he commenced his academic career. The college town, correspondingly to the Great City in Nyamnjoh's Mimboland, seemed to have everything. There was history, prestige, wealth and class. This is a source of happiness and excessive self-confidence. To the inexperienced and uninitiated, Thackeray argued, "...how pure and brilliant was that first sparkling draught of pleasure! —How the boy rushes at the cup, and with what a wild eagerness he drains it!...I hope there may be no degree of age or experience to which mortal may attain, when he shall become such a glum philosopher as not to be pleased by the sight of happy youth" (*Pendennis*, 128).

Thus begins Arthur Pendennis' journey into indulgent adulthood. His future as a student at either the University of Cambridge or the University of Oxford is unbelievably bright. His tastes is as imprudent and immoderate as that of a Beverly Hills divorcee. Student life is carefree merely because he does not know it can be otherwise. If he does not indeed have the world at his feet, in his eyes, he can see it in the distance. We are all not so lucky. Most children are not so blessed and this is a reflection of the democracy that is not there.

Whereas Pen, a westerner, lugs a trousseau to a prestigious university, Emmanuel Kwanga, an African from a nation well visited by westerners, journeys to town with the expectation that everything that can go wrong will go wrong. He has never been outside his village for any length of time. He has never seen electricity. His confidence is inversely proportional to that of the Calcutta born author's protagonist. "Oh, how I wish these learned men knew the mess into which they've pushed me. How I've become a prisoner without a crime" (9). The juxtaposition or opposition could not be more startling. While Kwanga lives for everyone in his village Pen is concerned only with himself. London and Nyamandem present two extremes. In this comparison we can see how one wealthy and powerful nation extends its control over another, all under the guise of polite assistance. Look at our schools, George Orwell exclaims when writing about another section of the British Empire. They are nothing more than "...factories for cheap clerks. We've never taught a single useful trade to the Indians. We daren't; frightened of the competition in industry" (Orwell 37). This is the same philosophy of the university professors who are more mindful of capital then intellectual curiosity.

What could be more repressive than a *Guillotine*? It limits people, keeping them silent and fearful and these limits extend to the last place one would rationally expect to see them; at the modern university. A place of learning is the last place one would expect a battle between chaos and order (20). What hurts the most is that the former seems to almost always overwhelm the latter. Nyamnjoh teaches confusion, or more to the point, illuminates with a withering spotlight the strange and frightening occurrences on the Cameroonian campus. Everything seems unsound. No one can be counted upon. *Souls Forgotten* is a novel of loved one's intentionally forsaken. The collective consciousness of the nation remains a source of fractured discord. The independent voice of the African remains unanswered, unfulfilled and, worst of all, unmentioned.

From their very origin literary texts have been motivated by this type of dissonance. They are written because it is too painful not to write them. The cost of repressing one's thoughts is immeasurable and creates so many spiritual problems that expressing one's conscience, wet with perspiration for all the world to see, is the only way to avoid going insane. Kwanga is put under severe psychological stress. Stronger boys would have collapsed under such pressure. His village depends on his success and his superiors (at the university) depend on his failure. This contradictory incompatibility can make a healthy mind schizophrenic. Surely this has something to do with why Nyamnjoh is a scholar at the University of Capetown instead of living in his own country of The Cameroons. "It is all hypocrisy!" cries the father of our hero Emmanuel Kwanga (27). The person who is truly unwilling to conform finds himself/herself in all kinds of trouble. Such bravery, almost begging to be a dead duck as opposed to being a live chicken, is embarked upon because there is no psychological alternative. The Algerian author Tahar Djaout once wrote, "Silence is death. If you are silent you are dead, And if you speak you are dead, So speak and die." (WEB). Djaout was assassinated in Northern Africa for supporting secularism and this sense of foreboding, of honesty having a permanent cost, of being an insignificant figure that is used or manipulated to further another person's purposes in a rigged game, propels a sense of uneasiness and foreboding over the terrain Nyamnjoh focuses his penetrating gaze upon. Abehema and The Great City bring with them a sense of tragedy and impending doom. The result is psychosis. It is enough to make even the most optimistic individual weep hot and bitter tears of rage.

The young in Africa in *Souls Forgotten* may not know it, but they are well on their way to incarceration. A journalist in California once said that "Prison is a world unto itself, like a game of Monopoly where the players don't understand the rules" (Mitford 4). How can they understand the rules when they are not written on paper? They are purposely opaque. They are intentionally malleable. Each step that a person takes through the campus is laden with changeability, contradictions and confusion. Nyamnjoh's novel, more than a political tract or a historical study, is an anthropologic postmortem which examines the psychic pain of a population in the throes of relentless agitation.

When Chapter Four begins, and Emmanuel wakes up after a fitful sleep beside his girlfriend Patience—the one he truly wants to marry and not Princess Tem who is his father's choice—he is a scared and frightened kid. Patience's voice "…sounded faint and faraway, as if from someone stranded in the muddy potholes across the road" (56). This is the language I am talking about. Nyamnjoh's text is always sad and forlorn. The characters always plagued with faults they cannot possibly overcome. It is as if life in Mimboland is precisely the opposite of the American fairytales children watch incessantly in Kansas City and Minneapolis on their portable DVD Players. The floor of the apartment is filed with rats. Emmanuel is trapped in a continual nightmare that is just like Post-traumatic stress disorder; his feet furiously peddling in the soft, wet earth without any traction as he makes a habit of going out to local bars to "consum[e] lethal brews drinks with fellow dropouts (58 – 59). Any youth has disappointments, but the severity of these bleak midwinter dreams is enough to terrify.

When reading one of Nyamnjoh's other novels, called *Mind Searching*, my initial thought was that someone would have to read Kafka, not for a reference point, but simply to cheer up. Emmanuel's relegation from the university was actually threatening his sanity. He would scream out in his sleep. He would walk in his sleep. "It was," in what I'm sure is an intentional biological comparison, "like watching life being sucked from a being" (62). The professors and administrators at his former university—those who have unscrupulously and without just cause thrown him out—are the parasites. The students are the hosts. The lifeblood, the very seminal fluid of Minmoland, is being harmed by the very people who should be helping and offering protection and insulation. Is it any wonder that when Emmanuel wakes up from his sleep he calls out to Patience "…the way a child calls out to its mother" (64)?

It is a sin to lock someone up in perpetual childhood. The gentle and the trustful, instead of moving forward, atrophy and move backwards. The word that Nyamnjoh likes to use, sarcastically, is "salubrity" or, more precisely, its inverse (Nyamnjoh 72). The city should be wholesome and favorable to one's health. That is what we tell young children that the world is all about. That is what they glean when they read Lewis Carroll's *Through the Looking Glass* and Kenneth Grahame's *The Wind in the Willows*. That is the way it should be. It is supposed to be about well being. Here in *Souls Forgotten* we have the way it is. In Nyamnjoh we have reality. The word the author uses is insalubrity and he uses it with the same biting anger that Tennessee Williams uses the word "mendacity" in *Cat on a Hot Tin Roof* to describe an almost unspeakable anger at being so fooled and so manipulated by the people that surround him (Nyamnjoh 72). Emmanuel's behavior, as his eyes open, reverts to the meekness and humility of a second, shocked childhood. He is aging prematurely. Alice, like a good Victorian girl, seeks order in the world around her. Her philosophy is to make sense and to make connections. The two, once again, are experiencing direct opposites. While Alice steps through the mirror that hangs above the mantelpiece and into to an alternative world that is divided into neatly organized squares, like a chessboard, Emmanuel steps into streets without names that are literally smeared with excrement. Heaps and heaps of human waste because this is the entity that is most common. The theme of the mirror keeps coming up again and again. He trims his beard in the mirror. Patience reapplies makeup with a handheld mirror in "…her crocodile skin handbag" (Nyamnjoh 86). Her newspaper, which she uses for her Civics and National Affairs course, is called the *Looking Glass* (Nyamnjoh 66). He is looking into the mirror for the efficient and predictable The Cameroons that only seems to exist in press releases and governmental bulletins. An educated, kind, and charitable student does not move forward to a faculty position or a life in the professional class. Just like the modern educational system, the person who genuinely wants to learn is placed upon a confusing, circular treadmill that is designed to diminish their spirit and their stamina.

The gap between theory and reality is the causation for the nation's collective psychosis. Everyone in Mimboland seems to be caught in some sort of a fog. Emmanuel calls this a "chemical reaction" which produces hallucinations, distortions and delusions (96). Medically speaking this may be a form of paranoia or schizophrenia. That is debatable. What is not debatable is that this trouble stems this sense of loss at the university, is symptomatic of a larger set of beliefs by which society orders reality. The idea is to render it unintelligible. No one ever taught him (or his people) just how corrupt things had become.

The more he pondered on his failures, the more confident Emmanuel became that his parents and Abehema would eventually understand that the modern world was far more of a delusion than their simplicity and innocence had permitted them to discover…They lived in the past with demoded ideas about education and opportunities. Though they weren't entirely to blame for their misconceptions of the changing circumstances, the cities and towns had tended to monopolise the race for civilisation, and to deny villages such as Abehema the right to share in the fruits of progress (102).

What the parents of our antihero do not know is that the University of Asieyam is compared to a hangman's noose (119). At play is a mechanism designed to separate the corrupt in the city from the impoverished in the country. The benefits of advantage are "baked" into the system. The people of Mimboland, Nyamnjoh tells us, go "…about their inactivities unquestionably like a people hypnotized or numbed by repression" (119). I would call them sheep. The society has so many problems that if one is not careful he/she can find themselves sipping alcohol and staring into the fireplace; afraid to speak too loudly because the penalty for uttering an unflattering remark is well more than anyone can afford.

What at first seems to be a treatise on the university student whose identity is being attacked quickly becomes a multi-layered novel which reveals that traditional African beliefs no longer belong or fit satisfactorily in a post-colonial world. The split between city and remote village is symptomatic of another problem, a bigger problem. If modernity has arrived, unasked for, what will become of the old ideas? Will the person who clings to them become "homeless"? Just as the immigrant novels of Upton Sinclair, Theodore Dreiser, Bernard Malamud and Amy Tan speaks of a clash of ideas here we have a similar conflict, but it is a conflict in reverse. Here the protagonist stays home and the game, or I would argue the problem, comes to him.

Colonial repression appears in the form of a poisonous gas emission in the territory near Abehema (*Souls Forgotten* 218). Like the December 1984 leak of gas in Bhophal, India in which metyl isocynate leaked and killed more than 20,000 people, tragedy arises from afar. The Union Carbide Corporation of Danbury, CT, now a subsidiary of the Dow Chemical Company, based in Midland, MI, created an international disaster in someone else's backyard. The old ideas and the old order are taken from someone else without even asking. Here in Africa the situation is little different. Merely two years later gas underneath a lake in The Cameroons explodes like a volcano. This explosion, one of the worst possible natural disasters to take place in sub-Saharan Africa or anywhere else, is of questionable source and it is this panic and disaster that Emmanuel encounters when he returns from the big city. One tragedy is not enough. He is homeless in more ways then one. The African in his twenties returns not in a triumph befitting a fairytale. He is not the prodigal son. Emmanuel comes home from one failure—an academic failure at the University of Asieyam—to be greeted by another even larger failure—a crushing or breaking of traditional African beliefs torn asunder under the cloud cover of chemically induced injury, illness and death. Surely a metaphor for more then one kind of calamity, Nyamnjoh describes the violent internal pressure "…as if someone had set fire to my, intestines, heart and lungs" (229).

The Lake Nyos disaster of August 21, 1986 has always been a bit of a mystery. This is part of the repression that Francis B. Nyamnjoh is trying to express in *Souls Forgotten*. Why did carbon dioxide exude from the lake near the Nigerian border, killing cattle, birds, and people indiscriminately? The question arises as whether or not this is a natural disaster. Is it an event brought about by the meddling of man or is it indeed the will of God? Nyamnjoh tells the reader of the "...unusualness of the past..." followed by the aberration of the present (247). One of the characters states that he fears something is wrong with everything (255). Anyone who reads and listens objectively realizes that there are so many layers of trouble that no one knows where to first focus their attention and begin to clean

Works Cited

Blaze, Michael Scott and Marybeth Gasman, Editors. *Booker T. Washington Rediscovered*, Johns Hopkins UP, 2012.

Bulhan, Hussein Abdilahi. *Frantz Fanon and the Psychology of Oppression*, Springer, 1985 (2004).

deBoer, Frederik. "Why We Should Fear University, Inc.: Against the Corporate Taming of the American College", *The New York Times*, 9 Sept, 2015.

Djaout, Tahar. www.goodreads.com/author/quotes/85960.Tahar_Djaout Accessed 10 Jan. 2016.

Express (L'), http://braungardt.trialectics.com/sciences/psychoanalysis/jacques-lacan/interview-jacques-lacan/ Accessed 11 Feb. 2016.

Gates, Henry Louis "Forty Acres and a Gap in Wealth" *New York Times* 18 Nov. 2007.

Ginsberg, Benjamin. *The Fall of the Faculty* Oxford U. P, 2013.

Harlan, Louis *Booker T. Washington: Volume I The Making of a Black Leader, 1856-1901* Oxford UP. 1975

McLaughlin, Becky, and Bob Coleman. *Everyday Theory: A Contemporary Reader* Pearson, 2005.

Mitford, Jessica. *Kind and Unusual Punishment: The Prison Business*. Alfred A. Knopf, 1973.

Nyamnjoh, Francis B. *Souls Forgotten*, Langaa-RPCIG, 2008.

_____. *Mind Searching* Langaa-RPCIG, 2007.

Orwell, George. *Burmese Days*. New Delhi: Heritage, 2006.

Sartre, Jean-Paul. Translated by Bernard Frechtman *What is Literature?* Philosophical Library. 1949.

Scott, Emmett J. and Lyman Beecher Stowe. *Booker T. Washington: Builder of a Civilization* (Illustrated Edition) Dodo P, 2008.

Thackeray, William Makepeace. *The History of Pendennis: His Fortunes and Misfortunes, His Friends and His Greatest Enemy,* CreateSpace, 2015.

Trimview and Greene "How We Got over: The Moral Teachings of the African-American Church on Business Ethics" *Business Ethics Quarterly,* vol. 7, no. 2, Mar 1997 pp. 133 – 147.

Washington, Booker T. *The Negro in the South; His economic progress in relation to his moral and religious development. Being the William Levi Bull lectures for the year 1907.* Citadel P, 1970.

_____. "The Colored Ministry; Its Defects and Needs" in *Christian Union*, Aug. 14, 1890.

Chapter 5

Nyamnjoh's *Homeless Waters:* Juvenile Rebellion and Old Age Recollection

Bill F. Ndi

Juxtaposing rebellion and recollection in this title and attributing each to a specific period of human development is a way of drawing attention, on the one hand, to the various periods when humans have to live by taking and executing orders from others to, on the other hand, when they have full autonomy to make critical appraisals of their youthful exuberance or apathy. Both exuberance and apathy could in themselves be manifestations of deeply rooted sociopolitical and psychological traumas and their consequences. These, as Francis B. Nyamnjoh's title, *Homeless Waters* indicates, push individuals to become homeless. It is in this vein that this chapter posits that every river has a source, a bed, two banks, and a mouth to empty itself into the ocean or other bigger body of water. When a river loses all or one of these—thus becoming homeless—it unleashes an unfriendly and deadly force like that in whose grip Nyamnjoh's protagonist, as a teenager, finds himself. The protagonist thus, like a river out of its bed, seeks balance between calm and rage, God and girls, work and pleasure, learning and mischief. While life can be well spiced if devoid of conflict and repression, it can also be acerbic with the said binary. The bearableness and unbearableness of belonging, of being in the chains of love and being free, underlie the conflict and repression which push many an African in general and many an Anglophone-Cameroonian in particular, like Ngoma, to master the art of resilience and of expressing the repressed.

The narrator's story becomes for the writer a guise by which means he tells a bigger tale of tyranny rocking his people and their refusal to cave in to such forces of oppression. How then is Ngoma's trajectory similar to that of a river overflowing its banks after a heavy downpour of rain? What are the sources of his troubles? What, like a river, are the main elements of Ngoma's existence that he has lost to letting out the unfriendly and deadly force responsible for the end of his own destined journey and education? Above all, do Ngoma's travails and resilience hide a bigger, national or, even maybe, an international tragedy? Carefully following the storyline, instances of repression—symbolic, rhetorical, personal, familial, societal—will probably reveal the potency of Nyamnjoh's figurative use of waters as the universal source of life, albeit, seminal fluids that produce life, but one pushed to vagrancy. Also, characters, their interactions with each other and their environment, the conflicts surrounding them and their fate as well as the writer's locus and concern for humanity will be brought to life.

Nyamnjoh's narrative seems to align with the representation of power relations and interactions from the micro familial level to the broader macro-societal, religious, and national level. The protagonist/narrator, Ngoma traces his relations beginning with his nuclear family. In the tradition of the bildungsroman, he gives the reader a foretaste of life in a family with just him, his mother, and sister long before Mother gets married to Lumawut. He tells how, "[t]ime came and dashed in bundles of happiness, which my sister and I consumed, as we grew innocent and pure" (2). He continues with his formative years as a schoolboy in elementary and secondary school. In a twist of infatuation, emotional overflow and youthful exuberance as well as sexual overindulgence while in college, Ngoma ends up in prison. Many years have passed since then and all of a sudden, his daughter begotten out of the ill-fated romance while still a teenager in college appears. This painful narrative is that of Ngoma who grows up not knowing his father and now his own daughter has also suffered the same fate as if stricken by some curse determined to cheat his lineage of tranquility. He also informs of his mother's travails as a single mother, a married woman and a divorcee. At the personal level, here are the elements that constitute the essence of Nyamnjoh's narrative in *Homeless Waters*. Nonetheless, Ngoma, as the narrator also establishes his relationship to the wider society. Nyamnjoh, by so-doing, fits the mold carved for him by Emmanuel Fru Doh (EFD). EFD points out that Nyamnjoh, as an Anglophone Cameroonian writer, through rebelliousness "battle[s] corruption and disturbing socio-political trends in society and their consequences on the human id, these works expose a tormented population totally submerged in the chaotic consequences of its misdemeanours"[sic] (70).

From what precedes, Ngoma starts extending his narration to the wider society when he is old enough to hear and understand the way adults would. He punctuates this episode with Mother telling them about the one man she had ever loved. The striking feature of Nyamnjoh's narrative is his bent on having his narrator tell the reader how he came to be trapped by and in a system(s) that he has little to no control of. His plight as a fatherless child results from nothing else but his grandfather's obstinate refusal to accept his daughter's own choice of husband and this, in spite of the fact that the two were madly in love. Mother, in her telling the story, takes a swipe at her father and the tradition which makes of any child born of a marriage not sanctioned by the parents and family's whims and caprices, theirs. She says thus:

> We would be married now if your grandfather had not behaved so rigidly. But your grandfather would not hear of any of his daughters getting married to a stranger, a "no man," someone without a base in the land...
> We thought we could lead father to change his mind by staying together and making children... But we were mistaken. Your grandfather warned us that any child we made out of our marriage belonged to him and the family. "A child belongs to he who owns the bed," he quoted the famous proverb of the land. (3)

This last note, our narrator records, strikes, wounds, and hurts more than all else. He comments on Mother's attitude; she shakes her head as one wounded by the wisdom of the land. Here, Nyamnjoh allows repressed feelings to loom large. He makes of *Homeless Waters* a testament of the expression of repressed feelings often buried or masked in youths through an outlandish exuberance that only age can guarantee an outlet for. It is, in short as Maxine L. Montgomery would have it, a tale of shared and personal pain often experienced by individuals as they deal with the consequences of horrific events (320). Ngoma's narration of his family relations with the broader society reminds the reader of Julia Kristeva's essay, *The Power of Horror: an Essay on Abjection.* Therein, Kriteva describes similar situations in the chapter: "Approaching Abjection" and underscores that such horrific and horrifying situations are those in which one is "neither subject nor object." Thus, she writes:

> There looms within abjection, one of those violent, dark revolts of being, directed against a threat that seems to emanate from an exorbitant outside or inside, ejected beyond the scope of the possible, the tolerable, the thinkable. It lies quite close, but it cannot be assimilated. It beseeches, worries, and fascinates, which nevertheless, does not let itself be seduced. Apprehensive desire turns aside; sickened, it rejects. A certainty protects it from the shameful—a certainty of which it is proud holds on to it. But simultaneously, just the same, that impetus, that spasm, that leap is drawn toward an elsewhere as tempting as it is condemned. Unflaggingly, like an inescapable boomerang, a vortex of summons and repulsion places the one haunted by it literally besides himself. (1)

This quote seems to be a perfect description of Nyamnjoh's plot. *Homeless Waters* addresses misery, injury, pain, suffering, and healing through time and space. This calls for a close examination of the plot of *Homeless Waters* to see how Nyamnjoh through his artistry unveils the aforementioned.

Ngoma takes the reader through his coming of age story. The reader follows him from when he is a boy growing up in Safang without concern of a father to when his mother finds him a stepfather and then they move to Bonfuma where he goes to primary school. He proves to be studious and excels in education. He is then sent off to college at Nsong. College seems to bring Ngoma into a new world of fancy. He meets other students (boys and girls) from bigger cities. It is in college where he gives in to his sexual fantasies and falls in love at first with Collette and mishandles this relationship by going for and ending up with Camille. The consequence of this poor behavior is Collette's exaction of revenge. She debunks Ngoma and Camille's scheme during an expulsion from school meant to discipline Ngoma for smoking on the school premises. She does everything to repress her feelings of anger and love turn hate until an appropriate opportunity presents itself. She does not fail to seize such opportunity to inflict pain to Ngoma and Camille. It is upon being expelled from school that Camille becomes the total unmaking of any serious dream Ngoma had ever nursed for a better future through educational achievement. She defrauds a letter which gives her permission to be with her mother. But she actually needs time to be with her new boyfriend Ngoma in Zintgraffstown. While there both Camille and Ngoma Richard, in the throes of reckless abandon, give in to their sexual desires and spend ten days locked in each other's hand and embrace. The result of satisfying this carnal desire is Camille's pregnancy which leads to both Camille and Ngoma Lumawut being definitively expelled from school. Ngoma ends up in juvenile prison wondering whatever became of Camille and his unborn child. At times he wondered whether the child was a boy or a girl. In the end, (which actually is the beginning of the story) Ngoma tells the reader about this child who had been born and given up for adoption. She was named Elizabeth-Paradise. Now grown up, her longing to reunite with her father before taking her last vows as a Reverend Sister with the Dominican Order spurs her to send a letter to her father. Ngoma tells of the arrival of the letter and his immediate reaction. He says:

> I was thrilled to be in the company of Elizabeth-Paradise, following the miraculous arrival of her letter inviting me to a meeting with "the daughter you have never met." Upon receipt of the mysterious letter, something had clicked, and I had, without thinking twice, abandoned the cattle on the hills and started trekking from Safang, through Bonfuma until I arrived in Jengjeng. There I took the first lorry I saw to Zintgraffstown, where I met the daughter I had never known. (161-162)

In the end, Ngoma is faced with a nightmarish past that he would have loved to bury. Yet, the coming into his life of Elizabeth-Paradise, the product of an ill-fated affair that forever ruined his academic ambition and life, vividly brings to life the way and manner in which he and Elizabeth-Paradise's mother, Camille, fell in love, their mischief, their expulsion from school, his subsequent detention at the juvenile center, his reluctance to take up teaching and, finally, his becoming a herdsboy. Ngoma's choice of becoming a herdsboy rather than a school teacher after his travails in juvenile corrections can be translated into Nyamnjoh's rebellion and espousal of nature. This rebellion and its expression are akin to that of the Romantics. His protagonist chooses nature over the promises of an artificial and material world in which the powerful are willing to crush, like his grandfather crushing his mother's and Camille's father crushing the dreams of the young. It is in no weak terms that Ngoma condemns the latter: "Camille's father, in arrogant bitterness, had declined anything to do with "a bastard baby" he says. The diction is marked by total disapprobation. The reader should recall that Ngoma had dreams. He was eager to learn as he owns up in his own words and tells of his academic prowess in the sciences, languages and the arts.

> Mathematics and French seemed to be the key subjects in the college. I found that my excellence in them almost automatically gave me a very easy time with the other disciplines. Subjects like English and English literature, History, Geography, as well as the rest of the sciences were scarcely a problem to me. I picked them up with my left hand, as one would say back home to denote that something was easy. This made me grow popular. And this popularity could be seen in the fact that every student in class knew my name, while I could hardly boast of knowing half the names in our class of ninety-six students. (38)

Yet, his experience as a young and intelligent man in such a tyrannical world spells nothing but doom for him. His upbringing exposes him to anti-socialization. When he is exposed to temptation reinforced by a process which Heidegger would call complete Europeanization of the earth and of man (15), he spirals out of control. It does not come therefore as a surprise when in the end— and in a twist of romantic rebellion—he chooses to abandon his childhood dream of wanting to be more "civilised[sic]—to eat and drink and breathe civilisation[sic] too" (14). He rejects or resigns before such a civilization. Civilization finally becomes his poisoned apple like the Industrial Revolution to the Romantics. Here, he is called, despite himself, to emulate Heidegger when he says, "…

indeed only the way back will lead us forward" (Heidegger 12). Over and above, his is a total embrace of Defoe's annotation on his copy of Francis Bacon's *Advancement of Human Learning* [1720s]. The annotation reads: "[a]dmirable therefore is the man who has chearfully[sic] past thro' life without the least desire of distinguishing himself" (qtd. in Backscheider Paula 3).

Furthermore, in the end, Nyamnjoh seems to build his novel on William Wordsworth's definition of poetry. As a Romantic, Wordsworth contends that poetry is "the spontaneous overflow of powerful feelings recollected in perfect tranquility." Nyamnjoh's shift from poetry to prose recollected when the protagonist has found total peace and tranquility in and with nature, being a herdsboy coming to terms with his own past and expressing powerful feelings, seems to extend Wordsworth's definition which like the old in his novelistic universe endeavors to stifle freedom of expression and desire in the name of tradition. So, in this seemingly and deceptively simple narrative under which Nyamnjoh docks, he addresses a number of human and social concerns in a setting that, on the one hand, tends to cling on to tradition, and on the other hand, would like to embrace modernity and its drive for materials. It is in this guise that concluding an examination on Nyamnjoh's handling of the narrative assemblage invites Kriteva's appreciation of the narrative as a cache for suffering. She asserts that:

> The narrative becomes a film always threatened with bursting. For when narrated identity is unbearable, when the boundary between subject and object is shaken, and when even the limit between inside and outside becomes uncertain, the narrative is what is challenged. (141)

Homeless Waters sets the tone, through a cast of multiple characters, for the acknowledgement of the unbearable. This is in keeping with Roland Barthes' precept of what characters and or individuals need to take advantage of. For Barthes, to acknowledge the unbearable is in and of itself an advantage. It signifies to the characters that they "must escape by whatever means, [they] establish within [themselves] the martial theater of Decision, of Action, of Outcome" (140-141). As such *Homeless Waters* pits characters who are infringed upon; each and every one of the characters sees his or her freedom taken hostage and he or she is left to be seen and not to be heard. In spite of these infringements, Nyamnjoh, through his characters, sits above their diagnosed pain and deception to evoke the unpalatable in an effort to keep disenfranchisement, torture, disillusionment, inequality, etc. at bay and gain for the "homeless" a voice that might someday be heard.

It is through Ngoma's disconcerting narrative that the protagonist/narrator voices all that which his society, with its own narrative, attempts to conceal and suppress. Ngoma as a character becomes the embodiment of an instructive awareness of an ill-fated relation between man, woman, child on the one hand and society with its tradition that challenges any rationale of logical thinking on the other hand. The first appearance of the narrator in his description of what life was for him as a child is enveloped with an air of innocence, purity and untamed freedom. This striking opening by the narrator is punctuated, like in music, with a flat note. This is most probably a hint to evoke suppressed childhood, thoughts, conflicts and repressed feelings. The narrator's desire to want to believe in the freedom he enjoyed as a child implies a psychological defense mechanism against the constraints and repressive forces that will compel citizens to put up appearances to please the whims and caprices of society. He is observant to the point where he does not miss the fact that "[w]e woke each day with smiles, as Mother strove to please us both" (Nyamnjoh 1). Could this strife to please be the result of fear of rebellion by Mother? Striving to please does not seem to be a natural human disposition and, as such, pushes for further question: why strive when it is naturally the responsibility of a parent to take care of and protect his/her young ones? Could his curiosity be the equivalent of the Heideggerian "concealed arrogance of a self-consciousness that banks on a self-invented *ratio* and its rationality"? (13)

Ngoma continues to draw attention to the dilemma of growing up without a father. He highlights that "…the presence of a father, imposing or not… we grew up without a father, without even contemplating the necessity of one, and without knowledge of his whereabouts" (Nyamnjoh 1). Such presence would have shielded the narrator from what he has carefully worded as "the tossing winds of adulthood" and he adds that "had our father been there as well, it's possible the situation would have been different. We might have sacrificed some of our happiness with a motherly touch for the presence of a father, imposing or not" (Nyamnjoh 1). This careful diction and imagery create a sense of wonder and doubt for the narrator does not really seem to come to terms with the fact that they were really "happy" (Nyamnjoh 1). His only consolation seems to be as he puts it, "maybe because we were still children—virgins … Maybe because Mother was always there converting our every worry into fantasies of a rosy future. Or maybe because Mother was the only person with whom we lived" (Nyamnjoh 1). Ngoma's recollections and thoughts here seem to highlight the fact that when people carry repressed feelings with them for too long, at one point they will have the need to let them out. Societies in which individuals live and evolve are not devoid of moral, ethical, legal, social, racial, religious, etc. values. Most of these values frown at and muzzle some desires that individuals would want to express, thus explaining why Mother has to convert "every worry into fantasies" (1). The result of this is that such individuals with repressed feelings, thoughts would have to withhold these desires; but for how long? When the outburst of emotions kicks in and overpowers the intellect, an outlet is created for long repressed feelings. Does Ngoma just let out these feelings with the same clouded vision of a rosy future?

These old age recollections open the doors for caustic criticism of the on-goings of the days of Ngoma's youth. The observant Ngoma talks of Mother's various suitors who came seeking her hand in marriage and went without Mother giving in. He also digs into the grapevine and pulls out stories of elopement, to marry even as a second wife, with young women as well as those who were already mothers and still wonders why, "marriage, it seemed, was a sought after institution" (Nyamnjoh 2). It is through this tale that the reader is informed of Mother's art of resisting what she considered to be adventurers taking advantage of women who desire marriage. Also, having been told the story of his origin, even as a child, Ngoma, it seems, becomes a nursery for rebellion. This seems to be in line with what Heidegger has to say: "[b]ut origin always comes to meet us from the future" (10). Though confused and unable to make sense of Mother's story, Ngoma reveals how the seeds of rebellion are already taking roots in him. He does not mince words. He says, "[i]n my child's mind, my grandfather had no right to an ambition that kept Mother away from the one person who made her happy, and would have made my sister and me normal children" (Nyamnjoh 4). The consequence of this is that Ngoma must have reckoned Mother's story accounts for the fact that he, Ngoma, is the product of a seminal fluid that has been rendered fatherless, homeless vagrant because of his grandfather's ambition to stop Mother from the right to choose whom she would have loved to marry. In the same vein, Ngoma seems to express his surprise as if to chide a senseless tradition that cheats its own daughters of their rightful place in society. Upon hearing all the stories leading up to his birth and his grandfather's blessing of Mother's womb for a baby boy, Ngoma states with mock irony that,

> [S]o I was made to understand. Boys continue the family line, something that even a girl with a Zulu name like Shaka cannot change. A tradition that must have perplexed my sister beyond words, as in many ways, there was little I could do that she wouldn't do ten times more and a hundred times better. (Nyamnjoh 5)

To Ngoma, it should be revolting for his sister who could do anything he could as a boy and still not be considered worthy of continuing the lineage. He tells the reader the now proverbial "what a man can do a woman can do and even better." If not, why should this tradition be perplexing? After going through his travails and not seeing his own daughter for more than 20 years, the reader comes across a Ngoma so willing to forfeit everything and go to this daughter he has never set eye on. He further espouses his daughter's choice of sisterhood/nunnery and he is quick to feel a deep sense of guilt as he alludes to the parable of the prodigal son when his daughter grants him forgiveness. In responding to this act of forgiving, he says, "I felt like an undeserving prodigal father… undeserving of her forgivingness and understanding" (161). He distances himself thus from the male dominated world of his grandparents who saw no fault in creating misery for their own daughters. With this distancing, the protagonist marks a radical shift from the traditional stance of oppressing females—a perspective which the author criticizes—to a more liberal acceptance of the wishes of females.

Furthermore, when Ngoma describes children's worldview, especially, how they would hang out on market days and benefit from the generosity of passers-by, he draws attention to children's sense of egalitarianism. He says, "[t]he tradition among us children was to divide equally amongst us anything that happened to fall our way" (Nyamnjoh 10). This claim by children developing their own tradition and the incident that follows are ways the author uses to point out that the old order changes to yield place to a new one and that even what is in the interest of all will never be espoused by all. The narrator tells of the rebelliousness of one of his peers kicking against tradition: "[i]nstead of behaving traditionally, this boy immediately threw the loaf into his mouth expanding like that of a python and snapped it shut to chew" (Nyamnjoh 10). The mention of a python here is figurative and underlines the destructive force of individuals who think of none but themselves and their bellies first. This is also an expression of a disgust at a few willing to hijack for themselves a system put to place to work in the interest of all. Nonetheless, Ngoma suggests in his telling of the story what those caught in the grip of a hijacker needs to do: "[o]ur furious lot fell on him and tore his mouth open, bringing out bits of smashed bread smeared with greedy saliva. Our shouts had brought our parents to their doors" (Nyamnjoh 10). Nyamnjoh would not dare, in an oppressive system he chides, to suggest directly that the greedy oppressors be beaten and deprived of their loot. It would be equivalent to calling calamity upon himself as a writer at worst and a reactionary subversive at best. Through this story, the reader can see and even learn from children that no one should be allowed to take over tradition, most especially one that is against an older and an oppressive one. The above mentioned imagery of a python needs to be further commented for, in Nyamnjoh's country of birth, the term "mboma," The Cameroons pidgin English for "python" is used to refer to the pot-bellied, greasy politicians in power who loot and spend lavishly on extra marital liaisons with young women the age of their granddaughters. This vice is certainly the object of Nyamnjoh's blatant criticism.

Ngoma is a child to whom much responsibility—that he does not fully understand—is given. However, one might ask at what cost? The effects of such charge on his id as well as his bewilderment are made evident from what the narrator says, "I tried to understand why I should be counted among those too old to eat, and why my grand-uncle kept urging me to take care of Mother and Shaka with statements such as, 'The wishes of children are like the wishes of kings.'?" (Nyamnjoh 9) He tells of the passage when Mother takes them visiting some kin in neighboring villages. He mentions his grand-uncle who is very fond of him and relays how this grand-uncle would always call him "brother" and would request that Ngoma, a child takes care of his own mother and elder sister. In requesting that Ngoma assumes such responsibility over his mother and elder sister, grand-uncle seems to be handing over the relay baton—of a female oppressive machine—to the youth to whom the future belongs. This act of senseless repression is to the dismay of the narrator. And the writer is careful to put what the grand-uncle considers 'words of wisdom' in single quotes as if to highlight the fact that Ngoma himself does not seem to see the wisdom in the words grand-uncle shares. He tells the reader:

> When we had been long with him and were about to return home, my grand-uncle would call me into his bedroom and share with me 'words of wisdom'. Then we would both come out and shake hands in the eyes of everyone. Finally he would ask me to take care of my daughter and granddaughter.
> 'Make sure you give them enough to eat and to do, "brother". Take care of them. (Nyamnjoh 9)

He curiously learns his mother is instead his daughter and his sister, his granddaughter. These responsibilities overwhelm Ngoma who suddenly becomes brother to a grand-uncle, father to his own mother, and grandfather to his elder sister, Shaka. In spite of the fact that Ngoma is overwhelmed by his responsibilities, it is with foresight that, when Mother breaks the news about her arrangement with Lumawut to move Ngoma and the elder sister, Shaka to Bonfuma, he and Shaka do not hesitate to ask respectively, "[W]hy must we go and live there with him?" and "Must we go to him, Mother?" (13).

These two seemingly naïve questions cushion both juvenile rebellion and old age recollection. Yet, it is with such excuses as: "it is difficult for the children to understand" (13) that the children's concerns are undermined for Mother and Lumawut's love is still in its infancy and blooms like a flower without blemish. Nonetheless, it is with a tinge of irony and sarcasm that the Narrator, after being cajoled by the mother who treats him with such terms of endearment as "Father," remarks: "I wanted to be more civilised[sic]—to eat and drink and breathe civilisation[sic] too" (14). This is just honeymoon phase and it is not yet over. And one wonders what would be the first spark of quarrel or disagreement between these two lovebirds whose match seems to be made in heaven? Who of the two would be the first to let his or her repressed feelings out? Above all else, how would the conflict be resolved? Are there any agents of resolution? Or, will the children's fears and concerns translate into the much dreaded nightmare journeying into the unknown? Even better still would it be as Paul Valery would have it when he says:

> [i]nterruption, incoherence, surprise are the ordinary conditions of our life. They have even become real needs for many people, whose minds are no longer fed by anything but sudden changes and constantly renewed stimuli. We can no longer bear anything that lasts. We no longer know how to make boredom bear fruit. So the whole question comes down to this: can the human mind master what the human mind has made? (Qtd. in Ricardo Gil Soeiro & Sofia Tavares, 101)

Besides, during the above mentioned episode and visits to Ngoma's grand-uncle, Nyamnjoh cleverly introduces one of the sore points of his country's colonial experience with conflicts, extortion, torture, and the First World War. This grand-uncle gives an insight into the German colonial adventure in Nyamnjoh's country of birth, The Cameroons. Germans as colonialists, terrorized the colonized so much so that many, many years after their departure, people are still weary of them as is the case with Ngoma's grand-uncle. Today, he would be diagnosed with Post-Traumatic Stress Disorder resulting from colonization. He would always warn the young Ngoma,

Beware of the Njangmans...' He always warned me against the Njangmans – which only much later I came to understand referred to the Germans – even though there were no Germans left. Because, as he would put it, 'The Njangmans, while withdrawing during the world war, tried to steal the Sacred Spitting Stone on the way to the palace, but the stone kept escaping back to its original location. And when they tried to set the palace on fire, the palace would not burn...' To him, the Njangmans were people to be watched at close range, and I had the duty of protecting Mother and Shaka from them, whom he was sure were still around. (Nyamnjoh 9)

It is through Ngoma's eyes that the reader has a view of the grand-uncle's perspective on the Germans. By introducing the story of the attempts to steal the spitting stone on the way to the palace, Nyamnjoh, a writer in the wake of neo-colonialism, skillfully debunks colonial rape, extortion, and theft. Could it be for this reason that EFD asserts that, "[t]heir [i.e. the writers'] goal is, first of all to show how the colonialist indoctrinated and misled them from their roots even before their independence, for which they had to struggle and in some cases are still struggling as is the case with Anglophone-Cameroon even today" (70)? The truth about colonialism is far from anything moral and neither does Nyamnjoh inculcate and push for virtue, nor does he offer reconstruction possibilities and representational models of his deconstructed and exposed historico-existential social factors of Mimboland reality. By so doing and paying absolute allegiance to the obscene and evil, Nyamnjoh's *Homeless Waters,* though not a war story per se, seems to be grounded in one of the tenets of writing a true war story as upheld by Tim O'brien who asserts, "[y]ou can tell a true war story by its absolute and uncompromising allegiance to obscenity and evil" (qtd. in Paul Budra and Zeitlin Michael 69). Nyamnjoh in his commitment *à la* Sartre indulges in a war aimed at exposing, through the voices of the victims of colonial repression such as Ngoma's grand-uncle, such ills that are all too often abandoned in the dustbin of history. This trend is one highlighted by EFD in his *Opus Magna* introducing Anglophone Cameroon Literature. In it, he states that "the general temper in Anglophone-Cameroon prose fiction is one of restlessness fuelled by a 100 society trapped at a cultural cross-roads with alienating trends stemming from conflicting colonial traditions" (69). It is therefore understandable that the Anglophone Cameroonian novelist like Nyamnjoh should cling to the tenets of a war story as highlighted above.

The characters are thus caught in the grip of forces, be them political, social, historical, cultural, etc. that pit them in a landscape akin to an oppressive battlefield in which the oppressed are bent on expressing all that which is repressed. It is no accident that the author carefully dedicates his novel "to mothering". Mother, in *Homeless Waters,* is not only the most oppressed character but the most effaced and silenced. Yet, the oppression, the effacement, and the silencing are not enough to clamp down on the castigation and expression of such ills. In the novel, the reader learns of most of her travails. These are mostly the result of a repressive society. The decisions she makes against such are all indication of her willingness to rather let out the repressed than allow the repressed in her to implode. In a society replete with individuals so keen on prying into people's private affairs, Mother does not allow gossips to oppress her to the point where she loses the deep seated warmth with which she always greets everyone. This warmth becomes her tool for rebellion and the object of Ngoma's recollection many, many years into his adulthood. In Ngoma's memory,

> Mother was tall and bubbling with life like a young banana tree growing near a spring. Like the ones down below in the fertile valleys that fed our village and beyond with their bumper harvests. She was kind, gentle, good and simply divine – this, I can still see, as I recollect my childhood, several decades into my adulthood.... In fact, I can't remember any cry of mine that went unattended, right from the time when I was a little baby in her arms, up to the age when the first shoots of reason sprouted out and set me wild with thirst for knowing. Harsh words were unknown to her. She greeted everyone with a warm smile. One that sprung from the depths of her heart and reached out – even to those neighbourhood[sic] gossips who stuck their noses like antennae into her most personal affairs. (Nyamnjoh 1)

The above brief remembrance of Mother paints rather a picture of a woman poised for rebellion against societal values which seem to be out to stifle any freedom that a woman should have or deserves to have in society. Thus, Mother works her way into "a being" and not in Kristeva's words, "ill-being" (140). She uses this act to echo what Joseph Addison states when he says, "[s]elf discipline is that which, next to virtue, truly and essentially raises one man [woman] above another" (WEB.).

Moreover, it is this self-discipline and determination to sit above trivialities that raise her above the women in her age group. The narrator draws attention to the fact that as the various young and self-confident suitors came, so did she give them a cold shoulder. The oblivious child who might not have noticed their coming and going now recalls,

> ... that Mother never appeared to have their time. Her determination to reign above trivial and trivialising[sic] variants of seduction gained her enormous popularity among the women of her age group. That was significant in neighbourhoods[sic] nourished by wild rumours[sic] fed by notorious rumour[sic] mongers about young beautiful girls ready to elope. Rumours[sic] further held that even women, who like Mother already had children, had run away by moonlight at the slightest opportunity to become second or third wives. Marriage, it seemed, was a sought after institution. (Nyamnjoh 2)

Again, the reader learns of Mother's position defying the above mentioned, very much "sought after institution". The narrator tells the reader, "[m]other remained steadfast and calm, giving no adventurer room to take advantage of her. She had learnt to fold and sit upon the risky advice of many who claimed to have her best interest at heart" (2). Besides, as she tells her children, Ngoma and Shaka of their father, she does not hesitate to take a swipe at the father's obstinacy in refusing her the opportunity to marry the love of her life. As a result of such persistent refusal, Mother did what she thought was right and went right ahead to having children (Ngoma and Shaka) with the undesired element. In consequence, her father lay claims to her children as dictated by traditional wisdom. By representing Mother thus, with her plight, Nyamnjoh vividly brings to mind the Heideggerian reflections on modes of conceptual representation. Heidegger holds that, "the mode of conceptual representation insinuates itself all too easily into a kind of human experience" (25). Hence, Nyamnjoh suggests that Mother's experience in this oppressive society in which she is set, has transformed her into what Julia Kristeva highlights when talking of "[s]uffering as the place of the subject". It is in this regard that she writes:

> Where it emerges, where it is differentiated, from chaos. An incandescent, unbearable limit between inside and outside, ego and other. The initial, fleeting grasp: "suffering," "fear," ultimate words sighting the crest where sense topples over into the senses, the "intimate" into "nerves." Being as ill-being. (140)

Further still, in testament of Mother's plight, the nature of Nyamnjoh's language mimic yet again, Heidegger who intends to bring readers face to face with the possibility of undergoing an experience with the expression of that which society oppresses (or as in the case of Heidegger with language). She undergoes an experience with a society that befalls her, strikes her, comes over her, overwhelms and transforms her (Heidegger 57).

In short the writer, in this instance, simply deconstructs her endurance, suffering, and her reception and resistance to the harsh blows dealt her by society. Even the writer's craft of expressing the repressed restrains him from naming a woman like Mother who, in her goodness and in spite of her sufferings, is representative of every other woman with plights similar to hers. Mother's effacement is replete with a sense of nagging frustration for the reader to quest if staying mute is a better way to hide repression, oppression and violence. In "A Dialogue on Language Between a Japanese and an Inquirer", Heidegger notes on subdued gestures, via the Japanese that, "[i]nconspicuities of this kind flow abundantly and hardly noticeable to ... [an] observer" (Heidegger 16). Over and above, the dedication of a narrative scarcely comes into the discussion and debate about a creative work of art. However, in Nyamnjoh's case, dedicating his work "to Mothering and Teaching" seems to intimate that the key role of teaching, consequently development, is dependent upon the woman though the male dominated society would rather eclipse her. This instance of Nyamnjoh taking up the fight against the oppression of women, must have prompted EFD's views that such writers are "matadors engaged in a battle to free the minds of the oppressed lot through the conflicts and the attendant outcome they paint" (70). To this I could add my voice, pointing out that they are out to shame the oppressor in the battle they are engaged in.

Mother turns out to be the exemplary role model thanks to whom the protagonist has a firsthand experience of what hard work, integrity, and wisdom represent. He muses on Mother's ability and the kind of society in which women are socially excluded and only allowed to be seen and never heard. This however, does not inhibit Mother from being an excellent father and mother. As such the narrator does not fail to decry the injustice in this type of society. He thus has this to say:

> Allowed, she would have joined even the men's society and out-saved quite a few of its members. But that would have been by men as an affront. It was a serious taboo to openly equate herself with any man, no matter how abnormally low his social status. She could do so in private, but never in public. [...] Mother doubling up masterfully as mother and father, I thought it terribly unjust for men to seek to dwarf women. (27)

Injustices such as the one denounced in the quote above, which tends towards dwarfing women, is further reiterated when Lumawut decides to get rid of Mother and has the corrupt councilors of Bonfuma, all backing him. The narrator wonders aloud: "What justice is there in this land! Lumawut and his new found love bribed them all! Corrupt beings they are, those councilors of Bonfuma!" (148) Here, Mother earns Ngoma's admiration and becomes the very person the narrator desires to contact "Before the law sanctions that [he is]I am a hooligan deserving immediate death, before [he]I drive[s] [himself]myself to death with painful thoughts, [he has]I have to write a letter to [his]my mother, [his]my sole parent" (164).

Such injustices, the author intimates, even if met with opposition from the women, the men seem not to pay attention to it. In a way,

Nyamnjoh's universe casts women expressing their repressed feelings in a male dominated society through their silence. This, to an extent, demonstrates the disdain these women have for what men uphold to be customary. Moreover, when these women are brewing their rebellion, and even among, and to the notice of, children, it is hardly noticeable by men lost in the cacophony generated by senseless, deafening, and boisterous clappings that leave them in hysteria. When Lumawut stands up lauding how supreme and irrevocable the customs and the ways of the land are, the observant narrator makes evident that,

> the notables (all men) agreed and applauded as they shook their heads. Not much clapping came from among the women and the children, this time. But this was hardly noticed, as the notables were loud and noisy in their response. (60)

From the above quote, "not much clapping" stresses disapprobation and Nyamnjoh seems to intimate that for any successful change to take place in this society, the oppressed i.e. women and children must to join forces in ushering in the change. Each time the opportunity presents itself, they have to show their opposition to these notables who oppress and refuse to notice them. He further draws the readers' attention to the fact that when talking about Mother in that same occasion, Lumawut talks of having "been living with a woman for a long long time…" (60). He does not name the woman. This avoidance of naming the woman in question i.e. Mother, immediately strikes the women as a deliberate effort to efface one of theirs. They seize this opportunity as their turn to express the dissatisfaction. They go ahead "to interrupt him with loud applause and ululations, interspaced the calling of Mother's name" (60). How else can women express clearly that which for too long has been repressed in them?

Shaka's desire to transcend her condition of a woman leads her to thirst after knowledge and not wait for it from men who would do everything to dwarf her. In a dialogue with her brother, Ngoma, she prides herself with the level of education she has attained by teaching herself. When the flabbergasted and bemused brother asks who was teaching her, her answer leaves no doubt that she is blazing a trail for women to express how fed-up they are with a system bent on repressing them. She tells him, responding to the question regarding who was teaching her: "[n]o one. I am teaching myself. I don't want any man teaching me how to read and write when they would not let me go to school…" (50). To this, her brother who does not only champion the woman's cause but castigate all that which is wrong with the tradition, lends support for her disappointment, saying: "… I could feel her anger and legitimate bitterness" (50). For Ngoma, this resentment is the legitimate expression of acrimony against a society that has so wronged its daughters in the name of senseless tradition.

Much could be written about each and every woman or girl in Nyamnjoh's universe. However, Collette, Camille, Shaka, Elizabeth Paradise, Jerusalem, the unnamed first, second or third wives of Lumawut's as well as Camille's mother are all victims of a male-dominated society that dictates the path women have to follow. Failure to do so becomes an invitation to ostracism, negation, and privation of all sorts. One wonders if Nyamnjoh, by having Elizabeth Paradise find solace in a convent, is advocating that women distance themselves from the machos' world to find peace where they dedicate their time and selves to spiritual quest and fulfillment or if he is simply concerned with the transcendental idea of being and belonging that goes beyond the substance. If the latter be the case, then Nyamnjoh is celebrating the woman at the transcendental level in this regard. Besides, the savory finality of the novel is the product of a woman's ingenuity and refusal to accept a truncated past as the narrator highlights:

> It was the ingenuity of Elizabeth-Paradise, her refusal to accept her truncated past, that had made possible my reunion with her, a few days before her final vows. It had taken over forty years for this to happen, but it was the greatest moment of my turbulent and disappointing life. (163)

Elizabeth-Paradise's indefatigable search for a father demonstrates her categorical refusal to find herself in the same uncomfortable shoes as her mother and father before her. She would rather channel her energy towards spiritual pursuit in a convent than unleash the deadly and unfriendly force unleashed by these two before her, and who ended up finding themselves in dire straits. She succeeds. And if the woman wins the day on the above celebratory note, what about the man?

Nyamnjoh presents the reader a cast of men from various walks of life. Some of them are anonymous i.e. they are either only talked about or they are nameless. Other male characters are characterized, named, identified by profession or trade. Either way, these men abet or move the actions of the plot, one way or another, towards juvenile rebellion and recollection in old age. Among the anonymous men in the cast are Mother's father, the protagonist's biological father, the numerous suitors who ventured in courting Mother to no avail, the nameless men of Safang youth groups, traders, and to an extent, Camille's father. Then we have Lumawut, Grand-uncle, Reverend Father Blackwater, Mr. Samba, Mabuh, Wutaseba Father Anthony, Ndida, Mr. France, Reverend Brother Jesus, the Doctor, and Reverend Brother Goodwood.

Lumawut is the epitome of the macho society in which the women and girls in Safang and Bonfuma are caught. Upon Lumawut's first encounter with mother, he does not let the opportunity to be the perfect gentleman slip off his hands. He starts by trying to win her children's love. He gives "Shaka two sets of earrings" (11). This becomes an opportunity for the writer to express his frustration at the outlandish and much cherished consumerism being forced upon his community from a very tender age. Though not the children's fault, the repressed feelings here are expressed through mother who is very keen on putting a check on and denouncing such consumerism. She declines Lumawuts offer of two sets of earrings for Shaka, arguing that her daughter has only two ears and to further make her point, she questions: "how many earrings can she wear? (11) Lumawut is unrelenting in his ploy to get closer to Mother. He offers her money. Mother, sensing the danger of accepting such an offer which on the surface seems inoffensive, does well to refuse. However, he explains it as a gesture of appreciation and nothing more. The explanation leaves Mother in a difficult position to refuse. With her acceptance of the offer, he promises to stop by again. This recollection becomes a tradition in due course, as the narrator tells the reader, Lumawut stops by every time he attended the market which was twice a week; stopping at Mother's house on his way to and from the market. Lumawut continues his ploy of winning over Mother with his bait of gifts: "each time he came he brought Mother and us various gifts" (12). Besides his bait of gifts, he does not relent in exploiting his talent as a good storyteller. This gets the children used to him. However, the writer through imagery and understatements foreshadows the relationship as one doomed to failure. It is the fact that such feelings in our narrator could not be readily expressed without consequences.

First, he talks of how Lumawut's friendship with Mother grew daily. The image of "garri soaked in cold water" as opposed to "garri" soaked in hot water is a hint at the temporal nature of such friendship. It must be noted that "garri" soaked in cold water for too long become mushy and unappetizing to eat because of the disgusting feel of it in the mouth. Again water scatters the "garri" grains that keep them together. On the contrary, had our young narrator conceived the friendship in terms of "garri soaked in hot water" then the finality of Lumawut's outrageous behavior and treatment of Mother just like he had done to his first wife would have come as a total surprise for "garri" soaked in hot water sticks together and can even serve as a binding glue.

Further still, when "Mother had introduced Lumawut to … grand-uncle (12) his reaction echoes through and understatement, "I think is putting my hand into a deep dark hole" (12) the impending doom of a failed relationship. Besides, upon this comment by grand-uncle, Nyamnjoh punctuates his story with the very first serious dialogue between Lumawut and Mother. Though it is reported by the narrator, we learn that Lumawut blames Mother "for surprising him" (12). Needless to point out that the outset of their relationship is a blame game. It thus brings to mind a quote from Heidegger highlighting that: "[t]he danger of our dialogues [is] hidden in language itself, not *what* [is] discussed nor the way in *which* we tried to do so" (4).

Again, when Lumawut shoves aside the blame and decides to go and see grand-uncle, he makes a choice of a gift for grand-uncle which speaks volumes as to the kind of relationship he is getting in to. He chooses a raincoat. Pointless to say this choice is symbolic for a raincoat is only used seasonally. This is as if he wishes to echo a protective gear that would brave the storm for as long as it lasts or again brave the rain storm he was scared of when he uttered his blame for having been surprised by Mother. When he meets with granduncle, he seems to have passed the litmus test. Yet, the narrator's diction only betrays his expression of repressed feelings. Talking of Lumawut, he says, he "looked firm and responsible" (12). This evokes his concern for appearance and reality. Lumawut is all about semblances of firmness and responsibility. But as the plot unfolds, the hallmarks of indecision and irresponsibility in Lumawut are all too apparent. This is highlighted when Ngoma narrates their arrival at Lumawut's compound upon moving to Bonfuma. His first wife, the narrator tells us, "…was wrapped in a thick cloth of anger [...] and welcomed none of us, not even her husband" (20). Her feeling of being betrayed, and back stabbed only find their expression in her silence; one which announces the raging storm that is brewing inside of her. The conflict having reached its apogee, Lumawut declines appeasing his first wife by going to plead to her in front of her parents for the poor treatment he has given her. This only sow the seeds of discontent in the young Ngoma who like every young person his age is strongly committed to following role models. He is thus pushed to express his disillusionment in Lumawut's behavior by pondering aloud, "[o]r perhaps his heart was beyond capture. Or maybe there was no heart to capture" (22).

Evidently, the heartless treatment Lumawut meted on his first wife could engender nothing but the revolting pain that the thought of it brings to bear upon Ngoma. Lumawut, as such, becomes a driving force that occasions most of the protagonist's actions and behavior. Lumawut's anti-role-model actions leave the narrator doubting seriously Lumawut's sincerity upon their arriving Bonfuma and discovering he has a wife and children. The narrator draws attention to his suspicion of Lumawut's insincerity: "[w]hether Lumawut had let Mother know that he was already married and she was coming to Bonfuma as a second wife, I can't say, but I doubt very much he did" (20). Lumawut's insincerity is even made more glaring by the first wife's epiphanic realization of her husband's prior misleading claims and excuses for staying away for long weeks and or the haste with which he had a new house built. When her husband brings home a new bride, she is awoken to the reality and says: "[n]ow

I understand all the trading up in the mountains. You stayed away for weeks saying marketing was adverse. Now I understand this new house you quickly built" (21). Her declaration reduces Lumawut, the man Ngoma looks up to, to a compulsive liar. With this, Ngoma's rebellion could be substantiated by Joseph Addison who famously said: "[n]othing that isn't a real crime makes a man appear so contemptible and little in the eyes of the world as inconsistency" (qtd. in Roger Fulton 31). Could this be any further from the truth when he comments that Lumawut "spoke like someone with his hands tied to his back" (24)? Certainly, no! for Ngoma has just heard this man tell the Headmaster explicitly that it is just a question of time before he begins falling out with Mother; most especially after he must "have learnt to fall out with her" (24). Lumawut is Nyamnjoh's poisoned fruit tree who delights in the practice of serial monogamy (polygamy) which to the writer is the trigger that ends harmonious relationships (65-66). He is not unaware of the ills caused by his mischief for, when he has to introduce Ngoma to a crowd gathered at his home for a feast he had organized, he has this to say: "[t]his young man is the one who has gone to learn so we may be cured of our original blindness that makes us see as if we didn't have eyes" (62). From this, it could be inferred that Lumawut is able to read 'rebellion' written on the wall and is quick to concede for the young like Ngoma constitute those to champion such rebellion which will herald the much desired change.

Also, at the early stages, Lumawut's make-beliefs to fulfil his desire and or lust for Mother's love, and subsequently marry and take her to Bonfuma warrant him bribing his way through in Safang. He joins the community development groups made up of young men though he rarely participates in any of their meetings. He only made sure his contributions were always in. The only occasion he happened to have been at one of their meetings was when they had to clear Mother's farm. The narrator seizes the opportunity in this instance to portray how mistaken the people of Safang describe Lumawut as "the most popular man in Safang" (13). Yet, the narrator jumps in with a diction that betrays the semblance of his art of pleasing: "he seemed to have learnt in his youth how to please" (13). Digging further down in Lumawut's character mineshaft, the narrator acquaints the reader of the geographical location of his compound situated at a significant distance between two rivers and the fact that he owned land on the banks of both rivers. This is a construct to express how opportunistic and how different from his peers Lumawut was. He is certainly blinded by sight as the narrator would have it. He underlines this when talking of Lumawut's friend Wutaseba who "sees what those [like Lumawut] blinded by sight can't" (28). Is it not the same blinding by sight that leads Camille's father to fail to realize that he is not only hurting his grandchild's father but the grandchild and its mother, his own daughter? The memory Ngoma takes to prison elucidates this: "At least she has tried and failed to make her father realise[sic] that she loves and cares for his prisoner. Looking at her as I am dragged away to prison, I feel I love her more than ever before" (164). Again this memory comforts in every measure the Aesopian view that, "[w]e hang the petty thieves and appoint the great ones to public office" (WEB).

Further, the author delves into the criticism of abuse of power in a polity that deprives hard working villagers of the rights to ownership of their lands. This accounts for the narrator's mock irony when he says, "[h]ard work alone did not guarantee land ownership, it was already a good sign for a village that was simply too populated to be interested in people who let grass flourish uninterruptedly" (18). In short, owning land is about who matters not about who inherits. It is a corrupt system in which bribery, cronyism, favoritism, and nepotism are the order of the day and Lumawut understands and plays by such rules. Even though he is an unwilling advocate to have Ngoma in school a year earlier than he is due, he gives free rein to bribing the headmaster to have the former admitted earlier than due. He uses his shrewdness in business as well as his sleight of hand of friendship by telling the Headmaster: "Just come to the house in the evening and we will fix it. [...] It is not today we are friends." These words followed by a pretentious act of taking his son away, push the Headmaster to stopping him with the question: "...are you too impatient to get your son admitted this year? (23) This is yet another one of Nyamnjoh's way of cleverly infusing in his writings such elements that will incur nefarious consequences upon being overtly critiqued. As such, one is tempted to ask the following questions along the line of Sartre's thinking of what constitutes literature. Is he not just injecting his feelings into the work? Is he not just allowing the words to take hold of the ideas, penetrate them, and metamorphose them? (18-19) The turn bribery has taken touches on every fabric of the society. Even attending a medical school becomes a business negotiation in which "[m]oney [...] a machine for the production of misery and unhappiness" (159) is the sole guarantor to have anyone trained as a doctor. So it does not come as a surprise that when the doctors finish their training after having used such dubious means to go through medical school, they would seek to recuperate their expenses rather than pay attention to medical ethics and the Hippocratic Oath. The narrator takes a swipe at bribery and its consequences in the medical profession. He says:

> Looking at the doctor during my examination, *I could see a money-minded medical practitioner in him*, (my emphasis) the sort who probably *went to medical school through bribery*, (my emphasis) and since completing his training, and *since completing training has been busy making back the millions he paid to get in.* (my emphasis) (155).

Yet again, through Ngoma's thickly layered narrative, Nyamnjoh reemphasizes his rebuke of a system marred by corruption in every section of life: institutional, judicial, medical, educational, etc. Ngoma finds out in the end that the only way out for him to succeed is to cede to the prevailing corruption, nepotism, and cronyism. These are the sore and thorny points of criticism the writer is out to drive home. Understood as such, it is no wonder Ngoma, such a bright and intelligent young man with a promising future should just surrender everything at the very first obstacle he encounters. He forfeits all as if to substantiate the author's advocacy for a society devoid of such corruption. It is also an evocation alluding to Chuang Tzu's parable, "Independence" in which the sage Tzu turns down a lucrative governmental position and would rather be a turtle wagging its tail in the mud. The wisdom in the choices Ngoma and Tzu make is clearly summed up in Elizabeth-Paradise's statement just before she summons her father to join hands in prayer. She says: "[o]ne person's cleverness is like shallow water that soon dries up" (166). In short societal wisdom falls short of Ngoma's and account for him sitting at long last telling stories he had long repressed for want of being a father and recounting such to his child. He underscores this saying:

Now, as I sit at the Dominican Convent in Zintgraffstown, under a mango tree heavy with fruit, telling Elizabeth-Paradise stories I would have loved to share with her, if I had had the opportunity of being her father in a normal way, my mind keeps going back to that fateful day at college, some forty years ago. (163)

Finally, the above fulfilment of wishful thinking would leave everyman having reached the innermost depth of his soul and contemplated his being and deeds to "[m]ake good use of the present, so as not to regret the past. And avoid keeping for tomorrow what you can do today. Sometimes there is no next time because what happened the first time" (166).

As I strive to draw this chapter to a conclusion, I cannot help borrowing from my teaching. I often come up with mnemonics derived from grouping letters of the alphabet, often the same letter repeated a number of times with that number prefixing the letters e.g. 4Cs, 4Ps, 4Is, 5Ps, etc. Evoking this in exploring juvenile rebellion and old age recollection brings to mind the 4Cs which stand for "Coincidences, Chances, Choices, and Consequences". The simple explanation of the 4Cs is that: "in life, there are no 'Coincidences', no 'Chances', only 'Choices' which people make and they have 'Consequences'." In Nyamnjoh's *Homeless Waters,* it is apparent that from the very beginning of the narrative right up to the moment that Ngoma falters in his relationship with Collette, and then gets involved in the similitude of bliss at the beginning of the novel, the novelist is busy enticing the reader with a bait which acts as a spell and sustains the readers' interest. This bait, the readers would naïvely take under the guise that the narrator is innocent. Having juxtaposed the idea of rebellion intrinsically linked to youthful exuberance marked by the Wordsworthian "spontaneous overflow of powerful feelings and recollected in perfect tranquility" (Web.) spurred by maturity, this chapter has carefully followed the narrative trajectory of the protagonist as well as those of other affiliated characters and their interactions and reactions in the face of challenges theretofore encountered. In so doing, the chapter has addressed a number of critical scholarly concerns while illuminating understanding of

Nyamnjoh's narrative as one engrained in the tradition of commitment that X-rays and makes visible the ugly face of society and societal repression at the origin of which are historical, social, political, cultural, psychological, economic, etc. forces. *Homeless Waters* aligns the presentation and representations of power relations and interactions as well as the effects and hard choices that such relations leave characters with; be it in real life or in the fictional universe therein depicted. It is in an attempt to contain the free and spontaneous expression of emotions and thoughts running contrary to traditional wisdom that *Homeless Waters* exposes the unbearableness of repression—akin to that in The Cameroons of today. The novel thus translates into underlying forces driving the will to strive and die for the freedom to expose the idea in which one believes even if it entails hoisting the dirty linen of that society for all to see.

Works Cited

Backscheider, Paula R. *Daniel Defoe: His Life,* The John Hopkins UP. 1989.
Barthes, Roland. *A Lover's Discourse* Translated by Richard Howard, Hill and Wang, 2001.
Budra, Paul and Zeitlin Michael, *Soldier Talk: The Vietnam War in Oral Narrative,* Indiana UP. 2004.
Fru Doh, Emmanuel. *Anglophone Cameroon Literature: An Introduction*, Lexington Books, 2015.
Fulton, Roger. *Common Sense Management,* Ten Speed P, 2009.
Heidegger, Martin. *On the Way to Language,* Translated by Peter D. Hertz HarperSanFrancisco, 1982.
Kristeva, Julia. *The Power of Horror: an Essay on Abjection.* Columbia UP. 1982.
Montgomery, Maxine L. "Re-membering the Forgotten War: Memory, History, and the Body in Toni Morrison's *Home*" *CLA Journal,* vol. LV. no 4, 2012, pp. 320-334.
Nyamnjoh, Francis B. *Homeless Waters,* Langaa-RPCIG, 2011.
O'brien, Tim. *The Things They Carried,* Houghton-Mifflin, 1990.
Sartre, J.P. *What is Literature?* Translated by Bernard Frechtman, Philosophical Library, 1949.

Soeiro, Ricardo Gil & Sofia Tavares. *Rethinking the Humanities: Paths and Challenges,* Cambridge Scholars, 2012.

Tzu, Chuang. "Independence" in Kennedy, X. J. & Gioia, Dana. *Backpack Literature,* (4th ed.), Pearson, 2010.

Wordsworth, William (1800) "Preface" to *Lyrical Ballads* qtd. in *Prefaces and Prologues.* Vol. XXXIX. The Harvard Classics, edited by Charles W. Eliot. P.F. Collier & Son, 1909–14; Bartleby.com, 2001. www.bartleby.com/39/. Accessed 27 June 2016.

Chapter 6

Rising from the Ashes: Conflict and Repression in Bill F. Ndi's Poetry

Antonio Jimenez-Munoz

Since Socrates' warning about song makers, poets have always had, over the centuries, to take the challenge of keeping up with their reputation for being capable to subvert and denounce oppression in spite of the muzzles in place to check the brazen who would dare to express the repressed. Some poets do so through an explicit rendering of conflictual images: through denunciations, vilifications or indictments on the oppressors. Rather than singing praise, they specifically stage conflict in their poems to capture their social role, since "washing one's hands of the conflict between the powerful and powerless means to side with the powerful, not to remain neutral" (Freire 102). In a similar vein, Bill F. Ndi's (Ndi) poetry thus provides a discursive space, in the nascent Anglophone Cameroon Literature, for the examination of the ways and manners in which poets would revive, in a dictatorship, the crushed and the repressed in a figurative language, structure, form, tone, imagery, etc. that gives them not only a new lease in life but the possibility of avoiding further oppression. These poems about repression from Ndi carry, with them, fruits of the anger and conflict that inspired them; the vile repression by the forces of regression in *La République du Cameroun*. The juicy appearance of the fruits of anger notwithstanding, a reading of the poems will not leave behind a bitter taste in the mouth of the oppressor, but the reader. Writing in a context whereby oppressive forces call the shots, pits the poet in a game of cats and mice, and marks the craft of the poet's art. Thus, Ndi devotes his art to the redemption of the oppressed not forgetting the oppressors to all of whom the poet presents old and new truths the latter have buried and or hidden away from the former who would emerge, from reading the poems, with a true sense of ennoblement as they see in the poems a reflection of their relationship to their oppressors.

Politicians and statesmen, when not the military, remind us constantly that conflict is a natural state among human beings, fuelled by the principle of economic and material scarcity. It is seemingly natural because the resources of our environment are limited and, thus, we are deemed to fight for them. Even early environmentalist economists perceived this as a precondition to human nature – in Europe and elsewhere: "Man has probably always worried about his environment because he was once totally dependent on it" (Fisher and Peterson 1). Nobel-prize winner Daniel Kahneman, explains that scarcity heavily determines our choices. Our view of the world, thus, is heavily determined by an implied lack of resources: scarcity captures the mind both when thinking "fast and when thinking slow" (Kahneman 31) and makes us see the world in a way which predates our choices. Following the rationale, conflict would be the natural state of men, and a poetry that attempted to subvert oppression would go against natural order. Poetry should be pure – rid of earthly entanglements.

Particularly African poets such as Ndi harshly reject that premise: scarcity does not justify oppression. Poets have interrogated the very tenets of their culture "precisely because they are a site of conflict, and precisely because the 'purity' of lyric address cannot be granted immunity" (Perrill 92). They are not without their arguments; due to technological advancements it is soon to be expected that, "the world can, in effect, get along without natural resources" (Solow 11). The role of poetry in questioning and reflecting upon conflict is thus doubly important. On the one hand, the fact that conflict may be naturally human does not make it morally desirable. On the other, technologically-fuelled sustained economic growth has not made this world fairer, safer, or again, one in which wealth is equitably distributed.

Technological advancement has been repeatedly hailed as the hallmark of progress and we must be reminded that repetition is the key to falsehood – and poetry its cure. No wonder John Maynard Keynes asserted, "the economic problem may be solved, or be at least within sight of solution, within a hundred years" (359). He further underscores that this "means that the economic problem is not – if we look into the future – the permanent problem of the human race" (Keynes 359). In any case, the competition brought by scarcity belongs to a world where the focus is almost exclusively on the material. In this regard, the supply of goods and services, the allocation of economic resources, and technological innovation become aspects of global governance that belong far away from individual psychology. Thus, we learn from Friedrich Nietzsche's aphorism 640, that "It is not conflict of opinions that has made history so violent but conflict of belief in opinions, that is to say conflict of convictions" (Nietzsche 200). As such, this falls within the subjective and the psychological. Karl Marx, likewise criticizing working classes for failing to perceive themselves as such, attacked the ideology imposed by economic superstructures and so does by bringing to the light that "life is not determined by consciousness but rather consciousness is determined by life" (Marx and Engels 15). As competition is a natural state of men, life seems necessarily conflictual: but material and psychological conflict are two very different approaches to interpreting reality. The status of poetry as an interpreter of life, ultimately, is what is at stake here. In the Western world, with very few exceptions of late, poets have refrained to comment on political or social issues, let alone stage conflict. A more recent school of poets in continents such as Africa gives us poems of conflict rather than of fruition: poetry is not the treatment of joy and triumph only. Conflict and despair are central subject matters, and if poets refrain from refracting this quintessential aspect of life they are failing to report on life significantly.

Literature falls within the purview of individual psychology or vice versa – we see the world through or eyes, for it to be read through someone's eyes too. This is particularly true of poetry in general and the poetry of Bill F. Ndi in particular. When a reader approaches a poem he or she listens to a voice that is half the voice of another, and yet the poem awakens sentiments to which readers are akin. Since the Romantic era, reading poetry has entailed reading outwardly so that it reverberates inwardly. This is a process in which the poet speaks to the reader in order to achieve a "great effect [...] both psychologically, and rhetorically, within a linguistic pattern of carefully balanced opposites" (Wolowsky 59). This opposition also encompasses the dichotomy between matter and soul, and between what is represented and what is longed for. The fact that a poem deals with the topic of anger, conflict, or vengeance in an oppressed society does not readily mean the text longs for them. On the contrary, it is often the case that a poem presents a given reality precisely to highlight the undesirability of the same and its ideas. Such is the case with John Keats's "On Death". Keats poem denies death as a psychological fear, rather than asserting the inevitability of eventual demise. He confronts death to life and—is precise to deny the unassailable preference of one over the other—reminds the reader that death may be considered a gift when compared with a miserable life. Thus, the poem sails around its real subject matter in a way that may be considered ironic. It presents death to discuss life. In one of the best theoretical works on the subject, Anne Mellor reminds us of Romantic irony which is not only a philosophical conception of the universe but also an artistic program. Thus she writes:

> Of course, romantic irony itself has more than one mode. The style of romantic irony varies from writer to writer. [...] But however distinctive the voice, a writer is a romantic ironist if and when his or her work commits itself enthusiastically both in content and form to a hovering or unresolved debate between a world of merely man-made being and a world of ontological becoming. (Mellor 187)

Poetry lies precisely within the tension between an artificial world, where scarcity and conflict are rife, and the moral idealization of the same. Hence the American modernist, Wallace Stevens rendered this in the first stanza of *The Man with the Blue Guitar*. The tension between reality and poetry are always resolved in favor of the latter, despite popular insistence on art to reflect life as accurately as possible. Wallace's poem reads:

> The man bent over his guitar,
> A shearsman of sorts. The day was green.
> They said, "You have a blue guitar,
> You do not play things as they are."
> The man replied, "Things as they are
> Are changed upon the blue guitar."
>
> And they said then, "But play, you must,

> A tune beyond us, yet ourselves,
> A tune upon the blue guitar
> Of things exactly as they are." (Stevens 61)

Poems are imperfect means of depicting reality because they aim at psychological connection, and not mere reflection of what there is. Their raison d'être is to mediate ideas, and not to transfer material things. As such, the relation of poems with life is not subject to contingencies: perhaps indirectly, but they manage to present things as they should be rather than as they are. For the reader, the constant adjustment between the pole of representation – what is presented – and the pole of interpretation – what the poem suggests – makes poetry different from any other kind of reading, and makes its interpretation less straightforward than other artistic discourses. In doing so, poetry inherently challenges received wisdom, and arouses any critical mind. Coming back to Nietzsche, doing so helps create a better, more knowledgeable society. Nietzsche highlights that:

> … if all those who have thought so highly of their convictions, brought to them sacrifices of every kind, and have not spared honour[sic], body or life in their service, had devoted only half their energy to investigating with what right they adhered to this or that conviction, by what path they had arrived at it, how peaceable a picture the history of mankind would present! How much more knowledge there would be!" (Nietzsche 200)

This building aspect of poetry – to make for a better, more knowledgeable society in which the poet is inserted – must not be overlooked when confronting a poem of conflict. Political denunciation and indictment do not stop at that, but strive for a better and fairer community. In other words, Modern Anglophone Cameroonian poetry complicates the aesthetical balance between the representation of destruction and hatred, and the suggestion for social construction and reconciliation. In increasingly challenging ways for the reader, it presents a more tangible reality so as to occlude the rationale of the poem. Often, it hides its suggestion behind what becomes its exact opposite. There is a trend in Cameroonian poetry written in English – in poets such as Bate Besong, Ba'billa Mutia, Bongasu Tanla Kishani, Gahlia Gwangwa'a, Nol Alembong, Ebini Christmas Atem, Peter W. Vakunta, or Emmanuel Fru Doh – to denounce in their poems the recurrent abuses of power, monetary exploitation of natural and human resources in their country (Jimenez-Munoz *in* Fishkin, Ankumah, and Ndi. *Fears, Doubts and joys of not Belonging* 34). In doing so, it may well be said that these militant poems become blunt, harsh and unrepentant – particularly to Western audiences, often oblivious to such dramatic circumstances – against those who vilified and exploited the country and its people. Besong's poems *Shame on the last vestiges of the geriatric politics of the Cameroon National Assembly* or *Why we laugh at politicians and give them names*, Vakunta's *Genocide* or *Eco-Terrorism*, of Doh's *Gang-Raped* or *The African Dinosaur* attest to such otherwise justified ruthlessness. Poems as these are necessarily conflictual because they respond to an all-encompassing threat and abuse: prima facie, they seem to respond to fire with fire, and to demand an eye for an eye.

However, perceiving the anger in these poems as their main means of expression would be superficial. It may well be true, in this case, that fury spurred these lines, but their suggestion and intention are more patriotic and redemptive than they may look at first glance. Besong angrily attacks Cameroonian politicians in order to highlight their disservice to their people. Also, he hopes that the situation is reversed. Vakunta depicts environmental abuse to promote man-made preservation of green areas. Doh shows brutality and abuse to chronicle their impact, but also to prevent future instances of such horrors. Again, these poets carefully present the reality of things as they are in order to promote things as they should be. No wonder, Doh in his *Anglophone Cameroon Literature: An Introduction*, emphasizes that, "Anglophone Cameroonian poets came to assume their authentic roles not only as seers and connoisseurs of nature and culture, but also as the voice of society, the downtrodden, rebels one might say" (138). Needless to underscore the fact that the end of the last century till the 2000s has been a very fertile period for Anglophone Cameroon poetry.

Undeniably one of the most productive and combatant authors in a younger generation of contemporary Anglophone Cameroonian literature is Ndi. Some of his poetry collections make explicit this vibrant animosity in their titles: *K'cracy, Trees in the Storm and other Poems* (2008), *Bleeding Red: Cameroon in Black and White* (2010), *Toil and Delivery* (2010), and *Waves of Anger* (2010) among others, while the more recent *Vestiges* (2013) and *Pride Aside and other Poems* (2016) seem to attune that angst and aim for more reflective, introspective, remembering poems. In effect, Ndi yokes in them, his practice of religious meditation with contemporary Anglophone poetic concerns. The proverbial saying holds that one should not judge a book by its cover, and neither by its title. This holds true for Ndi's poetry collections for neither do the former collections revel exclusively in violence and hatred, nor the latter embody the poet as detached from reality and his people. Within his means, and with different stylistic and literary devices as well as a distinct poetic voice, Ndi puts up a ferocious fight against injustice and the strong tendency of the Government of *La République du Cameroun* – if not other self-styled pan-African governments that have reduced their rule to the application of Machiavelli's practice of divide and rule, and of embracing the populace only to choke hold them as dangerous enemies to be eliminated. They thus become the true source of social disunion as they generate nothing but fear and not loved to govern abiding by the Machiavellian precept that: "One ought to be both feared and loved, but as it is difficult for the two to go together, it is much safer to be feared than loved, if one of the two has to be wanting" (Machiavelli qtd in Kocis, Robert 157). The social role of poetry, both for the schooled and not, remains strong within Ndi; being in many respects more formally risqué (i.e. an audacious venture into traditional forms) than in the previously mentioned poets. It is also the case that most of his poetry embeds a hopeful message within an uncompromising attack against what should not be. In effect, Ndi's poetry echoes and extends Lévi-Strauss's claim of, "myth as imaginary resolutions of real social contradictions" (qtd. in Terry Eagleton 97). Ndi's poems are not only imaginary resolutions of social contradictions but those for political, economic, as well as psychological contradictions. The poems seem to consist of deceptively clear and simple statements articulating oppression as the subject matter. This should come as no surprise from a poet who has been summed up as having, "… always belonged to the oppressed minority in his life's journey" (Doh, qtd. *in* Fishkin,

Ankumah, and Ndi 5). Ndi expresses the repressed in his poetry, in ways that differ from those of the aforementioned Anglophone Cameroonian writers. His poems are beautifully constructed, with attention paid to form, rhythm, symbolism, structure, diction, puns, form, repetition and inversions, etc. Thus the poems challenge and refresh his reader, tackling a range of questions extended to the metaphysical. This accounts for why the Australian poetess and critic, Maria Takolander would say of the collection *Toil and Delivery* to be "…a cryptic crossword puzzle […] marked by a strange energetic hybridity" (Foreword, *Toil and Delivery* ix).

In *K'cracy,* the opening poem, "Happy Birthday", already embodies some of these traits of his versification and arouses responses from the reader. First, it directly addresses a collective – a 'we', rather than a 'you' or 'them' – which deviates from the poet, and yet includes him. He cannot exclude himself for, with the oppressed he wears the same shoe and feels the same pinch. Secondly, it constantly presents and misrepresents its topic, so that the reader is forced to re-evaluate his or her own interpretation of the text as he or she reads. A key to unlocking the repressed he endeavors to express as a measure of conscientizing his reader. Finally, it includes grim images and calligraphic structure that, beyond attempting to startle the reader with their occasional coarseness, always call for redeeming action in the face of a better future. These grim images are certainly the ingredients with which Ndi crafts his poetry. And in this opening poem (reproduce here below in its entirety) we read,

HAPPY BIRTHDAY

❦ ❦

We need no broom!
!Ô   Ô!
We need a darkroom!
Today is a birthday
Not so ordinary a birthday
As it is a rarity of its kind
A day to everyman's mind
One celebrating
The birthing
Of a nation

> A nation
> With filth
> Filled
> And for this occasion
> Would in a procession
> All march down
> The store with or without gown
> And buy a broom
> And sweep away our nation's bloom!
> Being a wizard neither,
> Nor a street sweeper
> But one, like all, kept away from uphill
> By their broom and briar downhill
> Would all with zeal desire
> And sweep into the mire
> These legends our nation's
> Birthing engendered: passions!
> Passionate world champion,
> Champion of Corruption!
>
> (*K'cracy* 1)

Such a nation "With filth / Filled" and "Champion of corruption" will not thrive if the broom does away with all that is established. Speaking directly to Cameroonians, Ndi presents a potential call to violence, and reflects on its likely effects. The poet, who is not a "wizard" and not a "street sweeper" reflects the tension between action and consequence as tabula rasa which will also do away with that passion and bloom. The use of the broom as a double-edge tool – one to clean what is undesirable, but also to do it at the risk of losing a desirable part of what there is – is not only of the part of the people "kept away from uphill / By their broom and briar downhill" but also of the establishment. The broom, embodying violence and oppression, and often associated with witches and wizards cannot be the tool of choice for those seeking a sound revolution. Thus the poem's initial call to arms revolves around an emotional call to reject such violence and associates as resolution and denouement for the repressed. It expresses struggle, acting not only as a release and a key to unlock repression, but also as a way to express what the future may hold. In resolving conflict, if it can be done at all, the actors must resort to other strategies. This cast Ndi's poetry out of the scope of provinciality and transforms it into "a material act in a troubled world [...] conveyed with typical irony" (Takolander qtd. in Bill F. Ndi, Foreword, *Toil and Delivery* ix).

In addition, Ndi writes: "We need a darkroom!" And one needs wonder why a "darkroom". A darkroom is a place in which photographers capture and produce beautiful, and artistic images from negatives for eyes to revel on. It is his dire wish to have the image of the nation cured i.e. turn positive from its negatives viz. repression/oppression. Hence Emmanuel Fru Doh in discussing Ndi's "Social Angst and Humanist Vision..." asserts that, "Plato would have seen Ndi as a true poet focusing on people's emotion and thereby a perverter of morality and a deformer of minds besides all else" (qtd. *in* Fishkin, Ankumah, and Ndi 3). In effect Ndi keeps stretching the readers' ability to respond at every juncture in his poems.

Other poems such as "Letter to our deaf father of the nation: "Mr. Dict...."." exemplify Ndi's harshness to the oppressive monster and his machine. Ndi refrains from explicitly mentioning the deaf and certainly not dear dictator Paul Biya who is reminded that he will "live /die / (And Miserably / Too!). This is a subtle and ironic expression of the repression Cameroonians in general and Ndi in particular suffers or have suffered under the rule of "Mr. Dict...." Ndi's call is also an encouragement as well as an emotional appeal, for "Mr. Dict..." to give up ruling the country before he has no other choice but to meet his doom. It is a *modus operandi* for an honorable exit for "Mr. Dict...," who is a rather godly apple rotten at heart in Chaucerian terms. The lines read:

> Knowing that shimmering seal's
> Face, the rot in you conceals
> We would...
> Not in the woods...
> Hoot you down!
> Step down, renege the crown
> To hap your way under
> As we

> With our thorny
> Life of misery ...
> Do!
> Do, bury your mulishness! (*K'cracy* 4)

In the preceding lines, by combining language, religious and educational insight, Ndi appeals to "Mr. Dict..." to forfeit the oppression he has been and is visiting upon his subjects. He does not mince words to highlight the rot concealed beneath Mr. Dict's..." shimmering face. This is good reason for him to cut off from his elitist oppressive stance and forget his wrongs. Here above, Ndi seems to have further achieved what Ngugi wa Thiong'o, underscores in *Something Torn and New*. Talking of a similar situation lived by the Irish, he writes, "Language, religion, and education are to be deployed to achieve loss of memory and dismember the Irish [Cameroonian] elite from their parental social body" (21).

What is particularly interesting is the nature of the threat. Speaking for his people, the poet threatens to hoot down the dictator – not to shoot down – which calls for a non-violent exit to an otherwise oppressive dictatorship. Again, what seems to be a ruthless attack on dictatorship is a harsh – but never violent yet persuasive – call to action on the part of Biya. The expression of the sentiments of – particularly English-speaking – Cameroonians is effected in a way that facilitates building bridges out of oppression; like with the broom, it cannot be the tool to build a nation upon. The poet encourages those who have been silenced not to concentrate upon dictatorship-instilled violence, but to focus on both their hopes and aspirations instead. In this light, it is Ndi, the humanist at his best; arousing in his readers, responses that would allow them "to be" rather than "to do".

In "Hearing the Voiceless", poem in which the poet demonstrates that for one to prevail, he or she should let the voice of the voiceless remind them melodiously that "being favoured" comes through keen listening, the following lines stand out:

> The connection
> Of the Inner Voice
> And the voiceless, their voice

> Within telling their travail,
> Hopes and aspirations shall prevail
> In the like this melody is savoured [sic]

And thankfully hearing this sound I am favoured [sic]! (*K'cracy* 7)

In these lines, Ndi deploys a good number of literary devices viz. irony, paradox, simile, personification, rhyme, etc. which together stimulates the reader's generation of meaning from the poet's expression of the repressed in his poetic universe. Needless to emphasize that familiarity with literary techniques and conventions that Ndi employs in his poetry is that which govern his expression of the oppressed state he muses upon—hearing the inner voice of the voiceless—as well as the meaning made of the various poems (Eagleton 67).

Far from adhering to the pomposity of office, Ndi reveres poverty and simplicity in poems such as "The Wealth of Poverty" and in the title poem for the collection. "K'cracy" offers an allegory of the country as ruled by a self-fashioned shepherd – then farmer – whose submissive herd helped him remain in power. When eventually he faces trial, Ndi shifts focus from the ruler to the ruled while underlining a liberating perspective within which the oppressed clearly see themselves in relationship to their oppressors. Consequently, he writes:

> But this farmer cares less for his plants
> The shepherd's incarnate proves-he
> Yet, to the plants,
> Much for their "good state' cares-he.
> So droopily carry 'em smiles
> For their yearnings winning
> But homily carry herd and plants smiles
> For they longed not for the K'crats craving. (*K'cracy* 60)

The rank and file – the vast majority of the population who are not directly involved in office or the military – may have been unwarily passive to their subjugation in the past, but the essential fact is that their hopes and fears differ severely from the autocrat's incessant hungriness for power and control over these citizens. *K'cracy* is not the only volume in which Ndi champions resistance against tyranny and makes an effort to speak to the people as a whole. *Bleeding Red: Cameroon in Black and White* (2010) contains exacting denunciations of oppression, some of them in pidgin verse since, as the author's note reads, "Poetry is for all" (1). The opening poem, "Anthem for Essigang", historicizes the dire result of clannish pillaging and ravaging over the land and soul of too many Africans. This rousing or uplifting song identifies with the cause of the oppressed populace within a once upon a time grandiose house (nation, country, continent, etc.) now reduced to that of thieves and nothing more than an emblem of the tears of these oppressed lot. Ndi writes:

> My father's house that once all tongue could tell
> Has now become a house of thieves
> So the rest of the world can see
> The emblem of the tears of our people
> Clan of mbokos, clan of bandits
> With death and sadness in our store
> Thine be disgrace, thine be great shame
> And repudiation for evermore. (*Bleeding Red* 5)

This poem curiously mirrors or subverts the National Anthem of The Cameroons in rhythm and sound. Confer the last four lines of the above poem and the chorus of the anthem:

> *Chorus:*
> Land of Promise, land of Glory!
> Thou, of life and joy, our only store!
> Thine be honour, thine devotion,
> And deep endearment, for evermore. (Web.).

Ndi's poetry thus challenges the reader to heed Roman Ingarden who calls the reader "[to] bring to the work a certain pre-understanding, a dim context of belief and expectation within which the work's various features will be assessed" (qtd. in T. Eagleton 67).

The lexical field – thieves, tears, clan, death, sadness, disgrace, repudiation – speaks volumes about the contempt for the current situation of the "father's house" that represents the fatherland. However, the poem stops at the vilification of these plunderers, not because its main function ends there, but because it poses a repressed problem which can also be perceived in the poems hitherto analysed. By expressing a reality, the resolution of how such dire situations would be resolved is pending; it is precisely this construction, and not the destruction herewith advocated. Ndi portrays what captures his mind and passion. Running parallel to the sorry state of the country and most of Africa, which seems to be trapped into a neverending spiral of corruption, warfare, factional rivalry, and foreign-infused violence alongside religious fanaticism. The aforementioned poem is mirrored in a number of other compositions such as the deeply ironic "Peaceful Cameroon", where the persona confronts the ignorance of an Australian who unwisely assumes the country would be peaceful simply because it is never in the news (notably in the news about civil war, famine, religious fanaticism, factional violence, etc.). The poem progresses to denouncing how the country is peaceful but "with a head/ Whose wish is to see all were dead" (*Bleeding Red* 51). Notably, in "Once a Nation of Giants", he also depicts his people as slaves to foreign forces, "puppet masters" to the ruling oppressors, "bound / With shackles". The last two lines, however, reveal the real purpose of the poem; it is the still-distant future that captures the poet's mind than the here and now. So he draws attention to the fact that:

> Only the future would dig and bring to life
> Even when the years in millions have passed five. (*Bleeding Red* 43)

Hope for a better future in the face of adversity, however innocent it may look, cannot dispel that history remains with the oppressed for longer. For Ndi, forgiveness is not required at any stage, as hoping for the best does not entail oblivion. Atrocities may well not be responded to, but they need not be pardoned and or obliterated from the pages of history and collective memory. This negotiated way out of oppression does not include the necessity to forgive. Poems such as "Assassinating Democracy (Insurgence)" make it explicit. The poem denounces the erasure of the death of six Cameroonians, "gunned down /By the forces of regression" and denied by official history. In a postmodern twist the persona wishes an act of remembrance were made of this. It is particularly interesting how the poet – as a penman, not a gunman – situates the focus of the poem on celebration and stern stoicism until tyrannical dictatorship culture is overcome. Thus, the insurgence in the title becomes resistance rather than revolt:

> But, May, the month we screamed out
> "Mayday!"
> In quest for liberation from the chains of tyranny
> Deserves that attention worthy of any Victory.
> Martyrs are these six
> In this nation where no dead is a hero
> For what we live for is the here and now
> A less conducive one for a penman!
> Yet, I long for that day this Mayday
> Shall itself fit into our official commemorations!
> Our Martyrs' Mayday
> Victory over dictacracy! (*Bleeding Red* 15)

Situating the action in "May" the symbol of rebirth, i.e. full bloom of spring, the persona sets the tone for the shackles of oppression to be broken for "Victory over dictacracy!" to come.

Arguably the most consistent wrath on the part of the poet is echoed in the aptly-titled *Waves of Anger* (2010). Its preface beautifully sums up some of the aspects discussed: while the poet expresses "The weariness of life" it is "The moral degeneration of society his leitmotif" (*Waves* 9). The representation of reality in the poem serves to an ideal whose nature is moral. It is not to say, in this case, that the poet is moralistic, but that the poetic action firmly stems from moral values. Particularly in the case of Ndi, he is careful not to impose these to others, but to fiercely go against those who do put their interest before anyone else's. The wave as a purging agent is recurrent in poems such as "Waves That Save" and "Cleansing Waves", where they would "rid the nation of its pus /Sweeping all debris from mountains" (*Waves* 23). The language which these poems extol is more pungent, and more exacting, while at the same time more related to nature. The title poem uses nature-related lexicon to express a reality which, like the waves in the poems themselves, only attack at the very end:

> Running deeper than the slowest river
> From deep down the entrails rages anger
> By block headed heads birthed
> Baking all in the sun and staying in the shed
> And soliciting the world t'applaud their crime
> Waves cleanse by blowing in their eyes the brine. (*Waves* 22)

By using the poetic tactic of repressing its subject, the poems in *Waves* result perhaps in the most accomplished until his recent output. It is not the case that Ndi has suppressed his anger against oppression and tyranny – on the contrary, it is more powerful here precisely because its repression allows for a more powerful outburst, often released, as in the poem above, at the precise moment. The reader, rocked by the gentle sound of his words, is suddenly shocked by the suddenness of such violence, and the effect is even more convincing than in other more militant poems. These more reposed poems, such as "Of silence and Violence", are more successful as they become less vocative – they do not address Cameroonians directly – and more reflective. Because the reader enters these with a different frame of mind, it allows him/her to perceive Ndi's commitment to non-violence more clearly than in earlier pieces. The excerpt here below elucidates the claim:

> To thinking shouts the way to fend
> Where verbal violence is the trend
> Shoving active non-verbal non-violence
> The crown to wear without pretence
> Leaving it to speak a lot louder
> Than the thunderous cannons our murderer
> Fires in vain attempt to silent
> Our hearts drinking patience, sentient
> Active non-verbal non-violence
> Sailing in a waveless sea of silence

> And by the cool calm breeze caressed
> With truth and honesty pressed
> Justifying our action active
> Against the murderer's offensive. (*Waves* 32)

Bill F. Ndi's proposal for "non-verbal non-violence/ The crown to wear without pretence" against "the thunderous cannons our murderer/Fires in vain attempt to silent/Our hearts drinking patience.../ could be for the same reasons posited by Spencer who credits the school for being more powerful than the cannon for "better than the cannon it made conquest permanent. The cannon compels the body and the school bewitches the soul." (Spencer qtd. *In* Ngugi wa Thiong'o 21) And Ndi would rather have a lasting oppression free society/world occasioned by "... truth and honesty pressed/Justifying our action active/Against the murderer's offensive" (*Waves 32*).

Symbols help occlude the real focus of the poem. The unmistakably allegorical nature of poems such as "Purging the Marshes" symbolizes the land of the country as wetlands that need to be dredged of "their rotten dickheads", "rapists" and "murderers" so that its people can move on. Hence the following lines:

> Take the pleasure I do with the nation free of blisters:
> The rape, the land, the virgin and offspring gone
> All your relishes that have you undone. (*Waves* 24)

Perhaps in one uncommonly long piece for Ndi, the closing epic contained in "The Python's Trail" chronicles a fantasy that – despite the ironic emphasis of the poet for the text not to be taken "for any fiction" but " tale of the birth of a nation" – is more a meditative expressed desire than a tangible reality. Through such meditation, Ndi endeavors to apprehend God. By cleverly mixing kings, lands and religion, Ndi creates a rich texture that only resolves in the end. The connection with his earlier poems reveals that, far from reaching God's kingdom and fertile soils, the move of the Kom people after their king sacrifices his own life, entails a future that is akin to the past of modern-day The Cameroons. Hence:

> This is how the wave moved an angry saviour
> To sweep in front of a monarch his subjects' labour
> Taking the Kom people to the new found kingdom
> Where they've been waiting for God's kingdom to come.
>
> (*Waves* 109)

Furthermore, the pervasive representation of destruction – not only of violence but also of its aftermath – in Ndi's poems brings about the moment of creation, of building up upon the remnants of a broken land and society. His two most recent collections, *Vestiges* (2013) and *Pride Aside* (2016) explore the possibilities for such reconstruction from the spoils of destruction. The poems therein are presented with often striking and sensuous imagery. The former volume opens with a poem, "Our Rooftop Catacombs", which likens the poet and his fellow countrymen in the place of persecuted Christians under Roman tyranny. Despite being secluded in high places such as trees – also pointing to the East-West, North-South, (Francophone-Anglophone) cultural and linguistic divide in the country – what they manage to see from there is a barren land which, nevertheless will give life. And we read:

> With our people and their kin in ruin haplessly;
> Such flag bearers flag up the need for the big tree
> From which to see our abode blooms with leafless trees.
>
> (*Vestiges* 1)

Poems such as "Dictatorship" still reveal dry contempt on the part of the poet, but his increasing focus on the yes-men rather than on the head of state points at a political and social problem for national reconstruction. Those in power are aided by those who cannot return to their people as innocent. They have, just as many others, fallen for "demagogues [who] would blend and spice their sweet promises", but they are reminded that "those behind goat head do their own neglect" (*Vestiges* 6). Precisely at this point, when tyranny is about to be overthrown for a new freedom to be found, that is when men and women need to make their choice. In poems such as "Agony Free Freedom", Ndi tilts his attention towards social construction. Albeit fictional, his representation of reality becomes increasingly communal. What theorist Julian Jimenez notes of fiction is equally applicable here. According to him, literary creation has "proved an invaluable platform where community-models have been relentlessly tested, discarded or confirmed" as writers have "sought to formulate a kind of community that had not as yet existed" (Jimenez 2). Ndi's poems serve the purpose of experimenting a recreation from the ashes of oppression. Hence, he opposes those who think that "The worst still to come!" and conform to being oppressed, and those who should seek "The agony free freedom / Promised as a New Kingdom" (*Vestiges* 52). This poem like many others tend towards a moment of self-knowledge and oneness with some transcendent reality.

When, if, that time comes, it will be necessary for Cameroonians to be prepared. The social fracture in the country, however, is a more impending threat to future stability than military oppression. A figure such as Ndi, speaker of several of the languages at hand, and who regularly publishes in French and English, may become inspirational for such a process, if it ever comes. His most recent output, *Pride Aside and Other Poems* (2016) is a treatise on the necessity to delouse of pride (one of the seven deadly sins in Judeo-Christian doctrine) in order to create something new, and of the difficulties to do so. Sadly for the Cameroonian readership, and in spite of Ndi's tremendous output (at least 15 volumes of poetry), these poetic verve and apt denunciations are still pre-emptive: they have not still being given their opportunity as a community to thrive and prosper in absolute freedom. As these poems attest, that chance will come, and Ndi's poems may help better prepare his people to make that communal effort last in an oppression free society rebuilt from the ashes of the same.

Works Cited

Doh, Emmanuel Fru. "Bill Ndi's Social Angst and Humanist Vision: Politics, Alienation, and the Quest for Freedom in *K'cracy, Trees in the Storm, and Other Poems*" in *Fears, Doubts, and Joys of not Belonging*. Edited by Fishkin, Ankumah, and Ndi, Laanga RPCIG, 2014.

_____. *Anglophone Cameroon Literature: an Introduction*. Lexington, 2015.

Eagleton, Terry. *Literary Theory: an Introduction*. U of Minnesota P, 1998.

Fisher, A.C. and Peterson, F.M. "The Environment in Economics: A Survey" *Journal of Economic Literature* vol. 14, no.1, 1976, pp. 1-33.

Freire, Paulo. *The Politics of Education: Culture, Power, and Liberation*. Bergin and Garvey, 1998.

Jimenez Heffernan, Julian. "Introduction: Togetherness and its Discontents." in *Community in Twentieth-Century Fiction*. Edited by Paula Martín Salván, Gerardo Rodríguez Salas and Julián Jiménez Heffernan. Palgrave Macmillan, 2013, pp. 1-47.

Jimenez-Munoz, Antonio. "In Moments like These: Emmanuel Fru Doh and the Mirrors of Romanticism" *in Fears, Doubts and joys of not Belonging*. Edited by Fishkin, Ankumah, and Ndi, Laanga RPCIG, 2014.

Kahneman, Daniel. *Thinking, Fast and Slow*. Penguin, 2012.

Keynes, John M. *Essays in Persuasion 1750–1925*. Norton, 1963.

Kocis, Robert. *Mchiavelli Redeemed: Retrieving His Humanist Perspectives on Equality, Power, and Glory*. Lehigh UP, 1998.

Marx, Karl and Engels, Friedrich. *The German ideology*. International Publishers, 1970.

Mellor, Anne K. *English Romantic Irony*. Harvard UP, 1980.

Ndi, Bill F. *Pride Aside and Other Poems*. Langaa RPCIG, 2016.

_____. *Vestiges*. Laanga RPCIG, 2013.

_____. *Bleeding Red. Cameroon in Black and White*. Laanga RPCIG, 2010.

_____. *Waves of Anger*. PublishAmerica, 2010.

_____. *K'cracy, Trees in the Storm and other Poems*. Laanga RPCIG, 2008.

Nietzsche, Friedrich. *Human, All Too Human: A Book for Free Spirits*. Cambridge UP., 1996.

Perrill, Simon. "High Late-Modernists or Postmodernists?" in *The Cambridge Companion to British Poetry, 1945-2010*. Edited by Larrissy, Cambridge UP, 2016.

Solow, Robert M. "Is the End of the World at Hand?." *Challenge,* vol. 16, no. 1, 1973, pp. 39-50.

Stevens, Wallace. "The Man with the Blue Guitar." *English Poetry,* vol. 50, no. 2, 1937, p. 61.

wa Thiong'o, Ngugi. *Something Torn and New: An African Renaissance*, Civitas, 2009.

———————. *Decolonising the Mind: The Politics of Language in African Literature,* Heinemann, 1986.

Wolowsky, Shira. *The Art of Poetry: How to Read a Poem.* Oxford UP, 2008.

Chapter 7

Yearning for a Distance: Prophetic Narrative in Zora Neale Hurston's 1934 *Jonah's Gourd Vine*

Rhonda Collier

Most Macon and Lee County residents whip by Macedonia Baptist Church on Highway 14 east heading through Loachapoka, AL approximately 11 miles to Auburn, AL and miss the Alabama State Tourism marker that proclaims the following:

> Birthplace of Zora Neale Hurston
> Notasulga, Alabama
> Zora Neale Hurston (1891-1960)
> No, he couldn't leave Notasulga, where the train came puffing into the depot twice a day. No!! No!! He dropped everything and tore across the fields and came out as the last railroad cut just below the station. He sat down upon the embankment and waited!! Whaup, wahup!! "Opelika-black-and-dirty!! Opelika-black-and-dirty!! And around the bend came first the smoke stack, belching smoke and flames of fire. The drivers black-and-dirty." Then as she pulled into the station, the powerful whisper of steam. Starting off again, "Wolf coming! Wolf coming! Opelika-black-and-dirty! Auh-wah-hooon"—into the great away that gave John's feet such a yearning for distance. (Historical Marker qtd. from *Jonah's Gourd Vine*)

The marker is well placed and the extended quote from *Jonah's Gourd Vine* is extremely appropriate for an author who yearned to leave her Alabama roots behind[1] (Hurston 41). The church where her parents, Lucy Ann Potts and John Hurston met, Macedonia Baptist Church established 1885, Notasulga, AL, is in the front yard of a railroad track that continues to operate today. The "train" in the

---

[1] The quote from marker is taken from Zora Neale Hurston's *Jonah's Gourd Vine* (41).

excerpt is none other than Zora's "whale" in her prophetic narrative about the gifted main character John Buddy Pearson, modeled after Hurston's father, John Hurston. The train and whale references on the marker are lost to most visitors because, at best, even locals have only read Hurston's most popular novel *Their Eyes Were Watching God* (1937). Once emphasized in classes, many students at nearby Tuskegee University are amazed to learn that the "not-so-historic" Notasulga is only six miles from their national historic site campus.

Residents of Zora Neale Hurston's birthplace Notasulga, AL, dub the town "Not-As-Ugly" to help with the pronunciation of the town's name. Frequent misspellings, mispronunciations, and insider's joke perpetuate a continual misunderstanding of the small southern town as a site of literary production. Hurston's autobiography *Dust Tracks On a Road* (1942) further removes Notasulga, AL from American literary history by replacing it with her conceived hometown Eatonville, FL, where by all fictional accounts her life begins. Yet and still, Hurston's actual birthplace, Notasulga, remains one of the main settings in Hurston's first novel *Jonah's Gourd Vine (1934)* and thus claims its place as a part of the Harlem Renaissance's landscape of the South. Hurston's freshman novel is largely autobiographical and prophetic as she describes her main character's yearning for distance. Ironically, this yearning ultimately echoes a pattern that will follow Hurston's own life and death. In sync with one its popular misnomer, "Not-so-ugly" is not a tourist site like Eatonville, FL nor has it inspired an annual festival in Hurston's name. Yet, the Alabama State tourism historical marker's last phrase, "such a yearning for distance," explains how Hurston interprets her life and provides readers with a guide to her revisionist view of the biblical story of the prophet Jonah.

In the book of Jonah, one of the most popular books of the Old Testament, the story of an unwilling prophet is revealed. In the first of four chapters, God calls Jonah to travel to the city of Nineveh: "a capital city of an empire known for its cruelty in battle."[2] Jonah ignores God's order and elects to escape his hometown via a mariner's ship to the town of Tarshish (Jonah 1:3). However, God sends a storm that scares the fishermen, who immediately throw

---

[2] All biblical references are taken from the *Literary Study Bible, English Standard Version* (2007).

Jonah off their distressed ship. The most canonical part of the story occurs in the second chapter where Jonah remains three days in the belly of a big fish or "Jonah and the whale." During this time, he prays for his life and expresses gratitude for God's mercy. In the third chapter, armed with God's salvation, Jonah goes to Nineveh with a message from God to the sinful Ninevites. To Jonah's surprise, the Ninevites accept his prophetic message and turn from their evil ways. Finally, in the fourth chapter, an angry Jonah seeks distance from the Ninevites and waits for the city to self-destruct. As Jonah watches the city from a distance, God provides shade for him—the shade was a gourd vine that protected his head from the extreme heat of the arid city (Jonah 4:6). Given Jonah's anger and lack of compassion toward the Ninevites, God appoints a worm to attack the gourd vine so that it then withers and dies (Jonah 4:7-10). The final verses show the irony in the fact that Jonah is angry at the same compassion and mercy from God that frees him from the belly of the whale.

In *Jump at the Sun: Zora Neale Hurston's Comic Comedy* (1994), John Lowe uses the Jonah story to critique the comic nature of the Southern preacher and Hurston's depiction of his character flaws. He represents the gourd vine as the talent, skills and gifts needed to influence people. Lowe focuses on the worm as sexual malice that cuts down the preacher, John Buddy's gift to preach—his gourd vine (94). In contrast, Rita Dove, in her 2004 forward to *Jonah's Gourd Vine,* considers multiple possibilities for the worm that attacks the gourd vine—which she implies is Jonah himself. Dove proposes that general malice "burrows through the community" (xi) and brings John Buddy Pearson down. Deborah Plant in *Zora Neal Hurston: A Biography of the Spirit* (2007) acknowledges the ongoing argument among critics "[who] state that the key to understanding Hurston's life is to be found in her fiction and folklore work, not her autobiography" (104). In the end, Plant agrees that the novels do "give insight to Hurston's worldview" (104). Given that the main character is John Buddy Pearson, a preacher like Zora Neale Hurston's biological father John Hurston, Hurston's critique of Jonah becomes an interesting commentary of Southern religion and her own life.

Hurston's John is much more complicated than the Biblical Jonah, who most readers recall from the "Jonah and the Whale" story. Hurston's main character is a sinner who is called to do the right thing and in the end does not. In contrast, Jonah is a prophet who is reluctant to preach to a group of non-Jews, but fulfills his calling with a big push from God. Jonah's sin is his lack of sympathy for the Ninevites, but John Buddy's sin is an overwhelming lack of the empathy for his wife, children and parishioners. John's sin keep him from being a good father, husband and preacher. The ride in the frightening "black and dirty" metaphorical train from Opelika, AL is John Buddy's opportunity for rebirth and a chance at another life in a new place. Like Jonah's infamous whale, the "black and dirty train" carries the reluctant John Buddy to a place of salvation: Hurston's utopia—Eatonville, FL.

As the fictional John Buddy leaves Notasulga, AL behind, the novelist Hurston drops the town from her autobiography *Dust Tracks on a Road (1942)*. After moving the family from Notasulga, AL, Hurston's biological father became a preacher at Macedonia Baptist Church in Eatonville, FL, as well as a carpenter, businessman and eventually the mayor of the all black town. Minus "Notasulga roots," these facts about Florida and her father are proudly recanted in *Dust Tracks*. Predicting her own future and summarizing *Jonah Gourde Vine*, Hurston admits, "Some children are just bound to take after their fathers in spite of women's prayers" (*Dust Track on a Road* 32). Like her father, Hurston spent her own life searching for meaning and wandering from place to place. Her writings and research carried her to Harlem, NY, throughout the South, around the Caribbean, to Europe, and eventually to her unmarked grave in Florida. In 1973, the Pulitzer-prize winning author of *The Color Purple* Alice Walker uncovered Hurston's unmarked grave in Florida, but the family bible in Florida and Alabama census records showed that indeed Hurston's true birthplace was Notasulga, AL in 1891. It seems as if the Bible and the state of Alabama told the truth on Hurston, who wanted to escape both her age and birthplace. So it is not strange that the Bible would be the source of inspiration for a wandering preacher's daughter, novelist and anthropologist who, in terms of religion and religious practice, saw similarities in many great religions and these intersections were apparent in *Jonah's Gourd Vine*.

No doubt a result of her own desire to travel and study both African American and Caribbean culture, Hurston pays homage to

African cosmology and African American Christian traditions (Plant 126). The first line of the novel is a *signifying* nod to the orisha Chango, the Yoruba god of lightening, fire and thunder: "God was grumbling his thunder and playing the zig-zag lightning thru his fingers" (*Jonah's Gourd Vine* 1). Chango is the god of conflict and battle as he is known for yielding an axe. These lines also foreshadow the sexual passion and spiritual conflict that would define the main character John Buddy's life, who must decide if he will surrender to his sexual desire or remain faithful to his spiritual calling and his wife. Much like the historical marker's reference to "Opelika black-and-dirty" and the symbolic train's description as "belching smoke and flames of fires," Hurston's grumbling God sets the stage for the allegorical John who appears to represent the prophet Jonah in the Old Testament, as well as Hurston's father John Hurston from Notasulga, AL.

In *Jonah's Gourd Vine*, Hurston selects the characteristics of the Southern preacher and parallels them with the Jonah story. Indeed, she is more than familiar with the tenements of Christianity and the problems of trying to escape God's calling. In *Jonah's Gourd Vine*, Hurston's main character John Buddy Pearson must get to "Nineveh," wherever that might be or face a grumbling God's judgment. John Buddy's first journey is described as a water baptism accompanied by talking drums:

> John plunged on down to the Creek, singing a new song and stomping the beats. The Big Creek thundered among its rocks and whirled on down. So John sat on the foot-log and made some words so with the drums of the Creek...He stripped and carried his clothes across, then recrossed and plunged into the swift water and breasted strongly over (12).

Once John Buddy crosses over "da Big Creek," he encounters salvation— the opportunity for an education.

On the other side of the creek, John viewed literacy as his key to both spiritual and cultural empowerment: "This must be the school house that he heard about. Negro children learning how to read and write like white folks" (Hurston 13). Constructed nearly twenty years after Hurston's birth in Notasulga, the school that John Buddy refers to might have been one of the first Rosenwald schools in the nation, constructed in Macon and Lee County, AL. The mile markers for those schools are located on Highway 80 and Highway 14; Notasulga and Loachapoka, AL, respectively. Rosenwald school houses were a result of a collaboration between Booker T. Washington and Julius Rosenwald that began in 1912 and ended in 1932, two years before the publication of *Jonah's Gourd Vine*. Hurston gives a snapshot of impact of the Rosenwald schools as a part of the American landscape for educating Negro children in the South.[3]

Thus it is interesting that two years after the completion of *Jonah's Gourd Vine,* Hurston applied for and received a prestigious fellowship from the Julius Rosenwald Fund to attend Columbia University. Even as she wrote *Jonah's Gourd Vine*, she revealed her mother's advice to "jump at de sun." In *Dust Tracks on A Road*, Hurston describes her mother's hope that her spirit would always prevail and that she would take every opportunity to improve herself (13). Along those lines, the mission of the Rosenwald Fund was to improve the advancement of "Negro welfare." However, Hurston did not complete the Ph.D. and instead used the money to complete two plays and work on her most famous novel *Their Eyes Were Watching God* (1937). Advisors noted that she lacked discipline to engage in quiet study (Kaplan 165). Hurston creates a similar tension between the desire to learn and the desire to wander in *Jonah's Gourd Vine*. The character John Buddy wants to preach, but is unable to listen to the master teacher—God.

In *Jonah's Gourd Vine*, Hurston collapses her own desire for education with that of the main character John, who also represents her biological father. John's desire to learn and his attraction to Lucy mold him into a charismatic preacher. "She live over in Pottstown. Her folks done bought de old Cox place. She goes to school. Dey's big niggers" (Hurston 23). John wants to be one of those "big niggers." Being a "big nigger" implies status, power and upward mobility. John can accomplish this through the school and more

---

[3] Zora Neale Hurston was a 1934 recipient of the Julius Rosenwald Fund, whose mission was the advancement of "Negro welfare." Unfortunately, she did not complete a Ph.D. program at Columbia but did use the time and money to complete two plays and one novel including *Their Eyes Were Watching God (1937)*. Advisors noted she lacked discipline to engage in quiet study (Kaplan 165).

importantly through his calling to preach. The original title for *Jonah's Gourd Vine* was "Big Nigger," but Hurston reconsidered the title concerned with how it might be received by audiences (Lowe 87). This is especially pertinent considering Hurston's precarious role as artist versus activist in the 1930s. In *Dust Tracks* she opines: "Light came to me when I realized that I did not have to consider any racial group as a whole" (171). Pushing this line, Hurston does not shy away from using the term "big nigger" through out the novel, in fact she designates Tuskegee Institute's founder Booker T. Washington as one of the smartest men in the United States. The narrator proclaims:

> The wind said North. Trains said North....Ain't never been two sho 'nuff smart mens dese United States—Teddy Roosevelt and Booger T. Washington. Nigger so smart he et at de White house. Built uh great big ole school wuth uh thousand dollars, maybe mo'...Nigger invented de train... DuBois? Who is dat? 'Nother smart nigger? Man, he can't be smart ez Booger T.!... (148)

Ever the comic narrator, Hurston mirrors Booker T. thoughts in *Up from Slavery* (1915). In his seminal text, Washington claims: "The ministry was the profession that suffered the most—and still suffers, though there has been some great improvement—on account of not only ignorant but in many cases immoral men who claimed that they were "called to preach" (58). Hurston casts judgment on John Buddy, her father and other men of his type who are called to preach. Further, she aligns herself with the Washingtonian philosophy of racial uplift and industrial education that often found itself at odds with the Du Boisian view of racial progress in the twentieth century. Fascinated by the art of preaching, Hurston was more interested in observing culture than being an activist and was often criticized for her representation of black culture and speech. But, who could ignore "Booger T. Washington"? She admired Booker T. Washington's progress in education, and she accomplished this through travel, writing and self-reflection. In *Dust Tracks*, she notes "Booker T. Washington said once that you must not judge a man by the heights to which he has risen, but by the depths from which he came" (124). Not surprisingly, Hurston incorporates Booker T. Washington's philosophy that prefers "calls to some industrial occupation" (56). In *Jonah's Gourd Vine*, Hurston's illustrates bias toward John Buddy "the worker" versus the façade of John Buddy "the preacher." Obviously, Hurston found it humorous to posit her father's "bad character" against Booker T. Washington's "big character." As John Lowe points out in *Jump at the Sun: Zora Neale Hurston's Comic Comedy* (1994), John Buddy Pearson might be what is considered a "bad nigger" that he needs to be cut down to size not a "big nigger" who represents social progress (88). Hurston found the Christian calling culturally interesting, but more of a drama than anything she could ever personally experience. Hurston's drama involves John whose anger and inability to be faithful to his wife Lucy prevents him from receiving a true calling from God.

As John Buddy develops as a worker, the other characters in the novel describes him as a "battle-axe." This sharp description foreshadows his gift with words, his physical prowess, his call to preach; and yes, his needs to be cut down. This nickname embodies what Hurston calls in her linguistic essay, "Characteristics of Negro Expression" a "double-descriptive." John is "an axe" that is made for battle. The drama of *Jonah's Gourd Vine* unfolds:

> John won his first match pinning Nelse Watson from another camp to the ground, but his greatest stunt was picking up an axe by the very tip end of the helve and keeping the head on a level with his shoulder in his out-stretched arm. Coon could muscle out one axe, but John could balance two. **He could stand out like a cross, immobile for several seconds with an axe muscled out in each hand (my emphasis).** Next to showing muscle-power, John loved to tell stories. One night Do-dirty began, 'Y'all wanta heah some lies?' (61)

In this camp setting, Hurston highlights John's competitive nature and gift for telling tales. John is an axe yielding god with a magical tongue. He is like that "black and dirty" train from Opelika, and he is destined for exile. Hurston's character John Buddy may be read as the reluctant prophet Jonah and the train from Opelika as "the whale," and thus it is not hard to see that John has a lot to learn about being a true man of God. Hurston's language suggests a New

Testament transformation from the axe to the cross. Paralleling the figurative death, burial and resurrection of a man through the belly of the whale, the Jonah story is the precursor to the Christ story. John's lies, anger and infidelity buy his ticket from Notasulga, AL to salvation in Sanford, FL (Hurston's fictional version of Eatonville, FL). Master Alf sends him off, "John, distance is the only cure for certain diseases. Here's fifty dollars. There are lots of other towns in the world besides Notasulga, and there's several hours before midnight" (*Jonah's Gourd Vine* 99). John leaves Notasulga guilty of assaulting his brother-in-law and guilty of cheating on Lucy, his beloved wife and mother of his children.

Once Lucy, his wife, a fictional representation of Hurston's mother, arrives to their eventual home in Sanford, FL, John Buddy Pearson receives his call to preach. The "gourd vine" is rarely mentioned in popular reading of the Jonah story. Usually the focus is Jonah, who is trying to escape Nineveh; and the whale, who swallows Jonah. Rita Dove and John Lowe argue that John Buddy, who represents Hurston's father is the "gourd vine." In the text, the character Hattie notes: "Ah's cut down dat Jonah's gourd vine in a uh minute..." (xi). Yet, Hurston's description of "the battle axe" seems to note that John Buddy was the person who would chop some one down and the possibility that Lucy is the "gourd vine." In assigning signifiers, there is tension as to whether John Buddy was a good man, a strong man or a man who needed to be cut down. Applying the Bible example of Jonah, John Buddy has a chance to be better man. The same extends to the Washingtonian philosophy:

> I took my **axe** and led the way to the woods in order to relieve [the students] from any embarrassment, each afternoon after school I took my axe and led the way to the woods. When they saw that I was not afraid or ashamed to work, they began to assist with more enthusiasm. We kept at the work each afternoon, until we had cleared about twenty acres and had planted a crop. (Washington 99)

For the preacher John Buddy, the "axe" metaphor extends from the work camp to the church. Hurston offers that John Buddy is capable of building something great. The idea that he is a "gourd vine" who receives favor or protection of a special gift from God may be a possibility.

During the praise hymn, "He's a Battle Axe in de Time Uh Trouble," John is called to preach. Still popular today, this praise hymn is not considered a negro spiritual or gospel music, it is a poetic form from Africa that may praise any object, item or man not just God. The South African leader Shaka Zulu of the Zulu Nation was referred to as "the battle axe that excels over other battle-axes" in a similar praise hymn ("Praise Songs"). As an anthropologist, Hurston not only left her readers "dust tracks" and "belching trains," but she crossed "da creek" like her father John to reach other traditions that she then fused with Southern religious practice and folklore. Although the lyrics are not referenced in the text of "He's a Battle Axe" the song lyrics provide insight to John's skills:

> Chorus
> He'a battle axe (In the time of battle)
> He'a battle aze (In the time of battle)
> He'a batte axe (In the time of battle)
> Oh, he's (A shelter in the time of storm)
> Verse
> No man can do me like Jesus
> No a mumbling word he said
> Walk right down to Larzsus grave
> And raise him from the grave. ("He's A Battle Axe")

John Buddy is crowned "Battle Axe sho 'nuff-Hewin' down sinners tuh repentance" [Battle Axe sure enough helping down sinner to repentance] (111). John's words have the power to revive the lost soul and bring him to a new life. He is a man that can be counted on during a storm. Later Lucy coaches: "God don't call no man, John, turn 'im loose uh fool. Jus' you handle yo' members right and youse goin' tuh be uh sho 'nuff big nigger" [God don't call no man, John, Turn him loose you fool. Just you handle your members right and you are going to be a sure enough big nigger] (112). She warns that John that he must handle his members right in order to be a "big nigger." He has a gift—a calling if you will—that flourishes underneath Lucy's guidance, but he resents her instruction. Lucy suspects that John's gift is his gift with words and his power to persuade people, not necessary a calling from God. Later in *Dust Tracks*, Hurston would articulate her "universal female gospel" that all good traits and learning come from the mother's sides.

While there are many reading of the title *Jonah's Gourd Vine*, the female gospel perceives Lucy as "the gourd vine" and that John "the battle axe" chops her down. In *Dust Tracks*, Hurston implies that "the female gospel" is her mother's way of knowing the truth and understanding human behavior. Accordingly, the character Lucy's voice is a small but powerful voice of wisdom that surfaces in the text of Jonah; it is a voice that serves to protect John Buddy. Revisiting the Old Testament and God's instructions to Jonah to preach to the Ninevites, the gourd vine is only mentioned in the fourth and final chapter of the book: "Now the Lord God appointed a plant and made it come over Jonah, that it might shade over his head, to save him from his discomfort..." (Jonah 4:6). Indeed, in Hurston's tale, Lucy is the ever-loving always forgiving preacher's wife. However, in Jonah 4:8, God appointed a worm to attack the plant to teach Jonah a lesson. Literally, Lucy dies leaving John Buddy with no spiritual hope. John Lowe and Rita Dove do not take into account the novel as a framework for the real tension Hurston felt with her biological father. As the character Lucy is largely overlooked as the "gourd vine," both critics focus on the worm that attacks the gourd vine—John Pearson. Dove considers multiple possibilities for the worm, the character Hattie; or the general malice that "burrows through the community" (xi). Nonetheless, Lowe focuses on the worm as the sexual malice that cuts down John Buddy gift—the burgeoning ability to preach powerful sermons. Yet, a focus on the character Lucy broadens Trudier Harris's approach in *Saints and Sinners: Strong Black Women in African American Literature* in which archetypical women are pillars of strength, powerful ghosts or unbelievably saintly (10). In most cases of literature about African American women, Harris describes women as "suprahuman" (11). Hurston's Lucy provides readers with a female prophet who is an often silent, but powerful saint who also speaks from her death bed. As Toni Morrison's most famous work *Beloved* attests, Lucy is one of the truly beloved. In her own life, Hurston's was deeply affected by her mother's death, the manner in which it occurred, and how it was treated by her father.

Mirroring the Hurston's description of her own mother's death, Lucy Hurston, in *Dust Tracks on a Road*, a very ill Lucy Pearson dies after her husband John Buddy Pearson slaps her in the face. Lucy dies a victim of "The Battle Axe," but ends her life with a quiet sermon to John. The character Lucy rejects such traditional rites as having a pillow removed to die easy, removing glass to avoid seeing spirits leave, or covering a clock to stop time. She wanted her daughter to know that she is not afraid of death, but her requests are denied. The only request that the fictional Isis was able to honor was her mother's request to have Acts 26 near her side: "Go wash yuh face and turn tuh de Twenty-Sixth Chapter of de Acts fuh me" (130). While Hurston does not cite the verses of Act 26, this selection marks Apostle Paul's appeal for his life to King Agrippa (the last of the Herod dynasty) and a turn of scholarly interest for Hurston. The book of Act 26 provides the first documentation of the validity of Christianity in a court setting (338). Indeed, Lucy seems prepared to die and face any judgment for her actions as a Christian. Her message is for her husband John and the validity of his Christianity.

Hurston would have heard her father, John Hurston, preaching from the book of Acts and gained her own understanding of its relevance. The title "Jonah's Gourd Vine" indicates Hurston's desire to rewrite and question the Christian religion. She makes one reference Act 26 and does not explain this Biblical reference; however, in Acts 26, King Agrippa (the last King of the Herod dynasty) is almost persuaded to become a Christian (Act 26:28). Later Hurston would use her knowledge of scripture and research to work on a historical piece about Herod I, the first king in the Herod dynasty. Her approach to the Herod I biography was to debunk the idea of Herod as the evil King as depicted in her childhood studies (Plant 134-5). In *Zora Neale Hurston: A Biography of the Spirit* (2007), Deborah Plant notes: "Both in relation to *Jonah's* and to 'Herod the Great,' Hurston felt anxious about writing from a perspective that was contrary to popular opinion—specifically in relation to race, on the one hand, and religion, on the other" (137). In *Jonah Gourd Vine*, John's journey does not teach him any lessons. Zora demystifies the classic biblical story where Jonah emerges as a hero to the Ninevites people and most readers forget about the gourd vine. At times in the novel, the character John, like King Agrippa, is almost persuaded to change his behavior. Yet, in the end, move after move, "distance is not the cure for certain diseases."

The character John Buddy mourns Lucy's death but does not change his philandering ways. He continues to pursue sexual relationships and continues to break his commitments. God uses the gourd vine to teach Jonah a lesson about compassion. In Jonah 4:10, God speaks to Jonah: "You pity the plant, for which you did not labor, nor did you make it grow, which came into being in a night and perished in a night." In Hurston's *Jonah's Gourd Vine,* Rita Dove suggests that John Pearson is the vine or at least his talent is a "rapidly growing vine" (xi). She quotes "…Harris assures [Hattie], 'Ah'd cut down dat Jonah's gourd vine in minute, if Ah had all de say-so" (xi). This seems to refute the notion that Lucy is the gourd vine of the text. In fact, John is relieved at Lucy's death: "He was glad in his sadness" (136). He was free from Lucy's body, but not from her words or spirit. Hurston takes the most comic book of the bible, the master story if you will, to teach readers a lesson about distance and anger. Jonah is a man who tries to escape God, an impossibility which lands him in the belly of a whale; while John is a man who tries to escape his bad behavior which lands him on a train to Eatonville, FL. Hurston also considered the comic nature of her relationship with her father: a man she admired for his skills and accomplishments, and a man she resented for his inability to provide a stable life for her. However, she knew she was destined to become like her father. Hurston's humor is self-reflexive as she considers her own life and the influence of her mother—her own "gourd vine." In *Dust Tracks*, she confesses:

> I would wander off in the woods alone, following some inside urge to go places. This alarmed my mother a great deal. She used to say that she believed a woman who was an enemy of hers had sprinkled "travel dust" around the doorstep the day I was born…I don't know why it never occurred to connect my tendency with my father, who didn't have a thing on his mind but this town and the next one…Some children are just bound to take after their fathers in spite of women's prayers. (23)

Hurston's contentious homage to her father emerged in various ways in the text. The "black and dirty" that she describes train in Opelika ends the character John Pearson's life in Florida. Furthermore, John Pearson's last sermon, based on her observation of Black culture and her admiration for her father's craft, describes "de whistle of the de damnation train" as the character John Buddy exits from the congregation (180). The preacher John Buddy proclaims "When two trains of Time shall meet on de trestle/And wreck de burnin axles of de unformed ether" (181). Similar to Jonah's initial reaction, the train can be a powerful monster. In John's final sermon, the train becomes a well-placed message about Christ and connects to Hurston's initial train metaphor. John Pearson even manages to refer to the sea in the poetic sermon. He shouts:

> When Jesus shall place one foot on de neck of de sea, ha!
> One foot on dry land, ah
> When His chariot wheels shall be running hub-deep in fire
> He shall take His friends thru the open bosom of an un-clouded sky
> (*Jonah's Gourd Vine* 181)

Hurston carefully places the "ha"'s and the "ah"'s to capture a Southern preacher's rhythm. Furthermore, she drives home images of fire and power to define the nature of a Christian god. The sermon captures Hurston's message of Christ and judgment of her own father who like the character in the novel dies by being run-over by a train. The character John dies after having cheated on his third wife. He was killed by the "damnation train." The train that saved him from Notasulga and brought him to Florida, also kills him in a blink of an eye.

In *Jonah's Gourd Vine*, Hurston creates the backdrop for the lives of John Pearson and Lucy Pearson. The ultimate humor lies in "yearning for a distance" when in reality characters can not escape who they are and where they belong. The final lines of the praise song *Battle Axe* situate and frame John Pearson's character:

> When I get up in Heavean

I want you to be there too,
and when I cry out I been redeemed
I want you to say it too.
(I been redeemed)

Verse

There's one thing that I know I done wrong
I know I stayed in the wilderness
just a little too long.
(He's a shelter in the time of storm)
(He's a shelter in the time of storm)
(He's a shelter in the time of storm)
(He's a shelter in the time of storm) ("He's A Battle Axe")

It's seems impossible that John and Lucy will meet again. The novel suggests in John's own dream that "Somehow Lucy got lost from him, but there he was on a road—happy because the dead snake was behind him, but crying in his loneliness for Lucy" (185). The wilderness is a place of sin where John Pearson dwelled too long, but the conflict is that in spite of his sin he still yearns for salvation. He still has a gift. His final sermon asks for forgiveness and reconciliation. He preaches that all men need salvation because they will be judged in the end. The sermon has two implication in terms of Hurston's writing: 1) she forgives her father and 2) she was fascinated with her father's manner of speaking and wanted to emulate it in her writing. More than anything, Hurston was fascinated with religion and the "ways of Black folk." She had been encouraged to write about Eatonville –her muse. However, her relationship her father was not as clear. Most likely, she admired him from afar, but never really forgave him for how he treated her mother, the mistreatment she suffered at the hand of her stepmother, and his involvement with several women.

As *Jonah's Gourd Vine* was her first novel, Hurston had to write quickly about something she knew. She knew her father and his experience in Florida. She knew her Notasulga roots, and most likely grew up hearing stories about the family's journey from Notasulga, AL. John Hurston was one of those "Over da Creek niggers" and her mother Lucy was a more privileged Negro who lived in Notasulga on the Lee County side. *Jonah's Gourd Vine* explains the significance of "Over da Creek" as a paradigm for crossing over to a new way of thinking. The disease that John Pearson has is essentially a spiritual one. He dreams of Lucy, the creek, a snake and a crossroad; he wants to follow Lucy, but goes down the other road. Likewise, Hurston wants to follow her mother's advice but is doomed to follow her father's fate. Even in his dreams he can not achieve his desires. Zora Neale Hurston succeeds in describing the early twentieth century situation for Blacks in Macon and Lee County Alabama. When John Pearson is hit by a train, most readers feel sorry for him. He has tried to change, but he can not. The cure for some diseases is death.

Considering John Pearson's death and the alternate possibility that the Jonah story offers, Hurston's "cure for some diseases" is self-reflection not distance. Throughout the novel, there are moments when John Pearson takes responsibility for his behavior and makes corrections. For his final move, he chooses Pilgrim Rest where he marries Sally, and resolves to never cheat again. "Pilgrim Rest" is the symbolic place where the journey ends and there is no longer a "yearning for a distance." John Pearson, a "John Bunyan" of sorts in Hurston's version of *Pilgrim's Progress*, is merely an every man who encounters sin and looks for answers and a "shelter in a time of storm." For John Pearson, it is his new Cadillac and his visit to Oviedo, FL that seals his fate. The universe seems to work against him as he cheats with a woman named "Ora." It is not mistake that in Hebrew the word "ora" means "light"; while in Latin it means "pray." At her own risk, in *Jonah's Gourd Vine*, Hurston tackles the issues of religion, Black folklore and Black Southern speech. In *Dust Tracks*, she claims that "people need religion because the great masses fear life and its consequences" (201 version ed. Gates). Hurston chooses not to pray and relies on her own works and experiences to guide her life. In *Jonah's Gourd Vine*, Hurston magnifies the power of trains, automobiles and education to Black life at the beginning of the twentieth century. This excitement amplifies her personal decision to modify her birth date to the twentieth century. Why be left in ugly nineteenth-century Notasulga, when a beautiful life story can begin in Eatonville, FL, a all black town unmarked by a history of slavery or share cropping? The mention of Notasulga, AL only served to describe her parents in both *Dust Tracks* and *Jonah's Gourd Vine*, but her Notasulga birthplace did not define Zora Neale Hurston. Hurston uses *Jonah's Gourd Vine* to resolve her spiritual conflict with her father by showcasing a literal collision of tradition and modernity. John Hurston's traditional ways hold her back, but her desire to write about him inspire her creative genius. To remedy this autobiographical angst, she leaves the character John Pearson's foot twitching as the only sign of life after the train hits him. As the character John Pearson implies in the last sermon, she crosses boundaries, but leaves "one foot on dry land." Yet she could not forget her mother's influence. Hurston needed the prayer that her mother invoked in her life and yearned for the true friendship that would give the light she described in *Dust Tracks*. She was constantly searching for her mother's small voice and amplifying women's words in her texts. Hurston died with a few friends and refused her family's help. She was very poor and her final work on Herod the Great went unpublished. It seemed as if she had wandered too far from her familial and literary roots. Hurston's death and burial in St. Pierce, Florida in an unmarked grave and now the relatively obscure historical marker at Macedonia Baptist Church in Notasulga, AL, illustrate that the wandering instinct only hides prophets, preachers, messengers, and writers from the audiences who need them. The novel *Jonah's Gourd Vine* predicts Hurston's thirty year absence from the literary scene and the vacancy this absence created in American literary history for many years. Comically, Hurston was swallowed by a whale and was figuratively spit out preaching to a new group of readers. Her literary genius carried from her mother Lucy—her gourd vine—taught her to examine the truth and gave Hurston insight to understanding human behavior. As Hurston "jump[s] at de sun," new readers continue to catch her wherever she may be.

Works Cited

"Praise Song-African Literature." www.britannica.com/art/praise-song. Accessed 19 Oct 2016.

Harris, Trudier. *Saints, Sinners, Saviors: Strong Black Women in African American Literature*. Palgrave, 2001.

"He's A Battle Axe." www.allgospellyrics.com. 19 Oct 2016.

Hurston, Zora Neale. *Jonah's Gourd Vine.* Lippencott, 1934. Reprint. HarperCollins, 2008.

_____. *Dust Tracks On A Road.* Lippencott, 1942. Reprint. Ed. and intro. Robert Hemenway. U of Illinois P, 1984.

_____. *Dust Tracks On A Road.* Lippencott, 1942. Reprint. Foreword. Maya Angelou. Afterword, Bibliography, and Chronology. Henry Louis Gates. 1990. New York: Harper Collins, 1991.

Kaplan, Carla, Ed. *Zora Neale Hurston: A Life in Letters.* Doubleday, 2002.

Lowe, John. *Jump at the Sun: Zora Neale Hurston's Comic Comedy.* U of Illinois P, 1994.

Plant, Deborah. *Zora Neale Hurston: A Biography of the Spirit.* Praeger, 2007.

Washington, Booker T. *Up from Slavery.* Intro. John Hope Franklin. *Three Negro Classics.* Avon Books, 1965.

Chapter 8

The Plight of a Woman Expressed in Jing's Tale of an African Woman

Adaku T. Ankumah

African male writers have been criticized for supporting stereotypical portraits of women in Africa, their initial failures to create "authentic" female characters, women who are individuals and not defined in their relationships to men; women who have agency in their own lives to bring about changes. Those leading the way to unearthing the oppression tend to be females, with male authors generally criticized for their limited development of female characters. Chinua Achebe, for example, has been criticized for adopting a chauvinistic approach to depicting female characters, especially in his classic, *Things Fall Apart*. In *Contemporary African Literature and the Politics of Gender*, Florence Stratton takes to task not only critics to whom African women writers remain invisible but also African male writers who also create female characters who remain objects and not subjects. Her exemplars of this masculine tradition are Chinua Achebe and Ngugi wa Thiong'o who try to redress this issue in their later works, *Anthill of the Savannah* and *Devil on the Cross* respectively with female protagonists making a deliberate attempt to elevate the feminine over the masculine, though Stratton contends that the patriarchal framework of both stories are firmly in place. She credits women writers for "exposing biases and prejudices" in male writers and making gender an issue that must be dealt with openly and unreservedly by both writers and critics (176).

The unequal treatment of women leaves Katherine Frank to lament women who are "someone's daughter or wife or mother, shadowy figures who hover on the fringes of the plot, suckling infants, cooking, plaiting their hair." She also cites Kenneth Little's category of female stereotypes: "girlfriends or good-time girls, workers such as secretaries or clerks, wives and other make appendages, and prostitutes or courtesans" (14-15). Generally, one or two men will be singled out as exceptions to this bland portrayal, such as Sembène Ousmane in *God's Bits of Wood,* where the female is more in charge. Critics make a contrast between this male-dominated bias against female representation in literature to the "[militant] . . . new feminist novel" (Frank 15) in Africa. One female critic writes of these male authors that they "treat woman as peripheral to the larger exploration of man's experience" (Davies, qtd. in Nfah-Abenny 35) while women writers "break from the dominant male stance, by depicting *women and women's experiences* [author's emphasis], women's ways of knowing in womb's spaces and locations" (Nfah-Abbenyi 35-6).

Thomas Jing's name may not be a household name even among African literature fans and critics, but he is one such male writers who make women and their repression central to his work. Familiar with the oppression that comes from daring to express one's views in some African countries, Jing was born in The Cameroons and received his BA in History from the University of Yaoundé. After a teaching stint as a secondary school teacher, he obtained a Master's degree in translation from Canada and upon returning to The Cameroons, worked as senior translator, communications officer and head of archives at the Ministry of Fisheries and Animal Husbandry. He began his writing career writing for *The Cameroon Post* newspaper and *Cameroon Life* magazine, writing about issues in his homeland. As it happens in these countries, governments aim to suppress any opposition to their despotic regimes, and Jing left his country to go to South Africa, where he continued his writings, this time with the South African Lawyers for Human Rights. He left South Africa for Canada where he now resides and is finishing up his Ph.D. in Education. Thus, he writes from the position of one who understands what it means to be an outsider looking in; that remains the position of his female characters in *Tale of an African Woman.*

In his *Tale of an African Woman,* Jing joins a group of men called "men of goodwill" (Mariama Bâ, qtd. in Stratton 158) or male feminists, a term that is used to describe men who feel like John Brougher, founder of **MaleFeminists.com,** that men have a vital role to play to end gender inequalities. Brougher contends that "[w]omen deserve to be treated as equal human beings and it hurts every single one of us when that's not the case" ("Male Feminist"). Jing breaks the mold of female writers giving voice to their voiceless sisters as an African male who boldly assigns major roles to female characters in his 2007 novel wherein he narrates the impact of a curse on the village of Yakiri because their female ancestor Yaa is mistreated and denied justice as a woman. Other women who follow her do not fare any better until several generations later when one of her progeny, Yaya, appears on the scene by changing this culture of female repression and charting a new course for women to follow. This female is not just an ordinary protagonist; she becomes the president of a country.

In her keynote address on "Women and Creative Writing in Africa," the late Flora Nwapa urges African women writers in particular and also male writers in general to "break new ground by projecting the future of a female president" since, as she argues, the environment is ready for a female leader (96-7). She adds male writers because, as she notes towards the end of her essay, "[a] man can portray a powerful heroine as well as a woman can if he sets his mind to it and if he does not feel that portraying a strong heroine makes him less of a man" (98). Thomas Jing has responded to this call in his *Tale of an African Woman* as his narrator castigates the people of Bankim who did not act well in the face of the injustices and exclusionary acts which marginalized women. The village has maltreated women, but more particularly, one of its best. As a result of the injustice to their female ancestors, the village suffers total destruction from another group, leaving a remnant to seek a new location. Two relatives, trying to revive the old village, consult a medicine man about their future prospects. Using the old gnukwabe, the village "medicine man" as his mouthpiece, Jing conveys a number of important messages through this story: "The present more than the past will determine the future of your community, for if you sow injustice today, don't expect to harvest happiness and prosperity tomorrow" (92). Secondly, in response to their question that many of their ancestors didn't see female oppression as injustice, the old man responds, "When injustice lasts too long, it starts to look like justice" (92). The fact that the majority is satisfied with the status quo does not make it right, and as the old man notes, not everybody will be just, but the majority must be just or at least make justice the goal. Jing uses this powerful tale of women who refuse to be repressed, and though some of them died in the process, their refusal to be silenced paved the way for their progenitor to make it to the top.

The protagonist, Yaya, a female in the line of other trail-blazing women, is narrating her story to an Irish journalist who has travelled all the way from Ireland to Mungo to recount the story of "Her Excellency," a story which is not focused on the injustices, but a story of hope for the millions of women who still struggle with discrimination, persecution, and oppression. The protagonist herself is reluctant to add her story to a long list of stories of repression told by women in different centuries and in different parts of the world. Apart from her modesty, Yaya wonders how her story could make a dent in the often overlooked stories women have told for centuries. She remarks to her interviewer, "I don't think that the challenges I've faced are peculiar to me and so need to be recounted; nor am I even convinced that by recounting them, that'll make any great difference since the cries of women echo throughout generations and seem all through to have fallen only on deaf ears" (3). Her story may not be different from those of other women; in fact there are certainly horror stories far worse than hers, but the narrator promises that recounting hers will bring a difference, and that difference is spelled H O P E:

> Your story isn't about tears but rather about hope. Hope for millions of women across the world who tremble before their men as we talk, who live in constant fear and stoically face brutalities of the worse kind, women on the verge of giving up. For those women who have already fallen, your story will strengthen their resolve to stand up, and for those who feel like giving up, your account will provide them with the ammunition to continue to struggle. Hope is a powerful weapon. . . . (4)

One woman's success in places where women are still not enjoying the benefits of freedom to be what they want to be captures the resilience and the resistance of women. Fighting oppression and injustices against women, she notes, is a "collective responsibility" (4-5). In sharing her story with the rest of the world, she is inspiring her sisters who may be unable to articulate their oppressions, empowering them. Yaya assumes agency in recounting her story, for it is *her* story in *her* own words, including characters she considers important.

Some may argue whether there is a need for another story about the repression of women since women's issues have been highlighted not just in literature but in the media and in society in general, with the United Nations declaring the period 1975-1985 as the UN Decade for Women. This decade culminated with a 1985 conference on Women in Nairobi, Kenya, and another one ten years later in Beijing, China. In its efforts to fight for women's equality in all aspects, the UN merged its various agencies on women in 2010 to create a new agency called Gender Equality and the Empowerment of Women - or UN Women. Thus it appears women's issues have finally been recognized, and there is no need for another novel on this topic.

In addition to the proliferation of organizations addressing women's issues, African women have made remarkable progress in infiltrating into areas previously considered the prerogative of men. Earlier in 2014, Catherine Samba-Panza, a business woman, became the first female president of war-torn Central African Republic, joining the first female head of state of an African country and of Liberia, Ellen Johnson Sirleaf. The late Wangari Maathai, environmentalist and 2004 Nobel Peace Prize winner achieved what few men have accomplished with her prize. The first woman Chief Justice in Ghana is Georgina Theodora Wood, and there are female lawyers, doctors, engineers, professors, journalists, all over the continent. In addition, female writers have emerged from north, east, west, and south, and these have addressed the challenges women face in societies that are predominantly patriarchal.

The author is very much aware of the gains made in addressing gender inequalities, as the narrator notes:

> However, in spite of the tremendous progress realized, some members of the community continued to be left behind. Those most affected were women. More out of ignorance than malice, they were still being denied many things and their status did not quite reflect the overall progress of the society. (Jing 159)

He draws attention to the fact that more needs to be done because not all women have benefitted from the positive changes in society. Even in March 2014, there are some men who believe the cockpit is "no place for a woman." The man in question was on a WestJet flight from Calgary to Victoria, British Columbia, and revealed his sexism because the plane's pilot was a woman. He requested to be notified when "a fair lady is at the helm" next time so he would book another flight ("Note Left for Female Pilot"). Yes, progress has been made, but it is still slow for females. Jing chooses as Yaya, the last female descendant of Yaa, as the main character to challenge male hegemony in her culture.

Gender relations in Bankim, the ancestral village of the narrator does not support the glowing harmonious relationship that some purport existed between the sexes in pre-colonial Africa. Some critics argue that the traditional woman was free until colonialism when colonial masters brought with them their patriarchal construct of society. Obioma Nnaemeka calls this argument misleading since both sides tend to exaggerate the power women had during both times. In correction, she asserts:

> It may be more accurate to discuss women's power in *relative* terms by showing ways in which the intervention of the colonial period created a situation where the earlier *relatively* powerful positions held by women were *further* eroded by the introduction of new power paradigms and opportunities for acceding to power that are rooted in gender politics. (19)

On the contrary, Jing paints a picture of a society that privileges males over females and seriously stymies the growth and development of females who resist the status quo. In the light of the overarching goal for telling her story, Yaya begins with the story of her ancestor Yaa, a woman who embodies both aspects of repression and expression of her oppression by challenging the existing rules against female advancement. She came into the world with several strikes against her, for her father was killed by lightning one month before she was born, and her mother died after she was born. Her father Tadu was an enlightened member of the village, "a man of remarkable humility, integrity and genius" (8) whose wide travels had led him to sustainable agricultural practices which improved his yield, who knows how he would have raised his daughter. Given her father's stature in the village, the expectation after his premature death was for the wife to give birth to a male successor, a junior Tadu. Her birth was anticipated by the whole village as a huge crowd gathered around her hut, dancing as the talking drums sounded, "We want a male child" (10). As Mercy Oduyoye notes, the response to births in Akan society is the same: a female will give water to drink; a male is a "mighty man of valor"; thus the response is a "predominant expression of patriarchy" (87). A female child is unacceptable, especially since her father is dead and cannot produce males.

Does the repression of women come with a cost? The author suggests that the whole community suffers when one half is treated with "lack of gratitude, jealousy, injustice and outright meanness" (90). Women have made major contributions to the welfare of society, from domestic chores to marketplace, yet because of who they are, there are no signs to announce "Women at Work," as one comedienne notes (Chondra Pierce). To pay for all the work women do will bankrupt the national coffers of many countries. The most difficult part of Yaa's repression is the ingratitude shown to her by the very people that she helped. Yaa works hard after she acquires her own land, but again some women lash out at her: "She wants to show that she's hardworking and tireless"; "She thinks she's better than men" (41). When her hunting group goes for the annual expedition, she kills a lioness that attacks one of her male critics, Gombe. The rest of the men disappear, leaving her alone to fend off the lioness. Gombe dies, but without her intervention, he would have been torn apart instantly. The men go back home and keep quiet about her bravery, not even recommending her for an award.

Another outcome of the repression of women is seen in Yaa's mental breakdown. Female madness, critics tell us, is linked with repression and this connection with repression has been made by several writers. Fanon writes about the psychosis associated with colonialism, describing the colonizing condition as a "nervous condition." The madwoman is found in literature by women, as Sandra Gilbert and Susan Gubar demonstrate in their groundbreaking work *The Madwoman in the Attic*. Bertha Mason, a mixed ancestry woman (Creole and English) and first wife of Rochester in Charlotte Bronte's *Jane Eyre*, whose imprisonment in the attic of her marital home provides the title for the book. The hereditary insanity argument used by her husband aside, powerful and rebellious women like the big Bertha are a threat to patriarchy and must be kept in the attic as lunatics. This psychological meltdown, however, is not limited to western women, for in Tsitsi Dangarembga's *Nervous Conditions*, Nyasha, the "Europeanized" cousin of the protagonist, attempts to control her body by refusing to be controlled with food by her father, Babamakuru. Her anorexia is seen as protest, an "unconscious, inchoate and counterproductive protest without an effective language, voice or politics—but protest nonetheless" (Bordo, qtd. in Nfah-Abbenyi 69). Yaa's decline begins with this incidence of ingratitude of the villages, followed by her mother Chacha's death from a snake bite. In her moment of extreme loneliness after her mother's death and need for companionship, she is totally abandoned by all, including the women of her village. Instead of female solidarity as Yaa has enjoyed with her mother, she is abandoned as a pariah. As Nfah-Abbenyi notes, "women bring out the best in other women, listen to them, kindle their loves not only for living but for enjoying life" (93). However, in the absence of such camaraderie since no woman in the village befriends her, Yaa recoils into herself, withdraws from living in reality to create her own world of escape through madness.

The ultimate act of violence done to Yaa is her rape by the Tabih, an act which underscores gender inequality—male dominance and female powerlessness— and considered an abomination among the Bankim, especially where the victim of rape is a mad woman. Tabih, like the other men in the town, has been unable to dominate or overpower this woman who refuses to be subjected like the other women have. She has competed with men and humiliated them. In her right mind, she is a force to contend with, but in her insanity, Tabih, a leader who is supposed to protect his citizens, rapes one of the most vulnerable. The Tabih's abomination will bring untold hardships to the people of Bankim as the gnukwabe, the medicine man consulted to reveal the identity of the rapist will reveal. The village will be reduced to a rubble for their tolerating injustice for so long.

A major area of female oppression is the whole area of marriage, coupled with other domestic chores assigned to women. Thus women have been repressed and their aspirations killed because of the marriage and domesticity. In this culture, men enter into the contractual agreement on behalf of their daughters, and the mothers and daughters are kept in the dark about the arrangement. Tafon and Wirba's tall, beautiful daughter Mayemfon has nightmares about the arranged marriage, especially when she sees the future husband, a bad man that no one in her right frame of mind wants to marry in his own village, smeared with blood. She pleads with the mother to stop the negotiations for marriage, but she is as helpless as her daughter: "What do you expect me to tell him when I haven't been informed about the marriage.... You very well know that this matter doesn't involve women" (206). Mayemfom sees this forced marriage as the latest among many others to derail her future plans and "completely [ruin] her" (207). She has been forced out of school to take care of a relative's child. After the child grows up, Mayemfon tries to get back to school, but instead, she's given a piece of land to cultivate, for as her father tells her, "I can understand a boy going to school to come to the village and help in its development but a woman may wind up the property of another village" (207). Another opportunity presents itself for Mayemfon to work at a hospital. She submits her application, goes for an interview only to receive a lukewarm reception from her parents. Not all the females in the novel agree to this disruption of their lives. Yaa's friend Bishu has an older sister who is being forced into a similar situation with a man she does not like, and when the man shows up, a big fight breaks out, reminding Yaa of her mother's similar plight about fifteen years earlier. The next day, Bonsisi, the sister involved, has disappeared, nowhere to be found. Yaa surmises that she probably wants to "bring pressure to bear" on their father, to let him know that daughters cannot be disposed of to anybody the father chooses. Yaa draws this observation about practices that hinder female progress: "Traditions and customs should be meant to uplift people, not destroy them" (237). Unfortunately, this lesson is a hard one for society to learn.

Indeed, the repression of Yaa stems from the fact that she is too good, for she does not stay in her confined space, but she seeks new horizons as she ventures into areas reserved for men only. In most traditional cultures, there are gendered activities, marked for men only with females excluded from membership. She wants to be a goatherd at the age of ten, and joins the male goatherds who don't know whether to associate with her or not Although she hunts cane rats with them and engages in boyish activities with them, they still feel some other activities like wrestling are beyond the scope of women, and they laugh at the mere thought that she thinks she can compete against the weakest boy. Yet when they get tired of her nagging and put the weakest and smallest against her, Yaa humiliates him by putting him down on his back. Yaa thinks her victory will qualify her for participation in the initiation into manhood wrestling match. However, the Tabih or the leader of the Council of Elders informs her: "Do you know that you need to have balls to survive the physical activities required to select members of this society?" (19). Again, Yaa's exclusion is not based on any perceived weakness in her abilities but based on her gender.

Not only are women who are too good repressed, but also women who act independently of men, as is the case of Chacha, a friend of Yaa's mother, and the divorced childless woman who adopted Yaa after the death of her parents. A tall, tough and beautiful woman with a free spirit, Chacha challenges the notion of the woman as helpless and in need of males to stand on her feet. Her husband divorced her after years as a "barren woman," a view that is generally taken by African men that the woman is to blame in childless marriages. Yet scientific research reveals that men are equally at fault in some cases of infertility. Chacha does not accept responsibility for their lack of children; on the contrary, she blames the husband. The narrator notes she is not afraid of the council when she appears before them and uses logic to show them that she is not the party to blame for childlessness. Her syllogism is as follows:

    Major premise: Men who sleep around a whole lot get women pregnant;
    Minor premise: Her husband sleeps around a whole lot, and yet none of the women are pregnant;
    Conclusion: Her husband, not her, has infertility problem.

She diagnoses her husband's problem as having plenty liquid but without seeds and challenges the inherent sexism of the group: "The moment a person doesn't have two nuts swinging underneath, the person instantly become a fool in the eyes of this Council" (13). Even the men are amazed at the strength of her logic! As one writer notes, "The single woman who manages her affairs successfully without a man is an affront to patriarchy and a direct challenge to the so-called masculinity of men who want to 'possess' her" (Oduyoye 5). Indeed, Chacha has made it as an independent woman, "as if the community did not exist" (14) and even her detractors admit that the orphaned child will fare better in the care of such a hardworking woman.

The repression of women reaches a climax where education is concerned. In spite of the saying, "Educate a man and you educate an individual; educate a woman and you educate a village," women have been shortchanged where education is concerned because of patriarchy and even colonialism working together to keep women out of the classroom. As Tumbu, one of the men in Yakiri observes, "there can be no greater danger than sending a woman even to primary school" (300). Another man suggests that to educate a woman is to invest in another village's property since the woman will eventually get married. Readers of Tsitsi Dangarembga's *Nervous Conditions* cannot forget the chilling effects of Tambu's enigmatic opening words: "I was not sorry when my brother died" (1). Why would a young girl be so callous about a sibling's death? The narrator happens to be a female deprived of education so her brother could be educated. His death, therefore, becomes her opportunity to obtain an education. In a 2014 UNESCO Report about education, the author of the report, Pauline Rose, refers to the "global learning crisis" where disadvantaged, rural girls especially have difficulties getting places in schools. She notes the grim statistics facing girls in developing countries: All girls will not be easily accommodated in primary school until 2086, hence the author of the article's title, "The 70-Year Wait for Primary School." However, for secondary education, some of these girls fighting to get into elementary school may long be dead since it will not be until "the next century, 2111, before poor rural girls will all have places in secondary school, at the current levels of progress" (qtd. in Coughlin). There is still a gap between men's accessibility to the classroom and female's.

Yaya's acceptance into college after she makes straight A's on her college-entrance exam makes her a target of both male and female ridicule, leading her to withdrawing into herself. Not even her grandparents stand up for her initially. If a male student had achieved this distinction, it would have been cause for celebration in the entire village, a "great source of prestige" (294) for the village. However, this prestige, being "in the hands of a woman" dampened their celebration, turning it into a disappointment instead of an appointment with destiny: the first woman from Yakiri to go to college. Even her grandmother who is normally lucid cannot see a woman other than a wife and mother. Yaya expects the entire female community to celebrate her accomplishment and support her now, but they reject her. The opposition from men is even more caustic as one man, using a ridiculous malapropism, calls women's degrees "diseases" and does not see any difference between the two (300).

The repression of females is not carried out by males alone; the sad part is that females oppress other females to maintain the patriarchal values in place. Even the "midwives" who assisted her were enthusiastic initially, but when the leading one announced the birth of a baby girl, they all left disappointed. Mother and child were abandoned and the mother insulted for killing her husband. She died of grief, leaving a nameless baby behind. Eventually, the village will name the orphaned baby Yaa, which depending on the pronunciation, could mean loner or great one (11), and Yaa favors the latter pronunciation. As a preteen who wants to join an exclusively male group of goatherds, Yaa will be opposed most vehemently by women, one of whom asks, "Who does she think she is!" In the course of the Grand Migration of the village to their new settlement, Yakiri, the daughter of Yaa, Yabu, talks with her village people, upbraiding them about their "appalling treatment" of her mother in Bankim. She reminds them that "no human community could survive in the midst of prolonged injustice, especially one which tended to exclude others, not because they were bad but because they were of the "wrong" sex and too good" (81).

Just as there are women who hinder the progress of other women, Jing creates men who support the advancement of women and challenge unjust laws which limit some. Again these men like Asanbe and Ngufor are men of "integrity and intelligence," men who have the "reputation for fairness and perspicacity," men who have been around females long enough to know that if given the chance, women would excel at everything men did (20). Ngufor warns his male colleagues about tradition and its role: "We mustn't come across as a sentimental bunch only eager to uphold tradition, even when it doesn't serve our aims anymore. We mustn't forget that men put the tradition in place. So why should women even play by the rules they didn't contribute to formulate?" (20). The problem is not women's lack of ability; the problem stems from traditions put in place by men to prevent them from progressing. As Yaya admits, this "collection of habits" called tradition has become the major means of excluding women from advancement in society.

The most enthusiastic and vocal male supporter of female equality is none other than Father Sean, the young Irish priest who, in his twenties, left Ireland for Yakiri at the suggestion of one of Yakiri's sons studying in Oxford, England, Bernard Nso. It isn't coincidental that Father Sean agrees to settle in Yakiri, for at the founding of the village fifty years earlier, the gnukwabe who had been consulted by two cousins about their desire to make a fresh start from their old village Bankim after their mistreatment of one of theirs, Yaa, brought curses and destruction on them prophesies the arrival of a strange man to help them: "I also wish to tell you that your community will receive some assistance from a very strange man. He'll come from a very strange land...." (92). True to the prophecy, Father Sean is instrumental in the transformation of Yaya in the novel. This Irishman would be "good news for humanity" (97), especially for the village of Yakiri, a name which means "Yaa, we're very sorry" (95), a name meant to pacify their female ancestor Yaa and to begin a healing process.

Father Sean stands in stark contrast to the portrayal of the earlier colonizers like Achebe's Winterbottom in *Things Fall Apart* who claim hegemonic control over the colonized, seeing them as children to be raised by their all-knowing Parent. The colonial superiority pervades the novel, with the people of Umuofia seen as inferior to them. The must-read book for new arrivals is *The Pacification of the Primitive Tribes of the Lower Niger*. The Catholic priest does not read such a book; instead Nso gives him a manuscript titled *Origin of Yakiri* and a few words about building healthy relationships with the people: "[B]lond and Irish as you are, an African ceases to see these differences and considers you his or her own real brother if you give him or her good reasons to feel that way." Father is impressed by this bit of "African" wisdom: "In human relationships, they're more advanced than we are," he observes (101). Thus he is not on a "colonizing mission" to civilize the people as such; he is looking for ways to be accepted and to work alongside the people, for he believes development is best when it is collective (107). In fact, Father seems to be a precursor of the liberation theologians of the 1960s-1970s, Catholic priests in Latin America who responded to the Marxist liberation movements that wanted to right evils of repressive governments on behalf of the oppressed by aligning themselves to these marginalized people. To what would shock his predecessors, one of the first activities of the Catholic priest is a visit to the gnukwabe to observe how he treats a sick child. He does not prejudge the old man; he goes to observe, realizing that the old man loves his son as he says, just like Father's parents loved him. The traditional healer respects him, offers him a seat close to him and prepares food for a total stranger. He is amazed at the way the gnukwabe does things, so when his traveling companion, Kikakilaki, asks his opinion, he says, "I don't know what to think but if that's the way he uses his mystical power, it's a good thing" (146). Obviously, he doesn't endorse everything done by the old man, but he is ready to select practices which complement his own, such as the healing powers. This is a totally different mentality from that of other Europeans who populate the world of fiction and the real world.

The injustices in life do not escape Father Sean as he makes his way to Yakiri with a stop-over in Senegal and a visit to the island of Goree or to use the narrator's words, the "Slave House," the last holding place before African slaves crossed the Atlantic to their new homes in America and the Caribbean. This reminder of slavery triggers thoughts about injustices and persecution of one group by another. He ascribes these horrors as slavery and genocide to "mercantilist greed" and hate (109). As a priest trained to understand humans and move them from the "beastly" to their "saintly" side, he is very much aware of human failings and is ready to deal with female repression as one of these injustices found in society.

To insert females back into the village's life, Father allows for free expression of these women, offering the women of Yakiri the liberty to participate in the affairs of the village without being silenced by men. At his first press conference on plans for building a village school, Mbohti, a short woman nicknamed Malaria Butt because her butt trembles, shakes her butt to the dismay of the villagers. Father, however encourages her to "[s]hake it again," for a woman has a right to express herself (149-150). He incorporates women into the dance troupe he creates in response to Bernard Nso's advice to challenge the best dance troupe in the area. Even the music he composes for the occasion celebrates Yaa as the greatest ancestor (166).

Father Sean becomes Yaya's chief advocate in progressing through school, especially when Yaya excels in academics. He rewards Yaya's accomplishments when he orders her a rare pair of shoes at the end of her first semester in high school for her high performance. When Yaya came in first, beating young men in a traditional subject that men dominate, mathematics, Father and her grandparents were on hand to celebrate her accomplishments. When her grandfather wants to put a stop to Yaya's dream to go to college because of finances but more so because "the level of education she has attained is good enough for [her] to market [her] crops from the farm" (296); when the men of the village think that an educated woman, after pursuing further studies abroad will come "wearing high-heel shoes and a very short skirt, talk Mikari through her nostrils so that men shouldn't understand, sit down in the midst of men with her legs crossed, down more calabashes of palm wine than any man and smoke long cigarettes and puff smoke in their eyes" (299), Yaya sneaks out of bed early in the morning to consult with her mentor. Father Sean reassures her, "It'll take time here for people to understand the importance of educating women" (307). Father Sean promises to talk to her grandfather, assuring her that she will go to the university and become a great woman (307). He prepares her to focus on the intellectual and moral, but not the material aspects of boarding school life.

An obvious critique of Father's support of this young African woman is the idea that once again, it's the West that comes to the rescue of Africans, not Africans addressing these issues themselves. Is the author reinforcing the helplessness of Africans without

Western aid? It may appear so to those who think challenges to female oppression and a demand for equality by females is a Western phenomenon, as if African women need Westerners to come and reveal their problems to them. Some female writers initially resisted the label feminism for these reasons. As noted earlier, though, Father is not the typical Westerner who has a condescending attitude towards Africans. More importantly, Jing sees a connection between their oppression and oppression of women globally, in the larger context, not necessarily linking it to a white feminist movement, but to women in general and their struggles to overcome inequalities in society. Yaya does not advocate an isolationist approach to dealing with male domination and female repression, but neither does Yaya advocate a radical break with traditional society either. She still operates within her culture, but she entertains the idea of cultural hybridity:

> [A] culture which did not help people hold their own in the face of difficulties was not worth maintaining and I saw no harm for any group to borrow from other cultures to meet its own deficiencies. In that sense, I see cross-cultural fertilization as the way to the future. Once adopted, a new culture would provide a fresh source of inspiration and stimulus. (237)

She wants a society resulting from cultural crosspollination. According to her, there are intrinsically and extrinsically elements of goodness in every culture which, should each culture feed off these strengths, would make the world a desirable place to live in for all and not just for a portion.

Yaya handles female repression not by supporting open rebellion but by criticizing the parts of the culture that make female subjugation possible. Thus she shares with her friend Bishu, after her eldest sister's disappearance that "[at] some point, we must be daring enough to criticize our own society, without which our growth and development will be terribly stunted" (238). She leaves in place the societal and religious mores of her Roman Catholic community, though "[romance] of any kind was totally frowned upon and forbidden. Of course, not to talk of lovemaking!" (239). Yaya at this point is getting romantically involved with the male student she sees as her closest competitor, Forche. Yaya's relationship with Forche has been rough, especially when Yaya hears rumors supposedly started by him that Yaya is his wife. Her grandmother Wirba does not support a radical feminist viewpoint where heterosexual relations are concerned. Definitely not championing a western feminist ideology, she gives Yaya a lecture on male-female relationships:

> Now let me tell you something my dear child and make sure you retain it once and for all. If you have to discard your good man on grounds of a rumor you may wind up single. You've reacted solely with your emotions, without even using your head. I must tell you that this isn't the best way to proceed in life. (232)

Her grandmother buys into traditional notions of marriage as important to a woman, especially marriage to a man that the woman likes, not one chosen for her. She sees friendship as the basis to a good marriage and warns her granddaughter to begin a "fence-mending exercise" to ensure that another woman does not snatch her man. "A man," she notes, "is like a lion and the only way to tame a lion is to catch it, keep it, and know it before the crucial phase of taming it. . . . .It is good to be cautious with men but not to the point where you don't even want to get close to them" (234). Wirba avoids the extremes of Catholicism and traditionalism where men are concerned. She sees the nuns as "abnormal" women, having sacrificed their womanhood for a career; neither does she support the position of traditionalists like her husband who see women as "baby factories" (309). Yaa must go to college.

Though Thomas Jing's novel encompasses many aspects, including the historical, it is a coming-of-age story. Much has been written about the Bildungsroman, which has been hailed as one of Germany's contribution to literature. The term in its European setting is generally associated with males and considered a work that follows the development of a young boy "towards self-understanding and social responsibility" (Dilthey, qtd. in Summerfield 1). Though the masculine focus of the genre is evident in the first half of the twentieth century, their numbers increased in the second half of the century with women writers using the genre the most. Critics attribute the increase to the feminist movement of the 1960's (Feng 9). Feng notes the appropriation of the genre by ethnic women which departs from the linear trajectory of male version. Feng suggests that though some feminist scholars have re-defined the genre as it pertains to women, these women still follow a white, middle-class, female agenda, which is different from the agenda of ethnic or women of color (13).

Coming-of-age stories, though, are not a recent development in African literature. Camara Laye's *The African Child,* published in 1959, chronicles a young man's "growth from innocence to maturity against the background of traditional society" (Palmer 85). Tsitsi Dangarembga's *Nervous Conditions* which follows the maturation of a young girl, Tambu, as she attains an education and moves away from a naive acceptance of patriarchal authority of her uncle and the "Englishness" of her cousins who stayed in England to challenge her uncle's patriarchal and neocolonialist tendencies. The novelty about Jing's bildungsroman, though, is that unlike the other two mentioned, Camara Laye is a male writing about a male protagonist and Tsitsi Dangaremba, a female author, writes about a female protagonist. However, Thomas Jing is a male, writing about a female's coming-of-age story, and that makes this novel unique in that sense.

In their perspective of the female appropriation of this genre, most critics note the difference between the female and male uses of the genre. For example, Annis Pratt sees the "novel of development" as a "woman's Bildungsroman, but going in the opposite of the male genre in that the females grow down not up (qtd. *in* Summerfield & Downward 121). Another critic, Susan J Rosowski, shows similarity between the Bildungsroman and novel of awakening in that both recount "the attempts of a sensitive protagonist to learn the nature of the world, discover its meaning and pattern and acquire a philosophy of life" (120). However, Rosowski sees women's awakening as "an awakening to limitations" (qtd. *in* Summerfield & Downward 120). Jing does not project any such limitations on his protagonist, Yaya. In fact, Yaya's development follows the masculine upward trajectory, not downward, as she becomes president of her country. Does Jing's protagonist defy reality or is it another way for a male writer to ignore the realities of African women?

Thomas Jing, in the *Tale of an African Woman*, subverts the meta-narrative of female writers being a voice for numerous voiceless women in African traditional societies to create a group of female characters who dare to challenge the subjugation of women in their community and the female's lack of identity. They refuse to accept as normal the abnormal, for the author refuses to accept the continuing oppression of women as normal. In that sense, Jing sees the stagnation in society as a direct result of the injustice meted out to one half of the population. Any lasting changes to the subordinate position of women will involve men changing their orientation about women, men like Father Sean who seek "equality and justice for all."

Works Cited

Brougher, John. "I'm a Male Feminist. No, Seriously." Leading Women. CNN. 8 Oct. 2013. www.cnn.com/2013/10/08/opinion/im-a-male-feminist/. Accessed 13 Feb. 2014.

Coughlan, Sea. "The 70-Year Wait for Primary School." BBC 28 Jan. 2014. www.bbc.com/news/business-25811704. Accessed 3 Feb. 2014.

Feng, Pin-chia. *The Female* Bildungsroman *by Toni Morrison and Maxine Hong Kingston: A Postmodern Reading*. Peter Lang, 1998.

Frank, Katherine. "Women Without Men: The Feminist Novel in Africa." *Women in African Literature Today*. Eldred D. Jones, Eustace Palmer, and Marjorie Jones. Women in African Literature Today 15. James Currey, 1987, pp. 14-34.

Jing, Thomas. *Tale of an African Woman*. Langaa Research & Publishing CIG, 2007.

Nfah-Abbenyi, Juliana Makuchi. *Gender in African Women's Writing: Identity, Sexuality, and Difference.* Indiana UP, 1997.

Nnaemeka, Obioma, ed. *Sisterhood: Feminisms & Power: From Africa to the Diaspora.* Africa World, 1998.

Nwapa, Flora. "Women and Creative Writing in Africa." In *Sisterhood: Feminisms & Power: From Africa to the Diaspora*, pp. 89-99.

Oduyoye, Mercy Amba. *Daughters of Anowa: African Women & Patriarchy.* Orbis Books, 1995.

Palmer, Eustace. *An Introduction to the African Novel: A Critical Study of Twelve Books.* Africana, 1972.

Stratton, Florence. *Contemporary African Literature and the Politics of Gender.* Routledge, 1994

Rishoi, Christy. *From Girl to Woman: American Women's Coming-of-Age Narratives.* SUNY UP, 2003.

Chapter 9

Emmanuel Fru Doh's *Nomads: The Memoir of a Southern Cameroonian*: Censorship, Treachery, Instability and the Emergence of a Nation.

Benjamin Hart Fishkin

When *The Saturday Evening Post* was first published in the early nineteenth century, roughly at the time Andrew Jackson rose to prominence, the United States was perceived to be a simpler place. The family was something special, common people helped one another and the individual had a chance to survive, and even thrive, in a terrible world which had its share of corrupt leaders. It was not childish to be idealistic. The challenges, with hard work, were possible and future calamities, like the Civil War, were so far away that the nation existed in honeyed adolescence. The *Post*, over many years, chronicled this innocence and, like the Sankofar bird, looked backwards to an era that was past. It made sense and could be counted upon to provide both stability and order in the future. The rural Midwest had wholesomeness to it, a roughhewn quality that one could depend on, and now the only thing American culture can agree upon is that this iconic solid comfort is gone forever.

This feeling of a collective happiness, of a population that had no divisions, where the front doors of all in the community were always left unlocked is very similar to the methodically structured freedom British Southern Cameroons enjoyed before the terrible decision was made to connect Southern Cameroons and *La République du Cameroun*. Emmanuel Fru Doh, in his memoir *Nomads*, looks back with nostalgia to a time where police officers were friends of the public, just like in the mythology of Americana. There was a time once, he actually says, when "Life was good" (Doh 17). Electricity was cheap. Bank loans were plentiful. Parents focused on their kids. The establishment culture, for a brief shining moment, was methodical, precise and productive. What has become of this hope and transparency and how have these beneficial qualities become fractured and obliterated? (Doh 106) Like a weary married couple who stays together solely for the sake of the children, the two Cameroons stay together with the ties that bind the two together creating a piece of kabuki theater with stylized mischief and elaborate make-up. Doh reminds a population of this earlier period of happiness only to wind up weeping bitter tears at the fact that British Southern Cameroons has lost its ability to self-govern. Chaos now runs roughshod over order. At the hands of such western powers such as France and England, it has been pushed, pulled, prodded, manipulated, sutured and renamed to the point where even an author who was born there cannot distinguish mendacity from certainty.

Halfway through his memoir Doh states that "[p]eople take better care of their lawns than [President Paul] Biya does of [The] Cameroon[s]" (Doh 97). Does anybody wonder that there is scarcely a glimmer of hope for the restoration of British Southern Cameroons? What is repressed is a verbal and written accounting of what has been lost. There is no history. Ruinous and deleterious changes have erased it. Post-colonialism, despite publicly saying otherwise, presumes that free Africans are not capable of conducting such a forensic audit. Works like *Nomads* catalog an unpleasant reality and express what has been surreptitiously swept under the carpet; that no one with true power genuinely wants a united Cameroons. If one were looking for the real thing, Emmanuel Fru Doh will tell him/her not only where it went, but who has a vested interest in keeping it hidden.

Repression and surveillance are universal problems. The United States' embarrassment over the present disclosures by former Central Intelligence Agency (C.I.A.) employee Edward Snowden proves this. At issue is not that monitoring is taking place. That is presumed. The point of contention is to what extreme *La République du Cameroun* approaches the Orwellian Totalitarian autocracy. Doh believes that dysfunction is here and the nation torn asunder. Look at the problems in Liberia, a nation of free blacks which descended into a coup d'état and two civil wars. What about Sierra Leone, which became independent in 1961, only to have a general election in 1967 won by the opposition and then summarily dismissed by the ruling party, just like it happened in *La République du Cameroun* in 1992. Lest we forget the Peoples' Democratic Republic of Congo whose first democratically elected president (Pascal Lissouba) was removed by civil war funded by the French and led by former dictator Sassou Nguesso. This is what is meant by the author when he states "Who will accept that their enemies are members of their own nation's armed forces? (127) No wonder the identity of the Anglophone-Cameroon borders on a precipice that is as sharp as a razor blade; just a little push can cause it to freefall into insanity and madness.

Literature from its very origin has been a project of subversion resulting from oppression and repression. The question I am interested in is how does Emmanuel Fru Doh handle these issues differently than other writers in other parts of the world? Since Anglophone-Cameroon (formerly British Southern Cameroons) is compelled to deal with a history of repression and contemporary oppression, how does the narrator maintain his cultural, political, and spiritual individuality? Daily life seems to be a perpetual crisis in which no rational person can maintain his/her compusure.

Many years ago the famous singer Mahalia Jackson said "Blues are the songs of despair, but gospel songs are the songs of hope" (qtd. in Levine, 174). The big question is whether or not sub-Saharan Africa is so schizophrenic that it cannot tell one from the other. Jackson is the first gospel singer to sing at Carnegie Hall because God's music frees people. It restores them and makes them feel good. Who (other than God) will decide the song that will be upon the lips of the Anglophone-Cameroonian? Will it be a song that can be sung out loud? In *Nomads* "we are at a point where even human life no longer means anything" (Doh 97). Officers, in uniform, committ crimes "...slaughter innocent citizens on a daily basis without the police makingany arrests ever..." (Doh 97). There are some problems that one can never get over. Emmanuel Fru Doh's affection, devotion, and tender sentimental song quickly retreats into the bittersweet heartbreak of someone with a spirit disunited by divorce, seperation and desertion. His nation is being destroyed and it is being destroyed from afar. After nearly a decade of teaching at the University of Yaoundé, Doh joins the diaspora, traveling to the United States like so many Africans before him.

The predicament of the Anglophone-Cameroonian, much like peaceful protests that characterized the Civil Rghts movement in the Southern portion of the United States, is that she/he must take an intellectual approach towards finding a solution. What is needed is a spiritual approach. This is the way to fight the disgrace of secretly being reduced to the status of a nonentity in your own country. Instead of giving in to anger, one must resist the temptation to lash out at a loss of identity. Instead a conversion or transformation process must take place in which, according to T.S. Eliot, the mind will "… digest and transmute the passions which are its material" (qtd. in Warner 229). *Nomads* is a series of failed examples of possibility and purpose. Instead of pleasant remembrances we get a number of occurrences and events that are arranged and characterized by intimidation. In Chapter Nine of Doh's investigation a young couple is out shopping, well before the 6:00 PM curfew, and is detained by five soldiers with semiautomatic rifles. The young man is told to "lie down in the mud even as numerous young men idling around looked on" and the young woman reduced to tears (Doh 125). This is the type of tension, pressure, and conflict to which even the saintly are vulnerable. Even when a soldier literally steps on a prostate victim's shin, not a word is said in anger. This would be foolish in the presence of such overwhelming power. The task of the oppressed is neither to cringe nor retreat, but to construct a thought process that will surmount cultural, political, and religious attempts to keep them obsequious, obedient, and silent. This pyschological travail requires a written record of logic, aesthetics and ethics. The couple on the pavement needs a courageous philosophy; it needs a persistent culture. It needs a past.

Literature, and specifically Anglophone-Cameroon literature, is the mechanism of subversion whose power is superior to mob anger. The wand, bayonnet, cane, sword or sceptre of power is nothing but what a literary theorist would describe as an insecure and uneasy attempt to surveill. It is ludicrous in comparison to an unlimited discussion of knowledge, truth and human nature. This is how, via composing a history that cannot be thrown away, one rebels against and refutes a government "without standards" (Doh 145). The problems of The Cameroons, however, need more than refutation. They need to be traced back to their origin. What were once considered colonial problems, based in Western Europe, have now metastasized in a land far, far away and become hot iron forges for the African psyche. These unsettling enigmas—the unasked for diplomatic severing of a union into Anglophone and Francophone systems of management, are no longer British or French in nature. They have traveled across the South Atlantic Ocean, like a virus, to become internal, inherent problems that were never anticipated, contemplated or even considered at the Berlin Conference of 1884. What hurts the most is that the jailor looks just like the jailed. The language Emmanuel Fru Doh uses is "fusion" where the colonial culture and the indigineous culture mix together like a milkshake blended at high speed to produce a concoction that is terrifyingly homogoneous (Doh 96). Other Cameroonians have paradoxically picked up the tether of oppression and wielded it better than any foreigner. For Doh, the political sibling "practice[s] what the white man did to us decades before by not only killing Anglophones, but trying to turn them into Francophones" (149). This is the insecure attempt to surveill. It is succeeding. It is the intentional plan or strategy to keep one segment of the country in its place.

The rejection and the pain are palpable. It is with a heavy heart and a bitter realization that this emergent art form that needs a tractor-trailer sized infusion of faith and support grapples with a series of themes that are unique and peculiar to a region that changes names with the same frequency as others change socks. The literary text, not just Doh's but most of Anglophone-Cameroon literature, takes on a style that has been fermented, augured and aged in discord. The most incisive of these authors, to name a few, are Vakunta, Nyamnjoh, Ndi, Bate Besong, Linus Asong, Thomas Jing and Nkemngong Nkengasong. The art these figures produce is the opposite of a fine wine. The *Hobson's Choice* is that one must pay the cost of repressing and censoring oneself—with all of the spiritual problems inherent with keeping one's true opinion under wraps—or put these theses on paper and descend into a miasma that is Kafkaesque by comparison. Just as the language of Prague at the turn of the previous century was divided between Czech and German, sub-Saharan Africa in general, and The Cameroons in particular, must deal with a similar discrepancy that results in a surreal and a physchological brutality that far outpaces a physical beating. An unchecked bureaucracy thus overpowers and sends the mind of the Anglophone-Cameroonian spinning into an unasked for dream that is disorienting, terrifying, and of unlimited duration. In *Nomads*, Doh chronicles this dream as if he were a man walking in his sleep through a Kamerun divided unevenly between Britain and France. The smaller part was posessed by Britain and the larger by France (Doh 158). He prefers the term "cultural aliens" (Doh 159). However you term it the thrill, and solid comfort, are gone.

Literature is the most powerful incendiary device at the hand of the dissident. The individual author who writes about this part of the world realizes that his/her writings comprise a Anglophone Cameroonian literature that people in the western portion of Cameron feel compelled to contribute to, not because they want to but because they are obligated and compelled to. Not only because they are in pain under the subjugation of the Francophone-dominated regimes, but because not contributing will cause the English Speaking Cameroonian even more pain. They have to find a new government, a different civil service administration, a different educational system and a different police force. The cost of repressing one's thoughts, under these circumstances, is as immeasurable as it is universal. It creates so many spiritual problems, and is so disorienting and debilitating, that expressing one's conscience is the only effective means of cultural reconstruction. It is the only way to think clearly and simply in a nation that has lost its rearview mirror.

Instead of standing firmly and enjoying stability and groundedness, The Cameroons gets new names to paper over old failures. Emmanuel Fru Doh uses his memoir to expose this as a series of maneuvers and manipulations. By being called The Federal Republics of the Cameroons, The United Republic of the Cameroons, The Republic of Cameroon and *La République du Cameroun* by evading common sense and changing the name of Southern Cameroons to West Cameroon, half of the nation was bamboozled or "turned around".

> 'Something must be wrong here,' I mused to myself. I was determined, whenever I could make time, to talk to my father about all this, which seemed to be a plan just falling in place. He should know better given his age; they were the ones who were there when Cameroon was born. I was around, yes, but still too young to understand what was going on. Like virtuallly every

child, all I was interested in was the next thing with which to playcate my molars. What was all this about anyway? Why do they have to keep changing the name of our country for no obvious reason? I hated it because of the way it left me feeling empty and ungrounded. It would be interesting hearing how my father would explain this. (Doh 3 – 4)

How does a population stay intellectually vigorous while its government is doing somersaults to turn them into people with wooden and listless responses? They do not have a voice, and they are unable to react. Everyday encounters are a mess and everyone, even the likeminded, are strangers to them because they cannot risk taking someone into their confidence. This is very similar to an observation of Charles Dickens in *A Tale of Two Cities* where the most prolific Anglophone of all wonderfully remarks that a person can be lonely even in the largest of cities with people all around; "…every beating heart in the hundreds of thousands of breasts there, is, in some of its imaginings, a secret to the heart nearest it! Something of the awfulness, even of Death itself, is referable to this" (Dickens 8). This is the predicament of Judascious Fanda Yanda in Francis Nyamnjoh's *Mind Searching*. The need to stay alive, to stay involved, to stay connected to one's fellow citizen and to stay out of jail, is paramount to the point where Jeremy Bentham's nineteenth century prison need not be built in The Cameroons. It would be superflous. It would be redundant. The individual becomes his own constable and falls into the grip of the dictator by limiting himself and self-censoring himself or herself more effectively than anyone else can. One cannot express himself/herself and the ideas within his/her mind only have the free reign to move in a very small space that will never be memorialized, only rewritten.

Authors like Francis Nyamnjoh, Emmanuel Fru Doh, Linus Asong, Nkemngong Nkengasong, Bill F. Ndi and Thomas Jing focus on the titles of insiders and outsiders. Naturally the "insider" need not worry about expressing himself or herself. But he/she is in the minority and there is no guarantee that either will remain on the inside in the fluid world of African politics, lunching on the sumptuous "national cake" (Nyamnjoh "Commentary: [The] Cameroon[s]: A Country United by Ethnic Ambition and

Difference" 101). The fight for the cake can throw one out of the ring forever. This struggle for the national cake makes the world of outsides very volatile. This is a status that can quickly disappear. In Nyamnjoh's scholarly article, "Fiction and Reality of Mobility in Africa" there is a hierarchy, ordering or placement just like a financial portfolio of municipal bonds, that includes all of the criteria that can keep people out. Issues of race and class scarcely scratch the surface. All can turn people out. All can keep people silent. Doh takes this marginalization, segregates it linguistically and makes it sound like an elegy; "Anglophones are being treated as beggars outside their geographical space" (161). Unfortunately, those desperately seeking alms and lamenting their fate in comparison to the past before Southern Cameroons and *La République du Cameroun* were forced into a union in 1961 are everywhere. On December 29, 2013 in Cairo, for example, the Egyptian government arrested Al Jazeera journalists for having links with terrorist organizations and "...spreading false news..." (Web). Apparently both beauty and terror related charges are in the eye of the beholder. But what language does the beholder speak? The newspaperman and cameraman who gathers news for periodicals and television, is the outsider. The better he/she does his/her job the more danger they are in. These are the crimes of a rogue government, and they pertain to all rogue governments (not just Yaoundé and Cairo) all over the world.

The universality of this problem is what wrankles Emmanuel Fru Doh the most. You don't have to be an African to see it. This memoir seems errily familiar to any student of history and herein lies its importance. The sorrowful and the mournful seem to multiply exponentially and they are not limited by geographical borders. This is a problem everywhere and all governments are a mere step—when their perceived security is threatened—from crushing, silencing and placing their boot upon the throats of their very own people. The great fear is that of the individual humanist with agency, like the young couple out shopping or the reporters in Egypt, both of whom risk confinement and imprisonment, if need be, and refuse to stop voicing their opinions. "One would have thought they cared less about what was going on until one of the soldiers literally stepped with his boots on the shinn of the young man who had been rolling around in the mud with a stoical look on his face" (Doh 125). The police routinely reduce the Cameroonian to the status and perspective of swine. Doh's goal in *Nomads* is to transform the cultural identity of Anglophone-Cameroonians and to lift these individuals up out of the mud. This means changing western discourses so that no one is a master in someone else's house. No one is a farmer to someone else's livestock. What's more, this also means confronting Africans who *think* like westerners and eliminating their need to neutralize and dominate those in the linguistic minority. This political seasaw—with the Francophone getting more and more and the Anglophone getting less and less--is something that *La République du Cameroun*, the oppressor, is born into and encouraged to perpetuate. The Anglophone-Cameroon (British Southern Cameroons) under such a circumstance suffers tremendously, just as the Irish have suffereed at the hands of the British in Ireland, in the literature of James Joyce, or the Algerians have suffered at the hands of the French in Algeria, in the literature of Albert Camus. Moreso, than about a racial division, all of these are about power. Frantz Fanon in *Black Skin White Masks* states "When the Negro makes contact with the white world, a cetain sensitizing action takes place. If his psychic structure is weak, one observes a collapse of the ego. The black man stops being an *actional* person" (154). This "sensitizing" is how western education transforms the elite black class in Africa into diminuitive black men. Remember, all who are quarreling now in The Cameroons have Black skin. Who is telling the truth and who is issuing press releases? This is what social scientist James C. Scott calls the divergence between "...the public transcript and the hidden transcript..." (x). The distance between the alleged superiors and the allegged inferiors—just as the distance between circular rings within the cross-section of an oak or maple tree determines its age—is in direct proportion to The Cameroons' fear and unhappiness.

Domination does not discriminate. Attempts to change the social order occur everywhere and are dealt with in similar fashion, even in allegedly democratic countries. The thinker, the critic and the author who scrutinize pervasive power are all dealt with harshly. *Nomads* chronicles this selfishnessness and recklessness on the part of the powers that be and connects these events to wherever else on the globe they are occurring. The government demands silence and often officially/publicly, gets it. This is not reality and this, in and of itself, is not the whole story. What I am interested in is the subtext; the personal and what is not publicly expressed. A scholar like Scott, in *Domination and the Art of Resistance: Hidden Transcripts*, calls this being onstage. When an actor plays his/her part, it is a well rehearased public performace. In other words what is said is pruned, edited, polished and carefully calibrated. What is said offstage is contrastingly direct and organically instinctive, hot and volcanic. Peasants, prisoners, and pensioners are never truly or completely welcome to enter the narrative. Since they do not truly have their say, and everything they do say must be behind the back of the goverment, the aforementioned bold voice must be tamped down, muffled, diseminated, divided and doled out slowly at enormous pyschological and spiritual cost (Scott Preface xii). The diminishment of the human being in Anglophone Cameroon, Liberia, Sierra Leone, the Republic of Congo or the Central African Republic is important and comparable to the frosty relationship between the poor and subservient who have no powere and the rich and successful who wield it. The Cameroons is but one particularly painful chapter in a colonial mystery book where everyone knows who done it. The African is divided and on the margins. Scott calls this "public theater" but the proscenium arch can be erected anywhere (11). This is attested by the February 15, 2014 publication of *The Economist*, in which we read:

> [In China there is] ...a wider clampdown on free-thinking intellectuals. In December Zhang Xuezhong, a legal scholar, was dismissed from East China University of Political Science and Law in Shanghai after he published a series of articles defending the provisions of China's constitution. State media called such views a Western plot to overthrow the party. Also in December, Chen Hongguo, an academic at the Northwest University of Politics and Law in Xi'an, resigned. The university had objected, among other things, to his holding salons that discussed texts by Western philosophers such as John Stuart Mill. (40)

This above excerpt appeared more than two years ago in February of 2014 in *The Economist* magazine and it is not the only article in the publication that would have fit the bill. The British publication's exploration of academic freedom, entitled "Don't think, just teach", deals with topics that are now forbidden in the Chinese classroom—just as English is now forbidden in the some official documents. For example, a student may only be privy to a transcript that if written in French. Modernization is a symbolic papering over of ideas that we have seen before as far back as the fifties and sixties. This stance, called "a great regression," has resulted in the worst form of surveillance (*The Economist*, February 15, 2014, p. 40). The actor or actors find themselves hemmed in on all sides, obligated to deliver a "canned drama" where they must repress what they wish to express. The performer, like the Anglophone citizen depicted in Emmanuel Fru Doh's *Nomads*, is there to be silenced, manipulated, controlled and put "on the clock". A programmed speaker whose position is as precarious as the position of the Chinese academics. This is, quite literally, a command performance without the benefit of tuxedos and evening gowns. They must cede. They must think only in the privacy of their own minds while publicly disavowing themselves. There are concurrences between Emmanuel Fru Doh's work and Francis Nyamnjoh's *Mind Searching*. The most fundamental question, namely what scholar in the world would object to the teaching of John Stuart Mill, is never asked, let alone answered.

What we have here is a cross-section of The Cameroons that is mismanaged, dispirited and split by the structure of human language. *Nomads* is an insightful study that not only tells us that the nation is spiritually dead, but why this is so, how this has purposely been perpetrated, and by whom. The linguistic or cultural preference for French creates social separation. It is a weapon against any celebration of diversity. What comes to mind here, in comparison, is how a surgeon cuts the sternum and then pries the chest apart to reveal the heart when conducting an open-heart surgery. All of this is done internally with cold steel and precise incisions. Emmanuel Fru Doh is using his text as a historical document to pinpoint these penetrations, to tell us when they happened. These are the stages of collapse. Bill F. Ndi, in a blurb for Peter Vuteh Vakunta's *Straddling the Mungo: A Book of Poems in English and French*, comments that the nature of bilingualism in The Cameroons as "…a system where abuse and dereliction of duty have been given the leeway to run roughshod"

(Vakunta). Despite being part of the Constitution, bilingualism could not possibly prevail. Even in 1961 this was more a representation of unrestrained political fancy. It was a sentiment that fulfilled psychological belief, but did not deliver.

Fifty years on, the West still plays an influential role in the development of Africa. The players act covertly, surreptitiously and underhandedly. Their performances are often difficult to understand or to connect to a broader global diplomatic economic dispensation. Such intervention from afar is never asked for, nor is it ever publicized. The long reach of colonialism, although it is unlikely that anyone will come out one time and say it, still muddies the waters and weighs down the African with anticipatory fears. The first divide between reality and what is purported is the terrible truth about humanity that "…most people can be at ease in a foreign country only when they are disparaging the inhabitants" (Orwell 115). George Orwell wrote this in the thirties, but it is no less true today. Derision is part of the equation and it does not matter what is written down on paper. None can legislate human decency. Subjects are universally disrespected and humiliated so that they can be controlled. The literature of Anglophone Cameroon, led by authors like Emmanuel Fru Doh, peels back the curtain to reveal the consequences; sterile, unthinking, and empty vessels who no longer have an identity and for whom public language has become inadequate, scanty, deficient, and without the spark or flare that makes life worth living.

The nation that was once called Southern Cameroons in the early sixties went from a neatly structured efficency of transparent checks and balances to a country of fraud and waste where there were simply too many parts. It sets Doh's "brain racing" as he and his contemporaries see a financially strapped nation spend money at an alarming rate on governmental products that already exist (2). I am talking about official letterhead staionery, seals, stamps, coins and new police uniforms. All of this while the people are hungry and dying of common cold. Cameroonian mainstream political institutions could not care less about the promise of a partnership between both British and French influences. The importance of such an agreement was forgotten before the ink dried upon the paper. Doh, just a child at the time, was understandably worried and sharp enough to see that the future was bleak for those who were not part of the Francophone dominated system of management. "Even then, that was the last straw: the ultimate nominal destination seemed to ignore the fact that there were two Cameroons in the beginning and that got me concerned" (Doh 3). The word "concerned" is an understatement. What I would like this reader to grab here is the state of silent panic on the part of every thinker. It is worse than having a bad plan. The government has no plan neither for the present nor the future (97). If at all any, that dominant and perpetual of oppression may sound implausible, but Emmanuel Fru Doh tells us that "[The] Cameroon[s] is a mess, so much so that one has, virtually, to bribe even in a bank to deposit one's money into one's account; it is that bad" (98). No one complains at these malpractices and for that very reason this may be the absolute nadir or bottom of a burreacratic pit because, like dominoes, the Anglophone "flips" and/or falls in line so easily without objection. Homi Bhaba would call this mimicry, the worst form of camouflage where the "...effect of mimicy on the authority of colonial discourse is profound and disturbing. For in 'normalizing' the colonial state or subject, the dream of post-Enlightenment civility alienates its own language of liberty and produces another knowledge of its norms" (Bhaba 123). Who needs to bark orders and make demands of an external culture when West Cameroonians will eagerly acquiese, capitulate, and do it for free? His memoir looks at moments of loss of force, significance, and power without any promise that any of these problems will ever be remedied.

Once foreigners and inhabitants begin to mix freely the platform that falls away under the feet of the English speaking Cameroonian is autonomy. In a direct affront to the mental health of this portion of the population, the individual is forced to carry special papers of identification. This happened to Gandhi in South Africa, to Jews in Austria and Germany in the years leading up to World War II and was equally proposed by American presidential candidate Donald Trump (Gillman and J. Rushing *Daily Mail* November 21, 2015). These are old ideas of how to watch people and they do not go away. Only the names of the participants, and perhaps the technology used to mark them, seems to change. By the time the seventies roll around, Emmanuel Fru Doh shows us another downward step in the history of the nation while everyone's collective memory continues to fade.

By this time, however, it was no longer the West Cameroonian Police Force; it had now been adulterated with *La République's* tactics like the arbitrary arrest of citizens in the name of keeping the peace. Why were we to carry identification papers on our persons at all times as if we were in a state of emergency?...This approach to life was far ahead of its time, even for today's dastardly hour when murderous men go around killing innocent people because of differences in the beliefs they hold" (Doh 10 -11).

This is another step away from the ideal. The nation is quickly becoming a place the author's parents and grandparents would not recognize. The level of repression, or cleansing, is ratcheted up and *Nomads* becomes a series of unpleasant vignettes where the very geographical movement of the people becomes more difficult. People are pushed arbitrarily to the periphery. Nations (all over the world) must deal with a subjugated populace. This is what happens when books are pulled off of shelves and bits of language become forbidden. A society collapses when the free exchange of information, money, and merit is limited and as the memoir continues each jolt is more devastating than the one that precedes it.

As of this writing, new evidence of repression enters the news cycle and Emmanuel Fru Doh, I am certain, would not want any of it to go unnoticed. The important intellectual step here is to connect such occurrences and isolate the thread that serves as a conduit between them. *The New York Times*, on May 23, 2016, reports on its front page, below the fold, that Sheldon Adelson's recent acquisition of the *Las Vegas Review-Journal* is going to forever change the newspaper's editorial latitude. An article about a legal suit involving Mr. Adelson was

> [...] cut in half for the print edition on orders from the top editor, and the reporters were disturbed by editorial interference...With newspapers struggling to survive, it is not uncommon for wealthy businessmen to step in and buy them— Jeff Bezos with *The Washington Post*, for instance, and John Henry with *The Boston Globe*. Each case presents potential conflicts in

covering the owner's businesses, as well as concerns that the owner might attempt to influence coverage (Sydney Ember *New York Times* A1).

This is also an attempt to stifle expression. Whatever one's thoughts are about the casino business, should a newspaper conduct its investigative journalism any differently based upon who owns the periodical? Surely this is a moral lesson indicating the wide chasm between the way things should be and the way they really are. What Mr. Adelson wants one would imagine, he gets. In the subject of sub-Saharan study, what Paul Biya wants, he gets. If he wants a Francophone government that barely tolerates the Anglophone—after all as President of The Cameroons he spends most of his time in France and Switzerland, not London—he becomes the erector of the wall. Who, indeed, will pay for its construction?

Identification papers and newspaper coverage are only two of the many mechanisms that can restrain individual expression and development. When something sensible does not happen or is not talked about it is always because "…the big people in Yaoundé do not want it" (Doh 64). Where does that leave the general population? They wind up uninformed and unoriginal and this situation is exacerbated if they cannot share stories with their mother and father about a simpler and more idealistic time in Africa. The worst form of repression or limitation is that a tacit linguistic war has ruined family life in The Cameroons. There is no respect. There is no closeness. There is no unity. Today a child is adrift in his own community without the cohesion of sense of belonging that Doh makes the most compelling element of his memoir. The word I like to use to describe this is rudderless, and it is no accident. One cannot tell me that this is not a punishment enacted with intent.

Deeply engrained family problems are created by these conflicts and these sociological difficulties, which are more debilitating than economic ones, were not there before the 1884 Berlin Conference regulated colonial expansion. Such familial discords bring with them a volatility that often reaches beyond family boundaries. Look at the way Doh describes the Cameroons he remembers as a boy. "Buea was alive and we were happy children growing up as people without all of these ridiculous divisions now characterizing the nation:

"anglo," "frog," "enemies in the house," "come-no-go," "graffi," "sawa," and so on. When a person is considered an alien in his own fatherland and by his own people, then it becomes obvious the degree of lawlessness that is prevailing" (Doh 59-60). The later part of this quotation shows the divisiveness that appeared and increased as he got older. He continues "…we were kids growing up, and life was fun and we loved it" (Doh 60). All that was about to change and this is not the result of bad luck or an act of God. As a consequence of mainly "alien values" hierarchy had disappeared from the family, older siblings were less willing to assist their parents in the raising of their younger brothers and sisters, and these relationships became more difficult, with more fractures and more insults (Doh 59). Doh's unhappiness at what has happened is not at the physical arrival of the British and the French, but that this arrival has altered the unseen or invisible connective tissue that has supported and kept his people together.

When a society is repressed each individual is, or appears, isolated. Nothing isolates people more than obstructed, interrupted and controlled information. The establishment-culture did not have the same problems it has had since Southern Cameroons and *La République du Cameroun* were linked together. Things were transparent and families benefited from this transparency. Their thinking was clearer and their obstacles—there are always obstacles—could be planned for. Problems could be anticipated, bills could be paid and people could enjoy each other. Emmanuel Fru Doh reminds his reader of this high point in his hometown, and home country, but the tenor or spirit or uplift has been broken. *Nomads* sounds like a blues song telling of heartbreak. It is a look back at a special period of time, like one's youth, that can never be returned to except in the realm of the imagination. It is a story that the teller cannot quite get over no matter how painful. It always keeps pulling you back.

The famous linguist Noam Chomsky says, "If you don't like what someone has to say, argue with them" (Web.) Composing and publishing a book like *Nomads* may be the only way an author like Emmanuel Fru Doh may be able to mount an argument against the powers that be. If he spoke out loud in Yaoundé, where he once taught African Literature, he would be imprisoned, or worse. It has been nearly twenty years since Emmanuel Fru Doh taught in The

Cameroons and one does not need to be a crime-solving detective to figure out why. As things are he teaches at Century College in White Bear Lake, Minnesota, seven thousand miles from home. In such a politically charged environment as The Cameroons it is simply not possible to express oneself. He has instead agreed to write from afar, lobbing his text over the wall so that people at home may have their faint recollections secretly recharged, energized, and refurbished. Surely being a productive academic expatriate in the United States is preferable to living in a nation where the presidential election continues to be stolen from its rightful owners. John Fru Ndi should have been at one point now be the rightful President of The Cameroons, but that never was reality.

On the theme of theft, earlier this month on May 12, 2016, roughly one week after World Press Freedom Day, the Prime Minister of The Cameroons, Philomen Yang, confiscated a reporters' journalistic equipment. "CRTV reporter Teke Julius was covering a visit by Prime Minister Philomen Yang to a stadium construction site when reporters say Yang personally grabbed Julius' equipment and ordered it destroyed. Julius was then detained by the police for several hours" (Web. June 22, 2016). As a consequence, other journalists have vowed to boycott and blackout any news event involving the Prime Minister. This contentious streak involving authorities and the press is commonplace. It happened in the America that banned James Joyce's *Ulysses* in the 1920's and burned copies of the novel at the behest of the postal authorities. It happened during the Red Scare of the 1950's. It happened in the China of Mao Tse-tung and his successors, and it is happening in The Cameroons despite "independence" and protests to the contrary. A preoccupation with "…a comatose regime that had degenerated into a liability of the proletariat…" has stopped its own forward progress and endangered the mental health of the population, causing Emmanuel Fru Doh to produce such a justifiably venom filled book (108). The school "'…better than the cannon it made conquest permanent. The cannon compels the body and the school bewitches the soul'" (Ngugi 21). Life is out of balance and no longer makes sense. There is no oasis of tranquility except in the comforting illusion of one's mind.

Works Cited

Bhaba, Homi. *The Location of Culture.* Routledge Classics, 2004.

Dickens, Charles. *A Tale of Two Cities.* Dover, 2011.

"Don't Think, Just Teach: The party purges free thinkers but can it contain free thinking?" *The Economist.* 15 February 2014. <www.economist.com/news/china/21596571-party-purges-free-thinkers-can-it-contain-free-thinking-dont-think-just-teach>. 22 June 2016.

Ember, Sydney. "Adelson's Era: Do Billions Erode Press Freedom?" *The New York Times* 23 May 2016, natl. ed. A1+.

Fanon, Frantz. *Black Skin, White Masks.* Grove P, 1967.

Gillman, Ollie, and J. Taylor Rushing. "Pro-refugee Protest are Staged across the Nation amid Outrage at Trump for Agreeing with 'Nazi-like' Plan to Make US Muslims Register." *Mail Online.* Associated Newspaper, 21 Nov. 2015. <www.dailymail.co.uk/news/article-3328051/Pro-refugee-protests-nation-Donald-Trump-s-Nazi-plan-register-Muslims-Ben-Carson-call-people-fleeing-Syria-rabid-dogs.html>. 25 June 2016.

Kindzeka, Moki Jindzeka. "Cameroon Journalists Boycott Prime Minister Coverage" *Voice of America* 12 May 2016. <www.voanews.com/content/cameroon-journalists-boycott-prime-minister-coverage/3328560.html>. Accessed 25 June 2016.

Levine, Lawrence W. *Black Culture and Black Consciousness: African-American Thought From Slavery to Freedom.* Oxford UP, 1977.

"Noam Chomsky." BrainyQuote.com. Xplore Inc, 2016. www.brainyquote.com/quotes/quotes/n/noamchomsk447278.html Accessed 28 June 2016.

Nyamnjoh, Francis B. "Commentary: Cameroon: A Country United by Ethnic Ambition and Difference." *African Affairs* 98.390 (1999): 101-18.

_____. "Fiction and Reality of mobility in Africa." In *Citizenship Studies* 17.6-7 (2013): 653-80. *Taylor and Francis Online.* Routeledge, 9 Nov. 2013.

<www.tandfonline.com/doi/abs/10.1080/13621025.2013.834121>. Accessed 28 June 2016.

Nyamnjoh, Francis B. *Mind Searching*. Langaa RPCIG, 2007.

Orwell, George. *Burmese Days*. Heritage, 2006.

Scott, James C. *Domination and the Art of Resistance: Hidden Transcripts*. Yale UP. 1990.

Stelter, Briand and Ashley Fantz. "Jailed Al Jazeera journalists convicted in Egypt." *CNN World* 24 June 2014. www.cnn.com/2014/06/23/world/meast/egypt-al-jazeera-journalists-court/index.html Accessed 22 June 2016.

Vakunta, Peter W. *Straddling the Mungo: A Book of Poems in English and French*. Langaa RPCIG, 2009.

wa Thiong'o, Ngugi. *Something Torn and New: An African Renaissance*. Civitas, 2009.

Warner, Martin, *The Aesthetics of Argument* Oxford UP, 2016.

Chapter 10

Francis B. Nyamnjoh's *A Nose for Money:* Airing Devoiced Thoughts.

Bill F. Ndi

Airing one's thoughts in a context which guarantees freedom of speech and thoughts requires just the ability to speak or write to be forthright. However, in a context marked by repression and oppression, being forthright demands more than just the ability to speak and write. Also, mentioning repression and oppression entails that those caught in their web would undoubtedly seek avenues to air out their discontent in order to maintain their moral and psychological equilibrium. As a result, their subversion, their rebellion and their refusal to be mute in the face of wanton abuse of authority and power, would call for mechanisms which transcend basic language usage in speech and writing for practical purposes and intents. It is in this guise that exploring Francis B. Nyamnjoh's *A Nose for Money,* the present chapter would elucidate the *prison*, Land of Mimbo, in which nationals are trapped in a hapless condition that compels the writer, Francis B. Nyamnjoh, to subvert language in rebellion against the crushing weight of oppression or to reject the pain and sufferings brought about upon his people by the curtailing of basic freedoms. In the stead of the voice and thoughts of his people, the writer through this process not only shapes his own identity as a committed writer but also those of his fellow human beings asking for nothing more than freedom from constraints that drive them to the verge of insanity. On this note, how does the writer take up a fight that is another person's? How effective is the writer's fight for a cause from which the only benefit he reaps is mental or psychological satisfaction? Again, how do the repressed masses maintain their sanity? And finally, what tools do writers use to avoid falling prey to the repressive machine put in place by corrupt politicians and nitwitted leaders? Nyamnjoh depicts an unsettling clime, in which repression, oppression, and corruption are the order of the day. He paints a sordid tableau of the land of Mimbo, though not devoid of humor, with the sole goal of redressing the ills brought about by corrupt political, judicial, social, cultural, commercial, and economic practices. Such malpractices constitute the source of inspiration as well as the bricks with which are constructed the walls of Nyamnjoh's story, one in which he gives free rein to his repressed thoughts to resound louder than that of an authorized and paid praise singer or panegyrist.

Nyamnjoh's storyline is centered on the character of Prospère, a semi-literate Mimbolander whose wayward lifestyle takes him from poverty to prosperity. He is a true clone of the national on-goings in the land of Mimbo i.e. land of alcoholic beverages. This is Nyamnjoh's catchword for *La République du Cameroun*. It is true Mimboland could represent any post-colonial nation in Africa. Drawing upon onomastics, Nyamnjoh opens *A Nose for Money* with the protagonist's name: Prospère. By so doing, Nyamnjoh, like a practitioner of fine art, paints shades and hues of what the ordinary citizen would deem too dangerous to voice. This devoiced thought serves the writer as a *modus operandi* and a *modus Vivendi* and also sets the tone for Nyamnjoh's acerbic satire and irony which spice the work from start to finish. It is akin to what Alastair Fowler, in discussing Carlyle's satire and vilifying journalism aimed at the nation's masochism, points out. He makes known that Carlyle uses irony as "self protection". He further highlights that this "is secondary to his determined effort to get beyond the 'clothes' of institutions – beyond the nation's psychological defences[sic]" (300). Thus, irony, in Nyamnjoh's work, becomes both the engine and the driver of the story. For starters, Prospère, French for prosper, becomes Nyamnjoh's metaphor for everything that represents the antinomy of any form of prosperity or flourishing. This antinomic use of words, values, characters, and places becomes a shield screening such writer—readily styled by the powers that be as subversive—from the dangerous muzzle put in place to check not only people's thoughts but anything that is voiced against the corrupt who wield power. It is no surprise that one of the earliest reviewers of *A Nose for Money*, Primus Tazanu, highlights that

A Nose for Money is a synopsis of the lifestyles and experiences of the power drunk elite attached to the present political leadership in the land of Mimbo. It is a courageous book, a piece of venom calmly delivered in sugar cubes. With deep patriotism, strong sense of humour[sic] and exceptional talent, Nyamnjoh plunges very deep into the socio-economic and political world of Mimboland, revealing a festive world of deceit, opportunism, infidelity, insecurity, ignorance and a perfectly organised[sic] statecraft based on theft, insider-insider trading and secrecy. (Tezanu, "Africa's Power Elite…" WEB).

The aforementioned first word viz. Prospère, while setting the tone, also invokes and alludes to Shakespeare's Prospero. Like Shakespeare's Prospero who is overindulged in his quest for knowledge, Nyamnjoh's Prospère relentlessly pursues carnal and material pleasures while neglecting the *maladies* or unseen consequences such pleasures bring in their train. Such pursuit and its consequences become the source of his final tragedy. Prospère's name, in conjunction with the ensuing sentence, "Prospère pulled to a stop" (3), characterize and universalize *A Nose for Money*. The stop, to which he pulls, marks an end to a long and tedious crossing. The suddenness of this stop foreshadows the impending drama and tragedy that crowns the "festive world of deceit, opportunism, infidelity, insecurity, ignorance and a perfectly organised[sic] statecraft based on theft, insider-insider trading and secrecy" in the end of the novel (Tezanu, "Africa's Power Elite…").

In Mimboland, the trend to accumulate wealth is fraught with every crookish means possible and imaginable. It is but normal that Prospère, as well as the Honorable Minister, Matiba, should amass their riches through what one can, only to be polite, style as dubious means and circumstances. Nyamnjoh's castigation of this corrupt system through Prospère's tale becomes a calculated means of airing out unwanted views against what Ndi in *Mishaps and other poems* labels "state orchestrated perjury" (32), nepotism, and favoritism. Prospère's move to Nyamandem, the capital city, is to seek help from his tribesman who would facilitate the banking of his ill-gotten wealth without arousing suspicion. This is the practice of tribalism or so to speak an insidious form of primal racism. Giving epithets and accolades such as "Honourable" [sic] to the minister, Matiba, makes the reader to read in this character all else but honor. Such is Nyamnjoh's grounding of the characterization of Matiba into satire. He is the laughing stock of what honorables are. Besides, Nyamnjoh's choice of the Ministry headed by Matiba's hints at the writer's own desire to point out education and healthcare as two sectors which, if affected by the blatant and massive corruption running on the wheels of primitive racism, would indicate how deeply the gangrene of the said corruption has eaten into the fabric of the system. This position, Nyamnjoh argues, in his scholarly writing, along similar lines with Bourdieu that,

> the production, positioning and consumption of knowledge is far from a neutral, objective and disinterested process... mediated by hierarchies of humanity and human agency imposed by particular relations of power. (qtd. in "Potted Plants in Greenhouses").

Matiba is thus presented as an individual and or a child who would simply believe any tale told him. He does not verify the veracity of Prospère's tale about the origin of his wealth. Matiba is a symbolic representation of the state of the nation's education and health. Matiba occupies functions in the land that should reflect the two most important sectors on which the nation must rely for its smooth running as well as its future. His corrupt wheeling and dealings replicate the worst a nation has to offer and accounts for Nyamnjoh leaving the reader amidst the chaos lived by Matiba as well as all the other characters in the novel. The Prospère-Matiba duo exposes a journey into the heart of a system that, like the colonial system before independence, "represses where it should foster, tames instead of inspiring and enervates rather than strengthens" (qtd. in "Potted Plants in Greenhouses"). Such a system requires an expedient turn of the tide of events to bring about the harmony that the writer deems worthy of Mimbolanders whose creed of parvenus shamelessly bathe in a pool of sham and dishonesty. They have their priorities in reverse order. Nyamnjoh chastises such misplacements of priorities in his earlier novel, *Mind Searching* and seem to suggest just what he is putting to practice in *A Nose for Money*. In *Mind*

Searching he writes: "maybe he is one of those learned men who wrongly believe that western education is a prerequisite to good leadership. [...] Western education is the best means to become an academic simpleton, and a contextual misfit" (73). Matiba fits this mold perfectly well. With a minister of education like Matiba, only semi-literate individuals and contextual misfits like Prospère make it; for the system has an aversion for those who are well-educated, politically, socially, and morally alert.

Nyamnjoh, like most African writers, is fully aware that censorship of literary works has never been total but that it randomly targets individual writers whose works offend individuals in positions of power (Larson 121). Also, he is not blind to the punishment normally meted on any who would be brave enough to even attempt to out-smart, out-mouth or foul mouth the large number of corrupt Mimboland politicians. He uses the trial of Gaston Abanda to inform the reader of the judgment that any would get for dragging the President's name in the mud: "… twenty-five years, which is what you get for dragging the President's name in the mud" (135). Such politicians have institutionalized punitive measures, randomly targeting individual writers who offend them (Larson 121). Over and above, Nyamnjoh's scholarly work *Africa's Media: Democracy and the Politics of Belonging* explores the difficulties under which most African writers and media workers labor to carry out the activity and supports it with detailed examples from *La République du Cameroun,* his model for Mimboland. He thus has to devise means by which to craft his art or write within and against the dominant corrupt culture (Murphy 376). In his very first novel, an ethnographic novel, *Mind Searching,* Nyamnjoh displays his understanding of the repressive socio-cultural and political milieu from which he hails and intimates through a rhetorical question that "[c]ould I guess that in a highly repressive society, people think a lot, because thoughts happen to be the only safe way by which they can vent their frustrations and dissatisfaction with the authorities in place?" (68). This rhetorical question frees the author from the blame of making a declaration against any authority. While serving the purpose of shielding himself from any form of blame or the epidemic of repressive violence, Nyamnjoh allows his question to come across as a statement from an author who practices, or at least, is willing to practice that which he interrogates. This is comforted by James C. Scott's assertion that:

> As a formal matter, subordinate groups in these forms of domination have no political or civil rights ... The ideologies justifying domination of this kind include formal assumptions about inferiority and superiority which, in turn, find expression in certain rituals or etiquette regulating public contact between strata. (x-xi)

Consequently, Nyamnjoh, in his way to regulate public contact between strata, skillfully draws a cast of characters, depicts a setting as well as he employs various literary devices ranging from irony to euphemism with the overall effect of wry humor that would make an inattentive reader to laugh and laugh out his/her brains. It is the subtle technique of having the Cameroonian politician to laugh at his own foible, unconscious of the fact that he is the target of the ridiculousness therein upheld. It might be argued that the present breed of writers from the British Southern Cameroons use the same literary tradition as writers from other clime and time. Nonetheless, the ways in which they address the culprits and having these culprits blind to the fact that as they laugh at the ridiculousness of the situation exposed in their works, they are at the same time laughing at themselves, leave the critic with only few options amongst which a translation of novel uses of literary devices.

Nyamnjoh, in *A Nose for Money,* chooses to psychoanalyze not the victims of oppression but the oppressors. Instead of depicting the oppressed as victims and the oppressors as the all too powerful and unbeatable monsters, he resorts to casting the latter as true objects of the "laughing cry" at best and, at worst, objects of pity in the height of their tragedy. Nyamnjoh tightens the screws of oppression in this tragic circumstance by showing how family, the only source of comfort when all else is lost, turns out to be the very trigger for a disturbing and incomprehensible repression that death, and only death alone, can put an end to. Does this mean, for this life loving author, a tragic and pessimistic end for his beloved Mimboland? Or is he just playing by the rule highlighted by James C. Scott when he states that:

[...] slaves and serfs dare not contest the terms of their subordination openly. Behind the scenes though, they are likely to create and defend a social space in which offstage dissent to the official transcript of power relations is voiced. ... this social space takes or the specific content of dissent ... are unique as the particular culture and history of the actors in question require (x).

A Nose for Money is informed by both passion and commitment to the need for a vigorous and fundamental change that he so desires in the land of Mimbo. The end of the novel marks Prospère's end. Getting rid of Prospère, the fruit and product of a system that bars truth from being voiced, in the end is a subtle but much needed and refreshing way Nyamnjoh, as a writer, uses to take the reader on the path of that which has to be done for any real change to be effective in this land of Mimbo. Prospère, the opportunist, who would love to oppress the masses, and most especially women, as an integral part of the system rids himself of life by taking away his own life. In all, Prospère would have preferred the semblance of peace and harmony in which he would not "have others dictate what was good for him – at least, not when he could help it. When he made up his mind about something, he was bent on seeing it through" (56). Yet, when the truth hits him on the face like a lightning bolt, his pride, that has hitherto foreshadowed this moment, leads to his tragic fall. Prospère, who from the very beginning has been psycho-analyzed and portrayed in the light of a determined tyrant who would completely refuse to act as expected when he catches his wife cheating with a soldier, is now left to face the consequence of his obstinate and autocratic rule. In spite of advice from well-meaning friends, the narrator tells us he would decide against all odds:

> But he wasn't the sort of man to have others dictate what was good for him – at least, not when he could help it. When he made up his mind about something, he was bent on seeing it through. Few could dissuade him, perhaps the effect of the inadequate discipline and socialisation[sic] he received from his parents as a child. (156)

No matter how one would like to read the last sentence in the above quote, Nyamnjoh clearly makes a shift from novels published pre-independence and just immediately after independence. Pre- and post-independence works of art, Palmer contends, were "designed to express the strength, validity, and beauty of African life and culture" (ix). In *A Nose for Money,* Nyamnjoh is more concerned and inspired by the chaotic political, educational, social and economic climate in Mimboland post-independence. He leaves the reader with the notion that the inadequacies of colonial discipline and socialization account for such tyrannical behavior preponderant in the post-colonial African continent in general and The Cameroons in particular.

The setting casts the action and characters representation as caught in the grip of a metaphorical prison in which both the jailed and jailor are prisoners of different echelons. This brings to mind the now proverbial age old philosophical debate of the interdependency of slave and slave master. With a careful choice of character and profession for each, Nyamnjoh warrants his protagonist, Prospère, vertical, horizontal, and spatio-temporal movements. If one were to go by Prospère's, he is a driver. He starts off delivering alcohol to West Mimboland. Nyamnjoh exploits this driver's naiveté and ignorance to expose, through his horizontal, upward-downward and spatio-temporal movements, the scheming, machinations and exploitative machinery of the Mimboland government and its agents. It is through Prospère's eyes that the very first chapter of the novel brings to light the multiple ills, chaos, confusions, frustrations, and impending doom that loom over Mimboland. As a driver, his mobility depends on factors he scarcely has control over. It is in this guise that the narrator informs of the state of the roads during the rainy season. He spells out that "[i]t was always a nightmare, particularly for truckers like him" (3). Besides, Prospère's failure to heed to his wife's warning of an imminent downpour becomes an ominous sign of terrible things to come as along he is always forewarned yet ends up following the wrong path and regretting afterwards. "I'll pay greater attention to what she says next time," he muttered. Also, Rose's dissatisfaction with her husband's profession which she derisively qualifies as one which entails being "busy distributing drunkenness" (4) is suggestive of the writer's attitude towards the excessive use of alcohol in The Cameroons by politicians to numb the brains of any who would be critical of the pervasive bad governance therein.

The narrator tells the reader, in his probe into Prospère's mind, of the daily toils, travails, and tribulations of those "downtrodden or those rejected by city's promises" (7). He also shows that, in spite of their status of downtrodden these daring young men risk their lives daily in providing "Good Samaritan Services" (7). Nyamnjoh points out through this irony of situation how, through the process of hegemonization and power structuring, politicians have institutionalized and endorsed the ills and activities of these thieves, shoplifters, and burglars cum hawkers. The said activities become a no-go-area. Even though, to Propère, the reason for noninterference in the activities of the "sauveteurs" is fear of the repeat of history especially that of a 1940 massive strike that had seriously threatened French Colonialism and the narrator is quick to draw attention to the fact that,

> [w]hat Prospère didn't know was that the present government of Mimboland had decided never to touch the hawkers for another reason entirely. They saw hawking as a useful political weapon, not only because hawkers provided for the poor of the city, but also especially because their daily efforts to get by distracted and preoccupied the rich with matters of personal security (7).

This chaos as well as disorderliness becomes a manifestation of the political ill-will that leaves both poor and rich no real possibility of giving the government any trouble that could destabilize political misrule. Besides, a transliteration of the word "sauveteurs" from the French is lifeguard and reinforces the Nyamnjoh's subtle message of using this creed of unregulated merchants cum thugs as a rampart.

It is during Prospère's journey from rags to riches and encounter with the *Honourable* [sic] (emphasis mine) Matiba that he finally understands what, at the beginning of his stay in Nyamandem, was incomprehensible to him. In the course of this journey the reader has a clean sweep of Mimboland's "crimescape" through the eyes of a character whose fluidity of movement permits him to navigate through space and time as well as upward and downward the social ladder. Prospère's take on events at the beginning of the novel translates into that of ordinary folks whose dreams and aspirations like his can only come to fruition upon meeting with one of the "big wigs" in high office and upon their understanding of the guiding philosophy serving as an operating system and a lifestyle. Mimbolanders view themselves as victims in the "atmosphere of corruption and thirst for money..." (132) and would later understand that the normal route leading to successful business with the public service is indubitably informed by Prospère's example, who with "little left...by way of alternatives" (133) is

> [u]nable to do otherwise, and anxious to avoid blackmail of any kind, Prospère had allowed the goat to eat where it was tethered. They had become friends, and henceforth Matiba had tipped him off about this or that government contract and had provided him with vital insider information.... (170)

Matiba draws on his position as a government minister with knowledge of the prevalent corrupt business practices and the relationships successful businesses have with the government to caution Prospère on the inevitability of its blessings and assistance for any business in Mimboland to succeed.

It is thus implicit that, without government blessing, no businessman would succeed. So, what is the fate that would befall a writer who is out of favor with the government? This sneaky give and take exercise is a compelling reality Mimbolanders have to live with. Yet, in an ironic twist, Nyamnjoh has Matiba, confounding his belonging to the Freemasonry with the concept of a mason or builder. In actuality, Mimboland politicians, like those of The Cameroons, are nation wreckers. From the President through Ngomnsong to Matiba, the revolutionary who betrays the revolution for "the easy virtues of the stomach", it is evident that conceiving these "hungry vultures" as nation builders, borders on outright hypocrisy and or blatant lie. It is in this guise that the narrator reminds the reader that Matiba upon closing his deal with Prospère would, "now pay undivided attention to politics and nation tinkering" (133). This is clearly not the same as working in the interest of nation building. Prospère acquiesces many years after his initial encounter with Matiba. After having been tipped off on government contracts and after having had vital insider information provided him, all of these helped to propel him to the height of his wealth. It is in this vein that the author writes: "[t]hat's what allowing a goat to eat where it is tethered means," Prospère smiled; glad he hadn't learned it a minute too late" (170). Nonetheless, what Prospère seems to be comfortable with is exactly what the writer seems to intimate Mimbolanders ought to castigate and do away with. He has his protagonist state that: "[i]t pays to let a goat eat in peace, but it does you no good to try to chase it off" (170). Again, with Prospère's understanding of the Mimboland's governing logic, Nyamnjoh's character naming irony becomes even more evident for being tethered entails even Prospère's name or the idea of his name is holding him back just like everything else in Mimboland does tie people down.

To corroborate this authorial castigation, he makes it clear in an irony which draws attention to the fact that the result of Prospère's wealth is greeted by ugliness proportionate to his excessive richness. The narrator catches a glimpse of Prospère and reproduces a spiteful physical and a psychological portrait of him. Many years after he has been in the ugly business of "theft, insider-insider trading and secrecy," the author exposes the transformation so far undergone. It is an arresting moment of the physical mirroring the psychological and moral ugliness of the establishment debunked in *A Nose for Money*. That is why the reader comes across the following lines:

> Many years after establishing his own businesses, Prospère had lost the lean agile figure that used to make women call him handsome. Then they used to say he lacked only money to make himself a complete charmer. What an irony that his good looks should flee now that there was money in abundance to spend on the women! He would have liked to know that women could still love him because he was handsome, not only because he had a fat wallet (170).

With the beauty gone, and in spite of the availability of the complement missing at the beginning, i.e. money, the excessive fatness of the wallet replicating Prospère's physical fatness becomes the object of ridicule for the writer. Besides, Tezanu states:

> The interesting thing about the book is that it volunteers and sacrifices on behalf of the people, to act as a spy into the lives of politicians and their cronies. They deeply have the knowledge that their lifestyles may be provoking jealousy and spite from the populace (Tezanu, "Africa's Power Elite..." WEB).

This situational logic is akin to James C. Scott's in his attempt to make sense of class relations in a Malay village in which he highlights a certain contradiction in the kind of situational logic in that context. He makes evident that by confining his study to class relations alone:

> [i]t seemed the poor sang one tune when they were in the presence of the rich and another when they were among the poor. The rich too spoke one way to the poor and another among themselves. These were the grossest distinctions; many finer distinctions were discernible depending on the exact composition of the group talking and, of course, the issue in question. (ix)

The setting of the novel also expresses a thorny issue from the author's land of birth, The Cameroons: a phony union between East and West Cameroons on the eve of the independence of West Cameroon AKA British Southern Cameroons. Like modern day The Cameroons, Mimboland is a unitary state made up of East and West Mimboland. In situating the novel in Mimboland, Nyamnjoh carefully brings in not only the geographical divide but the prevailing linguistic divide and socio-political polarization between East and West Mimboland. The relationship between these two regions is not based on any concrete or loving relations between two formerly colonized peoples who share the desire to be together. When the reader comes across Prospère for the first time, it is in his stead as a delivery truck driver shuttling between East and West Mimboland. He establishes the bases of the relation between East and West Mimboland as he works for Mimboland Brewery Company (MBC). He only goes to West Mimboland to distribute and sell "drunkenness" to West Mimbolanders as Nyamnjoh's mouth piece,

Rose would have it. This subtle statement reveals the phony state of the union between the two Mimbolands. West Mimboland is a market for MBC based in East Mimboland. In this union, it is not hard to conjecture that West Mimbolanders are left in a perpetual state of stupor and confusion. West Mimboland becomes an excuse for crooks, thugs, and thieves as well as the ilk of the President, Mr. Ngomnsong, Gaston Abanda, Matiba and Prospère whose sources of riches as well as moral rectitude are not only questionable but dubious. Prospère uses this part of the country to justify the origin of their ill-gotten wealth. Even when the main proprietor of MBC, Gaston Abanda, is involved in a scam gone bad, Prospère meets Dieudonné in a bar where they carry out a conversation on the days happening in Sawang. Prospère chooses to hide his ignorance of what is in the newspaper by telling Dieudonné he "… was away in West Mimboland distributing beer" (61). Seemingly, this is to suggest that real news never reaches this part of the world.

The sour state of the union of The Cameroons is also reflected through all other forms of union apparent in the novel. The various marriages contracted and consummated are a reflection of a total sham and scam. The only real thing linking West and East Mimboland is the beer that Prospère delivers. West Mimboland seems to be left in oblivion and seems to serve the purpose of justifying anything from ignorance to the source of ill-gotten wealth of the rich East Mimbolanders. Mimboland's President is not only married to 4 wives, but he has mistresses everywhere in the nation! No doubt he adores people with Ngomnsong's stamina. Matiba, an ex-seminarian, is married to a wife never introduced to the reader, yet we know Marie-Claire is not only his secretary but his mistress with whom he hangs out. Going by Prospère's, as mentioned earlier, his fluidity warrants him to cross from one side of Mimboland into the other as well as his movement up and down the socio-political ladder. His relationships with women, as well as marriages from the first to the last, unveil themselves in the end as a real farce and calculated attempt at subverting the institution of marriage whose goal is to bring into a union, two loving individuals to live as one until death do them part.

Prospère's series of sham relationships and marriages is a glaring reflection of the contract of union between East and West

Mimboland. The novel comes out forcefully to reveal the questionable and inauthentic basis for any such union that ever was. After Prospère's first divorce with Rose, he begins his amorous adventures, which are plagued with a series of *maladies d'amour*, in the base neighborhood of Old Belle. He gravitates around the cheapest sex workers and newcomers to the city before venturing with one of the "top prostitutes" who "were patronised[sic] by the top men in society" (25). Upon arriving in Nyamandem, he has a fling with Matiba's secretary, Marie-Claire who would then afterwards "hook him up" with Charlotte, Prospère's first wife to be.

Nyamnjoh continues to cast marriage as a hollow sham through one of his most reprehensible characters, Fithang. After faking his way into marriage, he would not attend to any of the basic needs of his wife and children yet would beat them up if they dared to complain. This is the example that Prospère uses to legitimize his cruelty, insensitiveness, and meanness to women, be they girlfriends or prostitutes. However, Nyamnjoh unveils the fate that awaited Fithang in his recklessness (20). When he wakes up to calling his wife, "my darling," it is too late. Yet, without preaching, the appeal of this story to Prospère becomes the author's maneuvering gear to ready the reader for the drama to unfold in the end of the plot. Having learned from his boss, Fithang, Prospère manipulates women for his own gain (21). However, when he makes the mistake of approaching a "high class" prostitute, he receives the rebuke of his life. This prostitute with a dismissive, "I am not your type" (*25*) then goes on to telling Prospère how she has slept with dignitaries who have given her much more money than Prospère can afford.

In voicing the pitiful and unpalatable state of the Mimboland woman, Nyamnjoh skillfully steers clear of provoking the ire of many a feminist reader by not out rightly criticizing what most readers would hastily take for woman's involvement in her own plight and the ensuing stereotypes of women's philandering. In the cast of Prospère's wives, especially the first two whom Nyamnjoh portrays in the light of women enjoying the exploits of woman's liberation, their sexual libertinage becomes a money extorting venture. Is this a way for the author to question the essence of the feminist rebellion which has ever since been misconstrued even by women themselves? The women in Nyamnjoh's *A Nose for Money*, from every indication, form what Sean P. Hier, while discussing "sex as a social category," in his introduction to "Feminist Social Thought," dubs "a distinctive social group" (213). And this is much to the dismay of the tragic figure of Prospère at the end of his saga. This end immediately brings to mind the proverbial "had I known always comes last." Prospère's desired role for his wives all along has been for him to stage-manage them to live in his shadows, a desire which turns out to be all else but the fact that one can ascribe to what feminine nature is (Hier 213). However, in multiplying his marriages, Prospère hopes to pit each wife against the other. This fails as the wives come to an understanding of their collective position as women in Mimboland's social and political ruling relations and form instead an alliance. They come together and plot against their husband as a result of their common experience of Mimboland social oppression. By so doing, they reject Mimboland's education "that transforms people into unthinking zombies, kill their sociality, and numb their humanity even for their own children can hardly be relevant to social reproduction, let alone social transformation" (qtd. in "Potted Plants in Greenhouses"). Their plot is born of an interest in "eradicating or subverting" Mimboland's ascribed women's role (Hier 208). Men like Prospère, Matiba, Fithang, etc. may think they are running the show but how sadly mistaken are they for it is a woman's world!

Nyamnjoh brings the women's movement in the fictional land of Mimbo to trial. Even though these women have chosen libertinage over morality and virtue as well as they have had their way with Prospère whose impulses would have him oppress and oppress the world around him, their achievements have been geared towards an understanding of subjugation ever calling for a change. Their attempt at fighting such oppression is hinged on an equally immoral act which the writer - without starting a fight - simply brings up by getting these women to the court of Ngek, "a *Mungang man* that cures all kinds of illnesses" (182). He would have them confess their mischievous deeds. This act is a savvy way for the author, upon critically examining every aspect of his society, to point out how mistakes are made one after the other and even, at times, with the best intentions, the results always ends like Prospère's story. It is common knowledge that two wrongs never make a right. Nyamnjoh sets the moment of truth in *A Nose for Money* when the women have to admit that all along they have played the dirty game played by everyone who succeeds in Mimboland. It is no coincidence that the *Mungang man* points out to Prospère, in talking about Monique, the barren wife, now dead, that "her hands be free from dirty" (198). This echoes an earlier comment by the narrator who, talking of Prospère overbearing powers, indicates that in case he wanted to rid himself of any of his wives no judge in the country would rule against him for "he was a powerful man, and there was no court in the land that would decide against him in the event of divorce" (172). So, Mimboland is a place where the honest and law abiding are doomed to die while the dishonest crooks survive. Again, only the rich, having the right like Prospère, can bulldoze their way into the exclusive class of privileged "people whose nostrils and ears were conditioned to pick up only the smell and sound of waded notes" (157). Nyamnjoh, uses his diviners, Ngek, as well as Seng to penetrate the naked truth in Mimboland where the women like the men express total disinclination to love seriously. The presence of these clairvoyants seems to bolster Nyamnjoh's scholarly position vis-à-vis dominant Western epistemologies as opposed to African endogenous ones. They construct and voice thoughts about the unthinkable in a context which suffocates. They are brought in to resolve matters which a court run by corrupt judges cannot. They do not need to be bribed to have the truth or lie revealed.

Mimboland like *La République du Cameroun* has the most well-developed repressive system that can only be compared to the "rain clouds... circling the sun..." and "the heavens rumbling like a starving stomach" (3). This repressive system symbolized by the clouds foretells nothing good nor is the rumbling echoing the pangs of hunger the multitude are left with. Here, Nyamnjoh wraps his ominous signs of things to come in the rain clouds as well as the rumbling of the heavens. And this makes of the expression, "Mimboland/The Cameroons repression" a well suited prosaicism. Also, he carries on with a comparison that makes of the roads in Sawang more congested than a rubber plantation and only falls short of qualifying the roads a jungle. All the novelistic spaces, especially urban, repress and stifle rather than enables. This aspect of the novel brings to mind James C. Scotts' daring generalization on the disparity in power between dominant and subordinate. He claims that "the more the disparity… the more the public transcript of subordinates will take on a stereotyped, ritualistic cast. In other words, the more menacing the power, the thicker the mask" (3). Moreover, the lawlessness that reigns on the roads, for "seven out of every ten drivers on the road at the time knew next to nothing about the Highway Code…"(4), does nothing to help the repression. The combination of car infection and the potholes makes movement in Sawang a total nightmare. The road thus becomes Nyamnjoh's symbol for the "hard road to travel" in the country where even the road conditions can only be compared to those of the Gulag or the lower levels of Dante's *Inferno*. His other works, *The Travails of Dieudonné* & *Souls Forgotten* share this common trope of the road oppressing when and where reprieve is expected even from the environment. Therefore, how does one progress in this kind of a place?

In this context, Nyamnjoh's understanding that the "… ability to seek the truth has been crippled and overshadowed by prejudice and conceit." (*Mind Searching* 2), becomes what Zygmunt Bauman considers in "Foreword: On Being Light and Liquid" as a combination of these two elements. He easily navigates without being stopped, passing round obstacles, some of which he dissolves bearing and soaking his way through and emerging unscathed upon meeting with solids. This, in the words of Bauman, is "the extraordinary mobility of fluids [that] associates them with the idea of "lightness." We associate "lightness" or "weightlessness" with mobility and inconstancy: … the lighter we travel the easier and faster we move" (qtd. *in* Hier 298). With this, Nyamnjoh's *Mind Searching* hints that "[h]e must be careful what he says. May he be taken in good faith!" (59). Prospère devices his lightness by being economical with information about his past. Not even his wives know anything about his past which he claims he was once a businessman in the Republic of Kuti. Could this be Nyamnjoh's way of throwing light to his idea of freedom and the illusion of freedom? In *Mind Searching*, does he not say: "there is much to be gained in the illusion of freedom"? (68).

Furthermore, in *A Nose for Money*, Nyamnjoh touches on an argument he has raised in his scholarly works on colonial and colonizing epistemologies. He makes of the popular and more endogenous epistemology stronger and void of the weaknesses noted in colonial and colonizing epistemology. The latter epistemology is marked by limitation to appearances: the observable, the here and now, the ethnographic present, the quantifiable, etc. (cf. "Potted Plants in Greenhouses"). This argument is brought to light in *A Nose for Money* when Prospère, after having made the decision to keep his booty and leave Sawang for Nyamandem, chooses to go to his Village, Minka, and consult with Seng, the diviner. He has come to find out about his future. He impersonates and asks the old man a barrage of questions: "Is my path clear? Is there danger or there no danger?" (77). This episode gives Nyamnjoh the opportunity to regret the problems confronting endogenous epistemologies, represented in *A Nose for Money* by Seng. The narrator laments:

> Things have changed, and the quest for money had become everybody's business. The only problem was that charlatans had invaded this noble profession as well and people like Seng were getting more and more difficult to find. They had become an endangered species. (79)

Also, in the process of divination, Seng tells Prospère, passing for Dieudonné, that his problem is women and that Prospère has to be careful. Having voiced that which needs not be known by an intimate friend to "Dieudonné," Prospère now resolves never to let women be an obstacle in his life. He, however, does not give up the prospect of remarrying or that of calculated involvements with women even if it means further tortures. He falls victim of colonizing epistemology by rationalizing what Seng has told him. He comes up with a strategy of staying out of trouble by marrying two wives, so "in that way the one could compete with the other for his love, so that scandals like Rose's would cease to bother him" (85). Yet, as Seng makes it clear through Dieudonné, that if Prospère whom he has exhorted, does not heed his urgent appeals, it would be his funeral and warns: "the child who chooses to ignore the wisdom in grey hair has no one but himself to blame when trouble strikes" (177). The latter quote seems to be informed by Nyamnjoh's scholarship (cf. "Incompleteness: Frontier Africa and the Currency of Conviviality"). Were this claim true, then his fictional works as well as his scholarly works are informed by each other.

In the political *crimescape* that *La République du Cameroun* is, Nyamnjoh informs that ministerial appointments and de-appointments are all carefully criminally masterminded to avoid mass protest and political upheavals. Discussing the de-appointment of a West Mimboland minister, Mr. Ngomnsong, the writer informs that the decision to sack him from government is to avoid possible secession. The government manages West and East Mimboland as the men do their multiple wives. The President is careful not to allow secessionists take the slightest advantage to mudsling. He writes: "[n]ot wanting to give the West Mimboland Liberation Movement a cheap opportunity for easy propaganda and mudslinging, the president had kicked Ngomnsong out of the cabinet promptly" (144). This decision is rather an indication that the president in this case has worked out Ngomnsong's de-appointment in spite of the fact that he "adores men with his stamina" even though "a weakling of exceptional calibre[sic]" (144). This is a system in which the parameters for success are hardly defined.

In addition, in this criminally orchestrated polity, the president's strategy ensures that any journalist who dares to write anything against him or any of his ministers, one that's on seat or sacked like the notorious Ngomnsong, never writes anymore. This example of systematic suppression of voices in the land of Mimbo has Nyamnjoh introduce the fate of writers and all involved in press activities such as *The Shattered Mirror,* a West Mimboland satirical newspaper. A journalist of the named newspaper having with effrontery written a "stinker" considered even too radical for radical West Mimboland journalistic standards, is left with only the possibility of never writing again for, "the president hadn't simply ended with dismissing the minister, but had ensured that the journalist wrote no more" (146). This journalist, in dragging down and ridiculing the president's ideal, has provoked the president's rage because that which needs not be given voice to in a way that minimizes the stifling potential of the President's repressive machine has been attributed one. An approach which is far from the idolization of Africa found in the earliest generation of African novel (Palmer ix).

When Prospère is first introduced to the reader amidst the chaos and confusion in the city's crawling traffic, the narrator tells of him being angry and impatient. Such anger, coupled with impatience, is representative of those of the multitude of Cameroonians who find themselves tied or slowed down. Through the vivid description of the noon traffic, Nyamnjoh's metaphor for the chaos and confusion, he addresses issues of omnipresent corruption in Mimboland/*La République du Cameroun*. Therein, ironically, the officers in charge of enforcing the law are instead out to enforce corruption. This is what pushes Prospère, who is yet to outgrow his status of the ordinary Mimbolander, to fume "at the cab driver and policeman exchanging papers and money in front of him. He worked hard for his money, and didn't like the thought of passing it over to law enforcement agents for nothing other than the right to go home" (3). This weakness, exhibited by the cab driver, Prospère seems to blame on the ordinary Mimbolander/Cameroonian who does not loathe the idea of giving away his hard earned money. This form of oppression is not unique in the country. It is even evident in expected areas where nationals are treated with indignity and disrespect where they are supposed to be treated with dignity and respect.

The healthcare system also comes to mind in Nyamnjoh's universe when discussing the repression suffered by voices willing to be heard, helped, and guided. It is evident in the ways patients with sexually transmitted diseases are treated in hospitals. The author uses the peculiar case of patients with chronic gonorrhea to illustrate his point. He shows the patients in a hospital lobby waiting to be attended to and their growing impatience at the long and tortuous wait they are made to endure. The nurses have no sense of health privacy concerns, they divulge patients' illnesses to the hearing of everyone and treat the patients like "shit" (26).

Again, the patients are ridiculed by the same nurses who are supposed to administer care to them. Nyamnjoh captures such repressive instance through Prospère's souvenir of the last time he was in hospital and during which he made up his mind, "never again" (26) to step foot there. During a verbal exchange between a nurse and patients, one of the patients and the nurse almost get into a physical fight were it not for the timely intervention of other patients. At this juncture the patients realize that seeing the doctor is for another class of people in Mimboland as the most embittered of them says before leaving, "I'll visit a traditional doctor tomorrow since modern medicine does not seem to be for our type" (27). This alternative, here suggested by Nyamnjoh, is not in any way to accredit traditional medicine which oppresses in its own way as most of its city practitioners are quacks and charlatans who are infected by "the get-rich-quick mania which has cast a spell over the city" (28). Could this be another roundabout way, by the author, of making the body of ordinary Mimbolanders an experimental ground for those in power?

The abovementioned mania brings gossip in its train. Gossip occupies a central position in the conveyance of meaning as well as that of repressed voices. Fishkin reminds us:

> [Mimboland] is a Democratic post-colonial state in name only. This is accomplished not by clear rules and regulations but by obfuscation and a bifurcated national consciousness. Opacity seems to be everywhere, especially in the world of Post-Independence [Mimboland] Public Service. (185)

The writer reminds the reader on multiple occasions how "it was really against common sense to expect a goat not to eat where it was tethered" (170). So to speak, the public service is a grazing ground for the "civil servant" or explicitly belly servant.

In Mimboland, information is well filtered and only that which the powers that be would allow public access to any information. In this context the ordinary Mimbolander relies on gossip as source of information. It is no accident that in *A Nose for Money* the reader comes across stories like that of Gaston Abanda. When his deal with the Mammawese goes bad, the media only hints at it and gives no details, thus leaving the public to speculative rumors. The most glaring example used by Nyamnjoh to illustrate how in an overly repressed society gossip reveals itself as a much more potent source of information is in the discussion around Prospère's wealth. He brings to light Prospère's mastery of financial wizardry as he contemplates to send even "his youngest daughter abroad to master the white man's ruse" (174). Nyamnjoh's narrator draws attention to the fact that,

> There is no lie about it. Prospère was a very rich man. Some rated him among the five richest in the country. Others thought that he printed counterfeit money, which he mixed with good

notes and took to the bank. But those who wanted to appear more objective would ask why the police did nothing to track him down if it were true he counterfeited. Others claim his money came directly from the devil, with whom he had signed a pact to suck the lifeblood out of relatives and friends, whom he then turned into zombies to sweat and toil towards his personal enrichment. (174)

One would readily expect that in an economy and polity marked by accountability and transparency, one should be able, without the least iota of doubt, to trace the source of income of the wealthiest men in the land. However, since in Mimboland—like in *La République du Cameroun*—no one cares for accountability, not even the police would do something to investigate allegations of Prospère's counterfeiting practices. Everything in the land of Mimbo seems to be a maze. The above gossips and counter gossips in the quote make explicit their potency. A way for the writer to air out his thoughts deprived of voice. And were such thoughts allowed to be voiced, then everyone would have the same story of the malpractices of contract awards, of cronyism, of political corruption and of reciprocity that Nyamnjoh tersely puts as "scratch my back I scratch yours" (159).

A Nose for Money taps from endogenous oppression which hinders both physical human movements as well as those of thoughts. It illustrates that giving voice to thoughts that have been or are being repressed is a complex and multifaceted process which also requires complex and intricate means as well as skills to be effective. Nyamnjoh invades the hidden transcript in his stead as a repressed figure to successfully recreate a universe, woven around the idea of voicing the unpalatable, in which through metaphorization and characterization, encounters and counter-encounters allow the repressed in his physical world to be expressed, and humorously and ironically too, while giving him the opportunity to swim, with ease in the pool of a Jamaican proverb, "play fool to catch wise" (qtd. *in* Scott 3). Herein, Nyamnjoh is at his best in the fictionalization of what James C. Scott theorizes as the "Art of Resistance" which by far transcends DeBrabander's summary of this human endeavor as the "stoic virtue... carried out and achieved in the quiet fortress of the mind" (41). Nyamnjoh does exactly what in his first novel, *Mind Searching,* he makes his protagonist promise to do. He promises that: "if ever I decide to become a writer, I would have to write the way I think, even if this means writing only for myself" (67). Consequently, *A Nose for Money* is a reflection of this promise put to practice the transcription of his *stoic virtue*. He, by so doing, captures the identity of a repressive nation and gives voice to repressed thoughts. Little wonder some critics like Martin Evans have remarked that Nyamnjoh is keener on the practice and writing of sociology than creative fiction. His fiction is characterized by vocalizing his thoughts, deploring despicable societal on-goings.

Works cited

DeBrabander, Firmin. *Spinoza and the Stoics: Power Politics & the Passions.* Continuum International, 2008.

Evans, Martin. "*A Nose for Money,* by Francis B Nyamnjoh Review" in *The Review of African Political Economy* Vol. 34, no.111, 2007, pp. 211-212.

Fishkin, Benjamin H., Ankumah, Adaku T. & Ndi, Bill F. (eds.) *Fears, doubts and Joys of not Belonging.* Langaa RPCIG, 2013.

Fowler, Alastair. *A History of English Literature.* Havard UP, 1991.

Hier, Sean P. *Contemporary Sociological Thought: Themes and Theories.* Canadian Scholars' P, 2006.

Larson, Charles. *The Ordeal of the African Writer.* Zed Books, 2001.

Mufor, Atanga. *The Anglophone Cameroon Predicament.* Langaa RPCIG, 2011.

Murphy, Geraldine. "Olaudah Equiano, Accidental Tourist," *Eighteenth-Century Studies Vol. 27,* 1994, pp. 551-68. In Sollors.

Ndi, Bill F. *Mishaps and other poems.* Authorhouse, 2008.

Nyamnjoh, Francis B. *A Nose for Money.* 2nd ed. East African Educational Publishers, 2006,

_____. "'Potted Plants in Greenhouses': A Critical Reflection on the Resilience of Colonial Education in Africa." *Journal of Asian and African Studies,* vol. 47, no 2, 2012, pp. 129–154.

―――――――. *Mind Searching*. 2nd ed. Langaa RPCIG, 2007.

―――――――. *Africa's Media: Democracy and the Politics of Belonging*. Zed Books, 2005.

―――――――. "Incompleteness: Frontier Africa and the Currency of Conviviality", *Journal of Asian and African Studies* DOI: 10.1177/0021909615580867 http://jas.sagepub.com/content/early/2015/04/22/0021909615580867.full.pdf+html. Accessed 10 May 1025.

Palmer, Eustace. *An Introduction to the African Novel*. Africana Publishing, 1972.

Scott, James C. *Domination and the Art of Resistance: Hidden Transcripts*. Yale UP, 1992.

Tezanu, Primus. "Africa's Power Elite Castigated in Francis B. Nyamnjoh's *A Nose for Money*" 2007. www.nyamnjoh.com/page/5/. Accessed 25 Mar. 2014.

INDEX

A

Abuja 72
Achebe, Chinua 146, 158
Addison, Joseph 98, 105
Al Jazeera 172, 181
Alcoff.................................... 2, 20
Algiers.. 72
Amy Tan 82
Ankumah, Adaku T.12, 21, 49, 51, 52, 54, 55, 57, 64, 65, 115, 117, 119, 127, 128, 146, 203
Aristotle 54, 55, 61, 62, 64, 74
Asong, Linus 169, 171
Ateljevic 2, 20
Atwood, Margaret 67

B

Backscheider, Paula R. 90, 109
Barthes, Roland 91, 109
Bate Besong 115, 169
Bauman, Zygmunt.......... 197, 198
Belquin.. 6
Berlin Conference 169, 179
Bertha Mason......................... 152
Bhaba, Homi 181
Bhaba, Hommi 176
Bismarck 12
Biya, Paul 119, 120, 166, 178
Blaze, Michael 83
Booker T. Washington72-74, 83, 133, 135
Bourdieu 4, 5, 20, 186
Bowman, Paul 21

Budra, Paul 97, 110

C

Cairo................................. 72, 171
Camara Laye 162
Camus, Albert........................ 172
Castro-Gómez 3, 20
Catherine Samba-Panza...........150
Cerutti-Guldberg................... 3, 20
Charlotte Bronte 152
Chaucer 7
Chomsky 13, 180, 181

D

Dante..................................... 197
deBoer, Fredrik 66, 83
Deborah Plant 131, 139
DeBrabander, Firmin 203
Dewey 68, 71, 73
Dickens 7, 77, 171, 181
Dilthey.............................. 1, 162
Djaout, Tahar..................... 78, 83
Doh, Emmanuel Fru17, 20, 49, 51, 53, 57, 63, 64, 65, 86, 110, 115-119, 127, 128, 165-180
Downward..............................162
DuBois, W.E.B. 135
Dussel, Enrique 1-15, 20

E

Eagleton, Terry117, 121, 122, 127
Eberhard............................18, 21
Eliot, T.S...................... 110, 168
Elizabethan Literature 7

Ellen Johnson Sirleaf 150
Engels 113, 128
Euripides.......................... 54, 55

F

Fanon, Frantz 7, 12, 18, 21, 50, 64, 70, 83, 152, 173, 181

Feng.............................. 162, 163

Fishkin, Benjamin H. 12, 16, 21, 66, 115, 117, 119, 127, 128, 165, 201, 203

Fowler, Alastair 184, 203
France 12, 103, 166, 169, 178
Frank, Katherine 146, 147, 163
Freire 111, 128

G

Gates, Henry Louis 83
Georgina Theodora Wood...... 150
Ghisi 2, 21
Gilman 10, 21
Ginsberg, Benjamin . 66, 74, 76, 83
Grosfoguel 21

H

Hardy, Thomas 77
Harlan, Louis........................... 83
Harlem Renaissance 130
Harris, Trudier 138, 139, 140, 144
Heidegger 90, 93, 99, 100, 104, 110

Hier, Sean P. ... 195, 196, 198, 203
Holloway........... 11, 14, 16, 19, 21
Hurston, Zora Neale 129-144
Huxley, Aldous......................... 67

J

Jáuregui, Carlos 20
Jing, Thomas 146-150, 151, 157, 160-163, 169, 171

John Brougher 147
John Bunyan 143
Joyce, James 75, 172, 180

K

Kafka.................................... 79
Kahneman, Daniel 112, 128
Kaplan 134, 144
Keats, John 113
Kenneth Grahame 80
Kenneth Little........................ 146
Keynes, John Maynard 112, 128
Kierkegaard 1
Kinshasa 5
Kocis, Robert................... 117, 128
Kristeva, Julia........ 87, 98, 99, 110

L

Lacan, Jacques..................... 69, 70
Lake Nyos............... 13, 15, 18, 82
Larson, Charles 186, 187, 203
Levinas 1
Lewis Carroll........................... 80
Lowe, John 131, 134, 135, 136, 138, 144

Luanda.................................. 72

M

Machiavelli............................ 116
Magda.................................... 2
Mahalia Jackson 72, 167
Malamud, Bernard.................... 82
Mariama Bâ 147
Marx 1, 14, 113, 128
Mazrui 10, 21
McLaughlin, Becky........ 64, 70, 83
Mellor, Anne................... 114, 128
Mendieta, Eduardo................ 1, 20

Mind Searching 12, 79, 83, 171, 174, 181, 186, 187, 197, 203

Mona Lisa 11

Montgomery, Maxine L. 110

Mufor Atanga 203

Murphy, Geraldine 203

Mutia, Ba'bila 115

N

Ndi, Bill F. 12, 21, 49, 52-59, 64, 65, 85, 111-128, 169, 171, 175, 180, 183, 185, 203

Nfah-Abbenyi 147, 152, 163

Nfar-Abbenyi 59, 65

Nietzsche, Friedrich 113, 115, 128

Nkengasong, Nkemngong 169, 171

Norman Rockwell 69

Nwapa, Flora 148, 164

Nyamnjoh, Francis B. 1, 3, 5, 7, 16, 17, 18, 19, 21, 55, 64-110, 169, 171, 174, 181-204

O

Obioma Nnaemeka 151

O'brien, Tim 110

Oduyoye, Mercy 151, 155, 164

Oedipus 53, 54, 55, 57, 61, 65

Orwell, George 67, 78, 83, 175, 181

Oxford Street 7

P

Palmer, Eustace 162-164, 189, 200, 203

Perrill, Simon 112, 128

Plant, Deborah 131, 132, 139, 144

Plato 74, 119

Pratt, Annis 162

Pulitzer 132

R

Racine 7

Ranciere 8, 21

Ricardo Gil Soeiro 96

Ricoeur, Paul 1, 20

Rishoi, Christy 164

Rita Dove 131, 136, 138, 140

Rosenwald 133, 134

Rosowski, Susan J. 162

S

Sandra Gilbert 152

Sankofar 72, 165

Santos, Boaventura de Sousa 15, 21

Sardar 2, 21

Sartre, Jean-Paul 67, 83, 97, 107, 110

Schutte, Ofelia 3, 20, 21

Scott, James C. 51, 65, 74, 83, 173, 174, 181, 187, 188, 192, 202, 203

SDF 5, 6, 8, 16, 18

Sékou Touré 50

Shaka Zulu 137

Shakespeare 7, 185

Sophocles 54, 55, 57, 65

Spencer, Edmund 125

Stratton, Florence ... 146, 147, 164

Summerfield 162

Susan Gubar 152

T

Tavares, Sofia 96, 110

Tennessee Williams 80

Tezanu, Primus 185, 192, 204

Thackeray, William Makepeace. 69, 76, 77, 83

Theodore Dreiser 82

transmodernity 2, 7, 11, 13, 16, 17, 20

Tsitsi Dangarembga. 152, 156, 162

Tunis.. 72

U

United Nations....................... 149

Upton Sinclair 82

V

Vachon 18

Vakunta, Peter W. 49-58,   61-65, 115, 116, 169, 175, 181

W

wa Thiong'o, Ngugi 120, 125, 128, 146, 181

Walker, Alice........................... 132

Wallace, Stevens 114, 128

Wangari Maathai 150

Waterloo 8, 14

West Cameroon 170, 193

Wolowsky 113, 128

Wordsworth, William 90, 110

X

Xenophon................................. 74

Y

Yamoussoukro 72

Yaoundé 5, 72, 147, 167, 172, 178, 180

Yondo Black 5, 8, 15

Z

Zeitlin Michael 97, 110

www.ingramcontent.com/pod-product-compliance
Lightning Source LLC
Chambersburg PA
CBHW010719300426
44115CB00020B/2962